Tomato Soup

Arty-Pants

2022

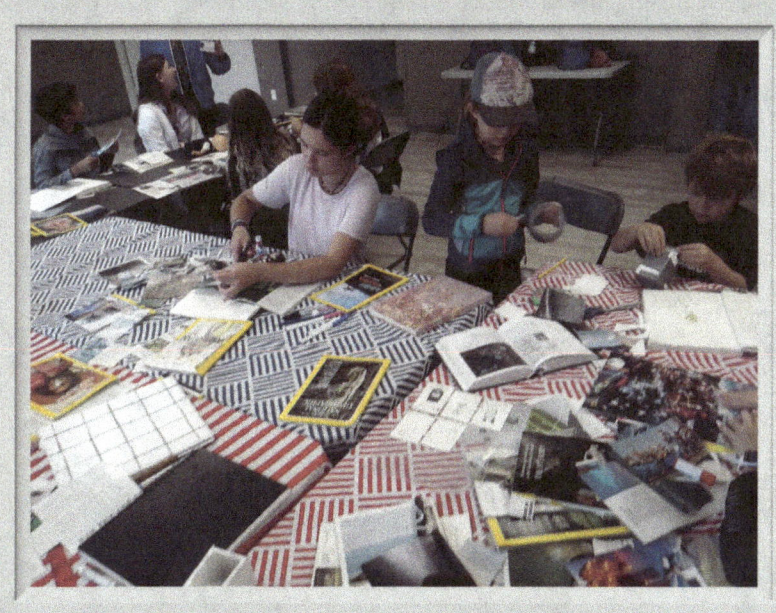

Tomato Soup

Arty-Pants

2022

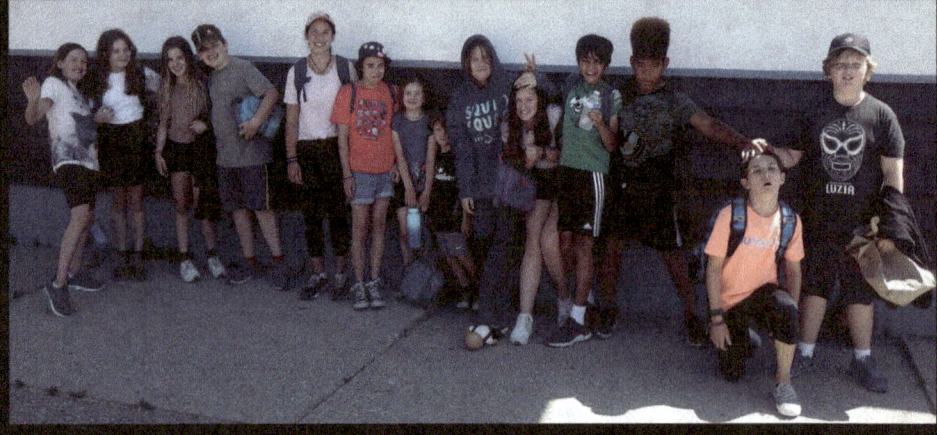

© 2022 Arty-Pants.

All artwork is © by the individual artists.

Book Design and editing by Blaise Kolodychuk

Tomato Pie was photographed by:

Matthew, Stella, Mabel and Blaise

TABLE OF CONTENTS

Ben ·· pg. 5

Sock Story ·· pg. 14

Genevieve ·· pg. 19

Gus ·· pg. 29

Hazel ·· pg. 39

Kate ·· pg. 53

Chicken Wings ····································· pg. 64

Mabel ·· pg. 67

Matthew ··· pg. 77

Max ·· pg. 85

Rhiannon ·· pg. 91

Declan ··· pg. 99

Sam ·· pg. 107

Sarah ·· pg. 119

Sophie ··· pg. 131

Stella ·· pg. 145

Tomato Pie ··· pg. 155

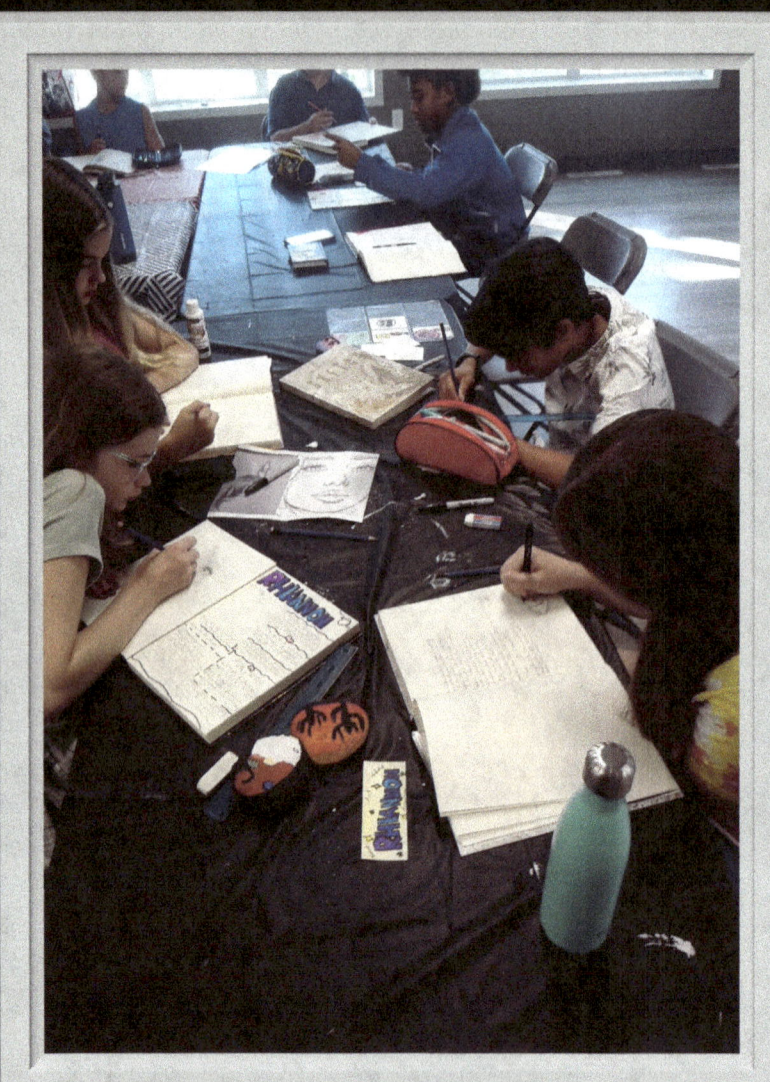

Ben's SUPER COOL

SKETCHBOOK OF AWESOMENESS, SUPERIORITY, INTRIGUE, MYSTIQUE, AND THREE-HUNDRED SEVENTY-EIGHT OTHER ADJECTIVES THAT I WON'T BOTHER TO LIST HERE, SO INSTEAD HERE'S A DRAWING OF A CUTE, ALBEIT TINY CAT:

MEOW!

ANYHOW, IF YOU LIKED THAT SKETCH, YOU'LL PROBABLY LIKE MY OTHER ONES AS WELL. OR NOT. MAYBE YOU'RE A WEIRDO WHO ONLY LIKES CATS AND LITERALLY NOTHING ELSE. OH WELL, THERE WILL OTHER LIFEFORMS THAT WILL ENJOY MY ART. MAYBE. IF YOU WOULD LIKE TO SEE IT THOUGH, TURN THIS COVER VIA YOUR HANDS, PAWS, HOOVES, OR THE EQUIVALENT IN YOUR SPECIES. TELEPATHY AND/OR WITCHCRAFT

Ben

From Blaispedia, the paid encyclopedia

INFO

Benjamin Peter James Bradley Moon is a human* who was born on October 20th, 2006 in Vancouver, BC. Ben's favourite color is #2172b8 and his favourite animals are cats.

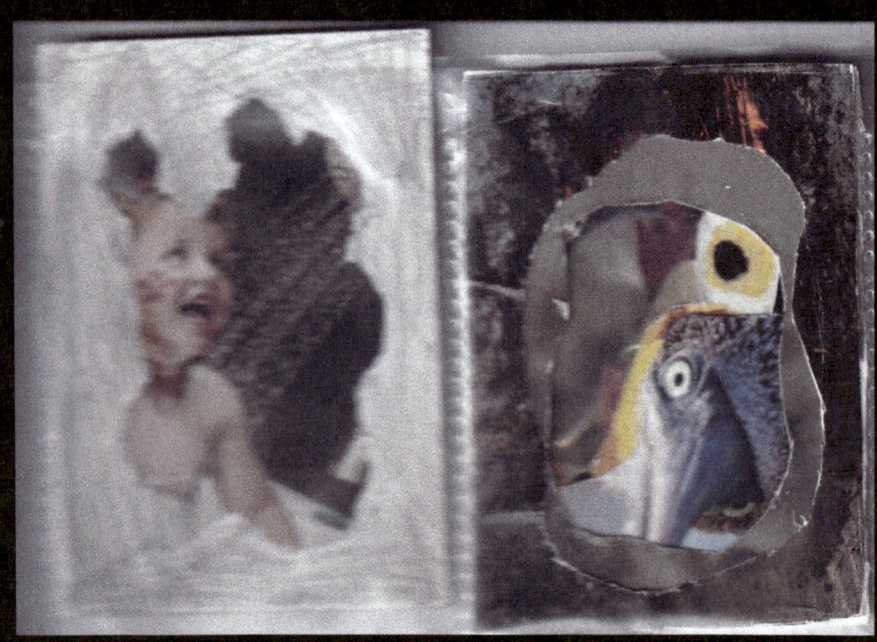

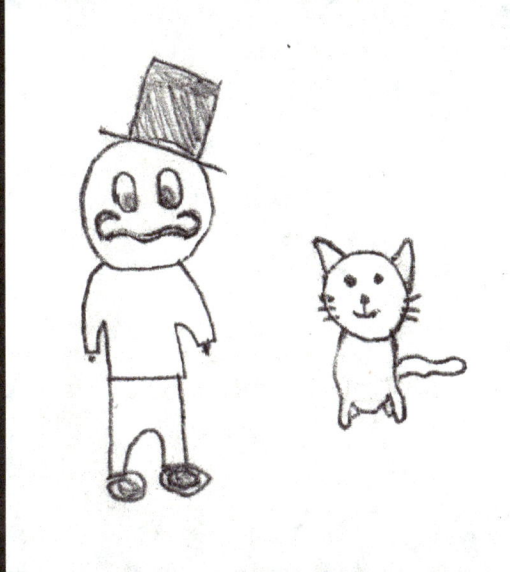

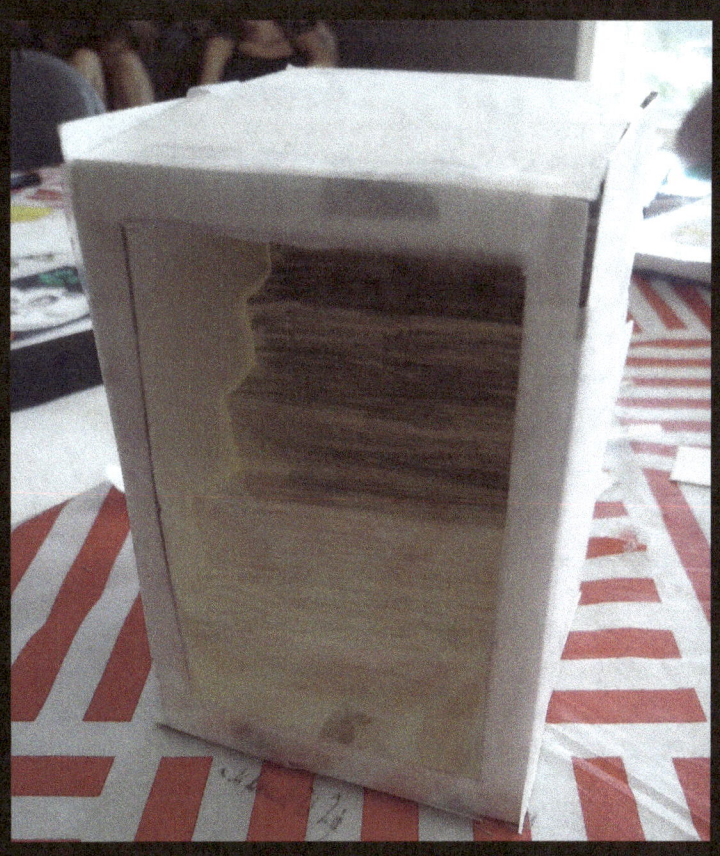

Ben's song about Blaise's face

Your face
Your face

Your face is a tiny fluffy purple bunny rabbit stuffed with cheese
Your face is a tiny fluffy purple bunny rabbit stuffed with bees
Your face is a tiny fluffy purple bunny rabbit stuffed with knees
Your face is a tiny fluffy purple bunny rabbit, that's your face.

Your face
Your face is a tiny fluffy bunny rabbit
Your face
Your face is a tiny fluffy bunny
Your face
Your face is a tiny fluffy bunny rabbit
Your face is a bunny
Yeah that's your face

Your face is a tiny fluffy purple bunny rabbit stuffed with cheese (Lots of cheese)
Your face is a tiny fluffy purple bunny rabbit stuffed with bees (Tons of bees)
Your face is a tiny fluffy purple bunny rabbit stuffed with knees (All the knees)
Your face is a tiny fluffy purple bunny rabbit, that's your face. (Your face is WEIRD)

Your face
It smells like a cat
Your face
It moves like a bat
Your face (your face)
It eats lots of cheese
Your face (your face)
It's shaped like your keys (You'll never be able to unlock your front door again, ha!)

Your face
Your face is a tiny fluffy bunny rabbit
Your face
Your face is a tiny fluffy bunny
Your face
Your face is a tiny fluffy bunny rabbit
Your face is a bunny
Yeah that's your face (Yeah that's your face)
Yeah that's your face (Yeah that's your face)
Yeah that's your face (Yeah that's your face)
Yeah that's your face face face face

Your face is a tiny fluffy purple bunny rabbit stuffed with cheese
Your face is a tiny fluffy purple bunny rabbit stuffed with bees
Your face is a tiny fluffy purple bunny rabbit stuffed with knees
Your face is a tiny fluffy purple bunny rabbit, that's your face

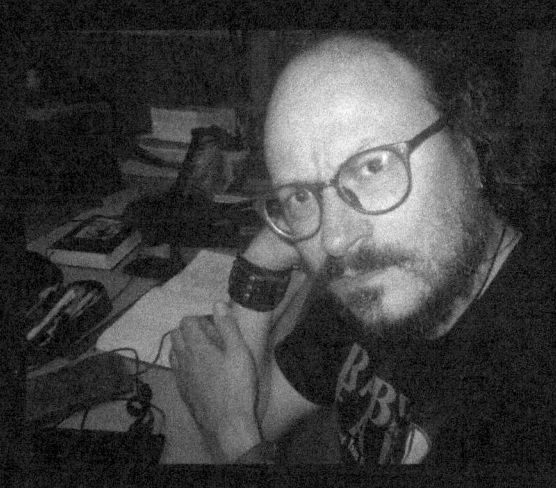

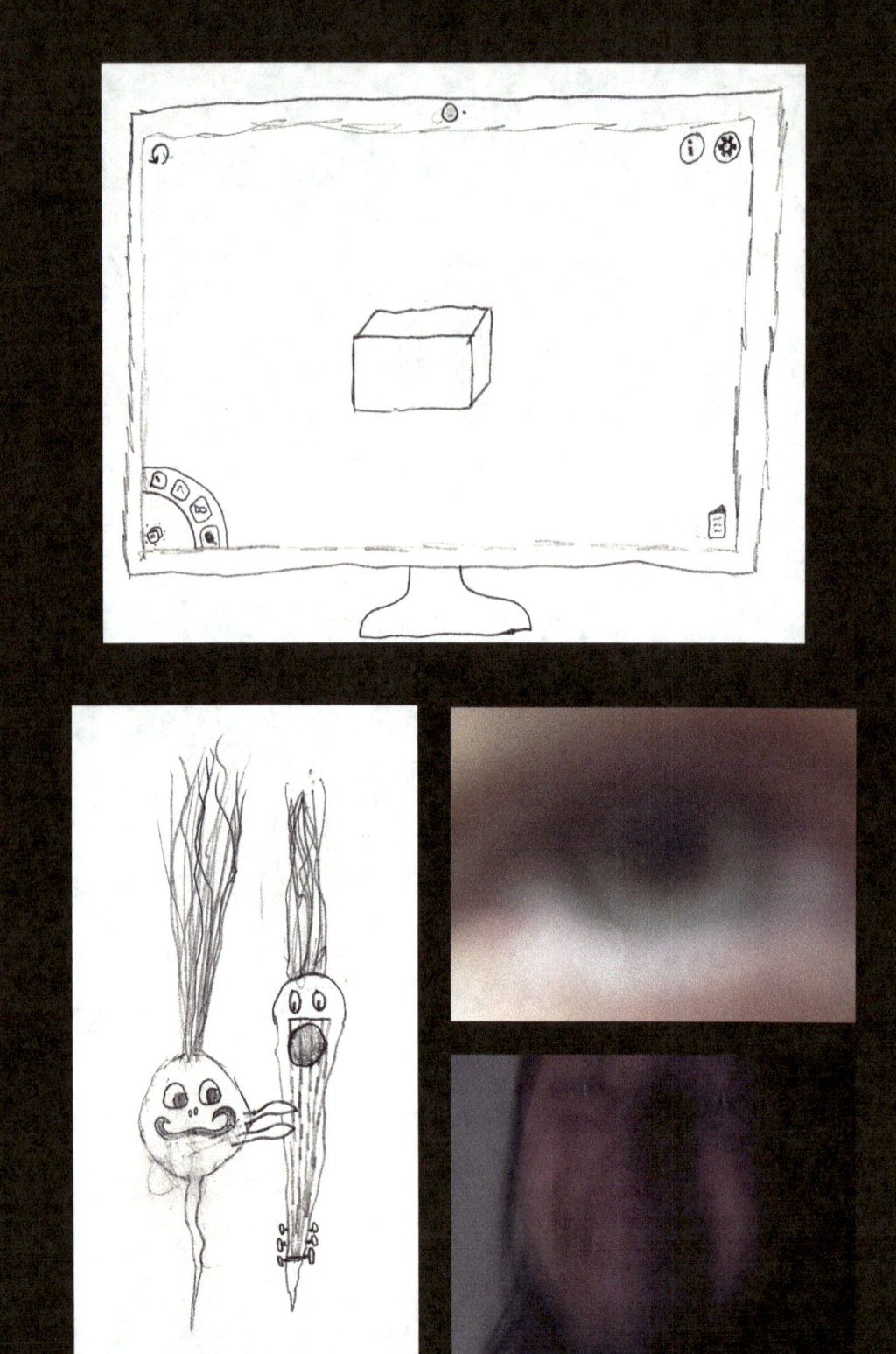

Once there was a kitten named 'Boggy' who went and talked to his friend Mr. Floorboard. Mr. Floorboard was next to nothing at all but he was green with red spots. All of the sudden, the flowers came and attacked them with the power of singing vegetables. They all went home and ate stopwatches for brunch. It didn't matter that one of them was turning lime green; they just kept on folding the windows into miniature caricatures of themselves. WatchyMcWatchFace the Stopwatch was in a jar of pickles bigger than Mt. Everest yet as small as an ant. The paper folded into a can of beans, put on pants, and glitched into the underworld. "Whoops!" she exclaimed audibly, rotating like bacon.

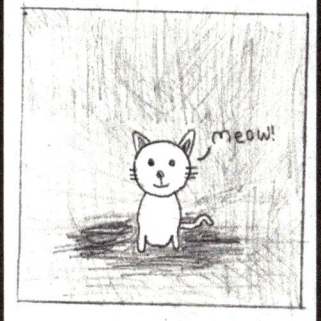

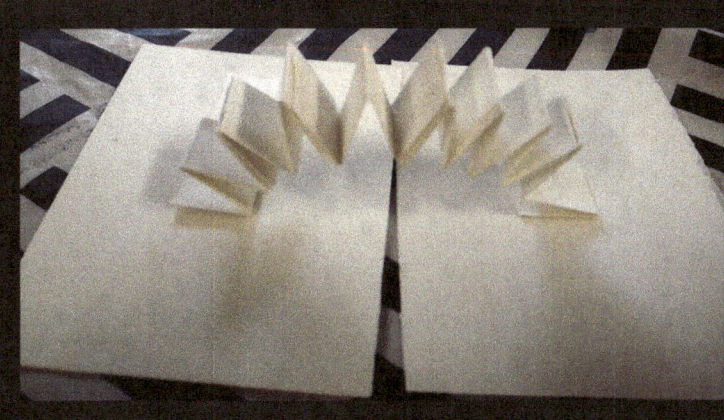

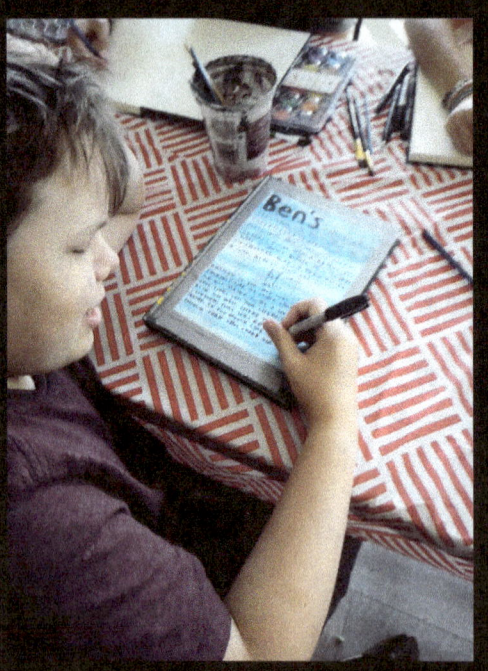
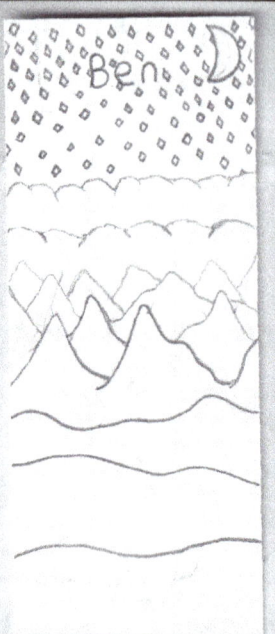

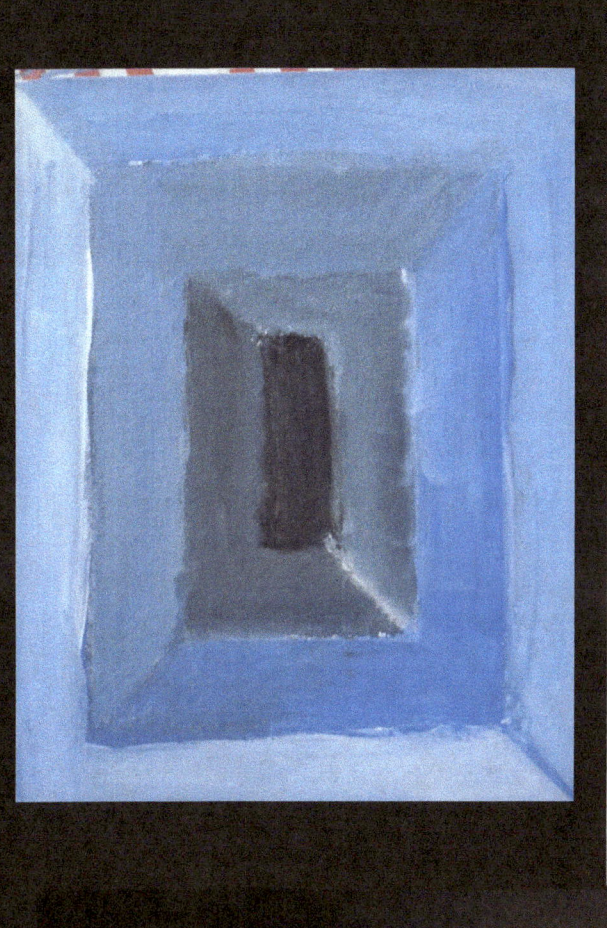
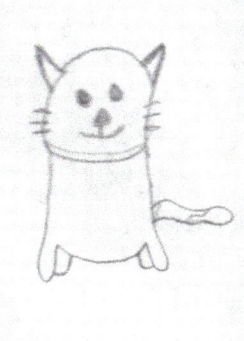
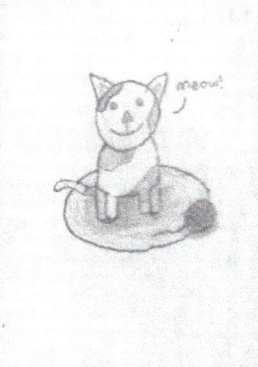

A SOCK STORY
Realized By Ben Moon

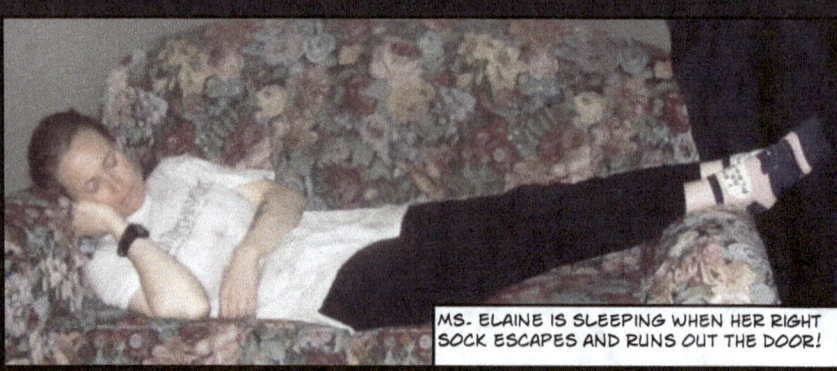

MS. ELAINE IS SLEEPING WHEN HER RIGHT SOCK ESCAPES AND RUNS OUT THE DOOR!

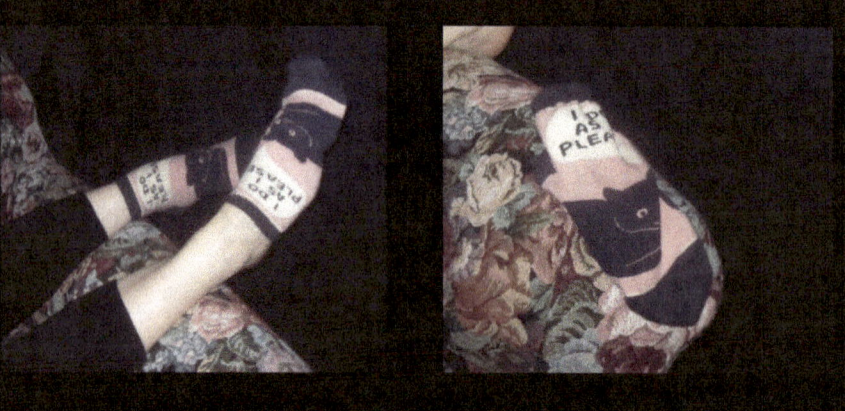

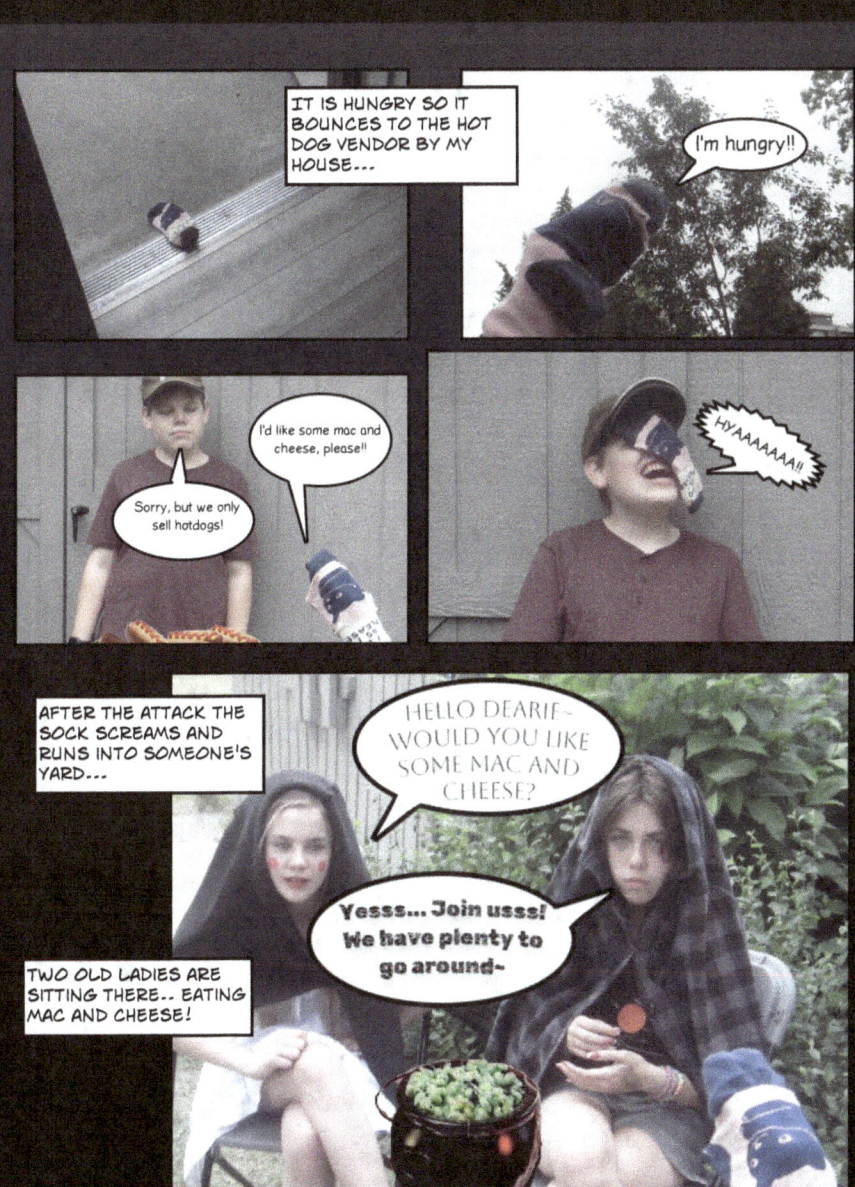

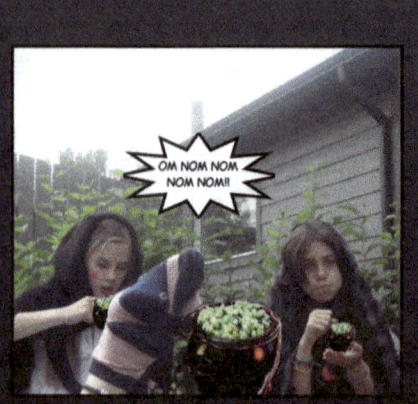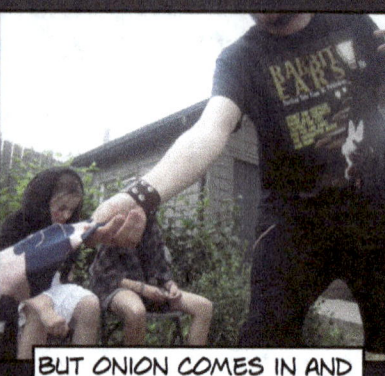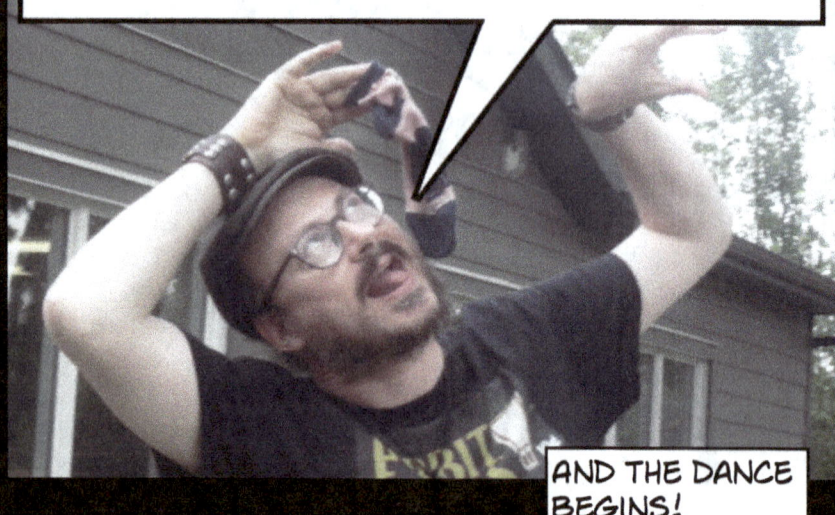

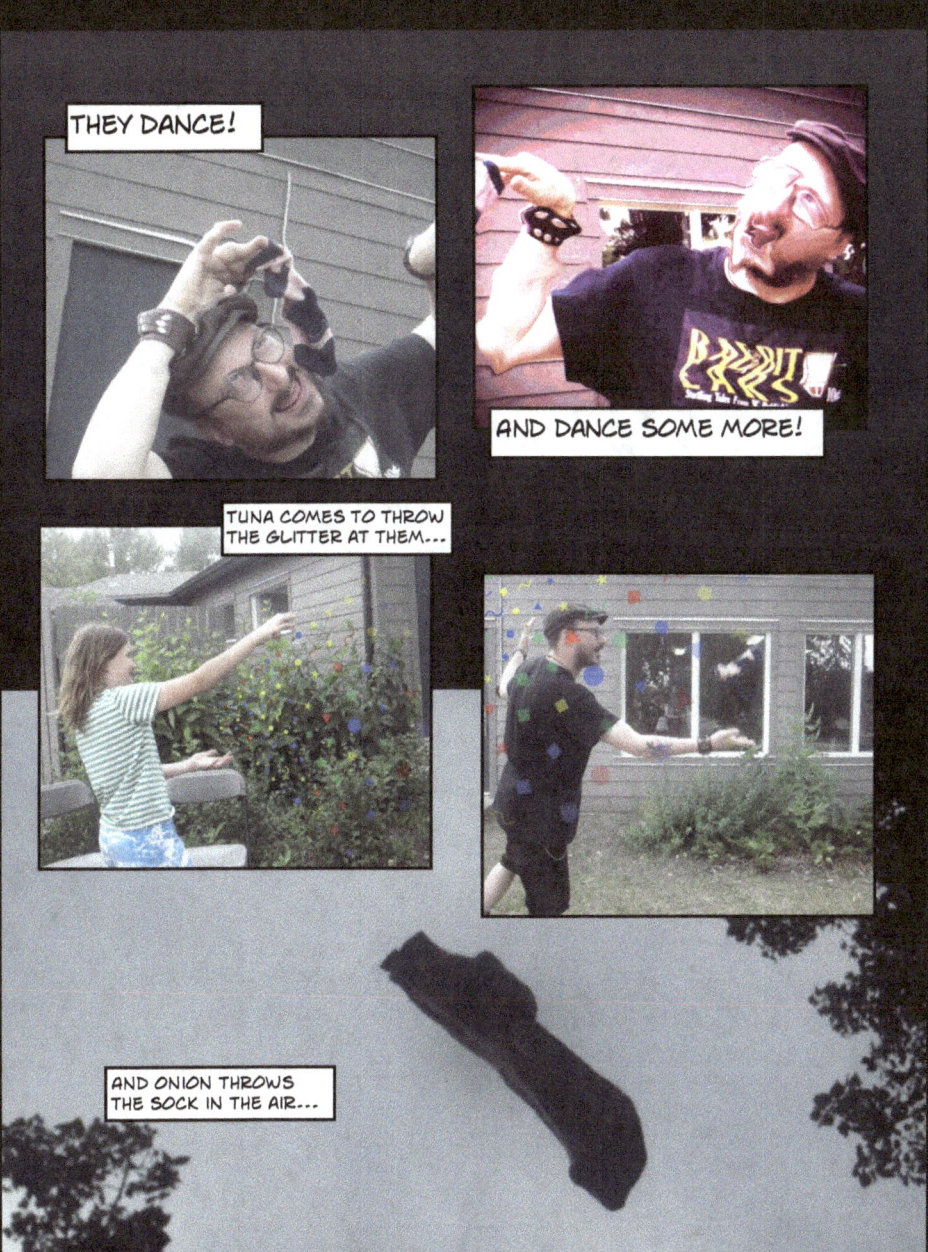

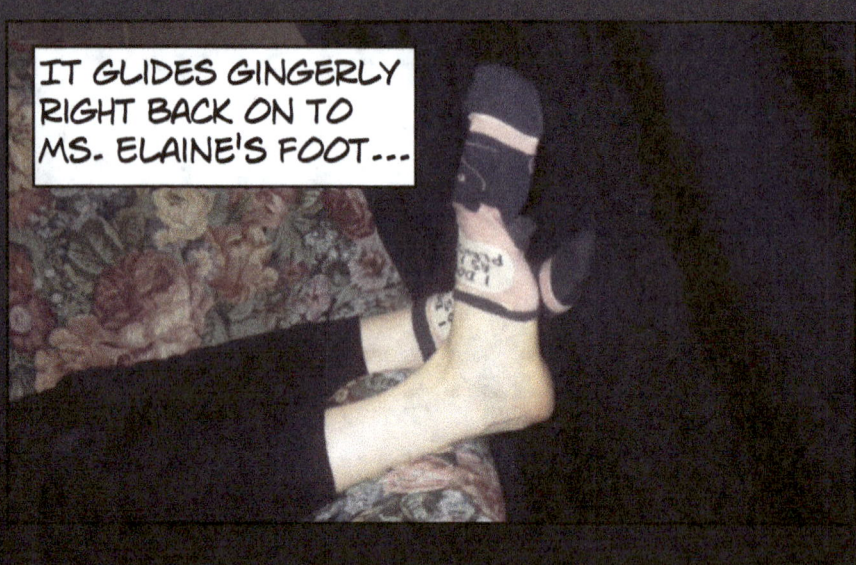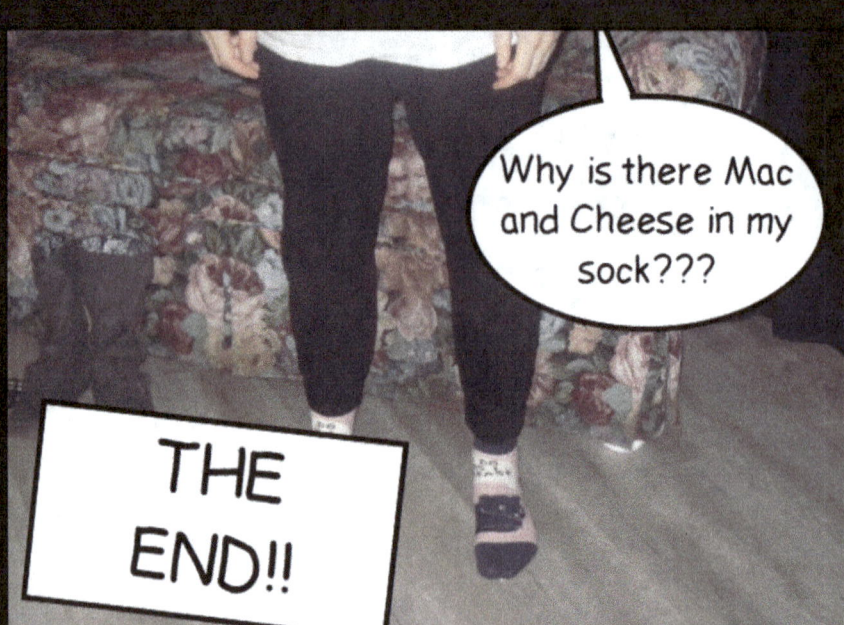

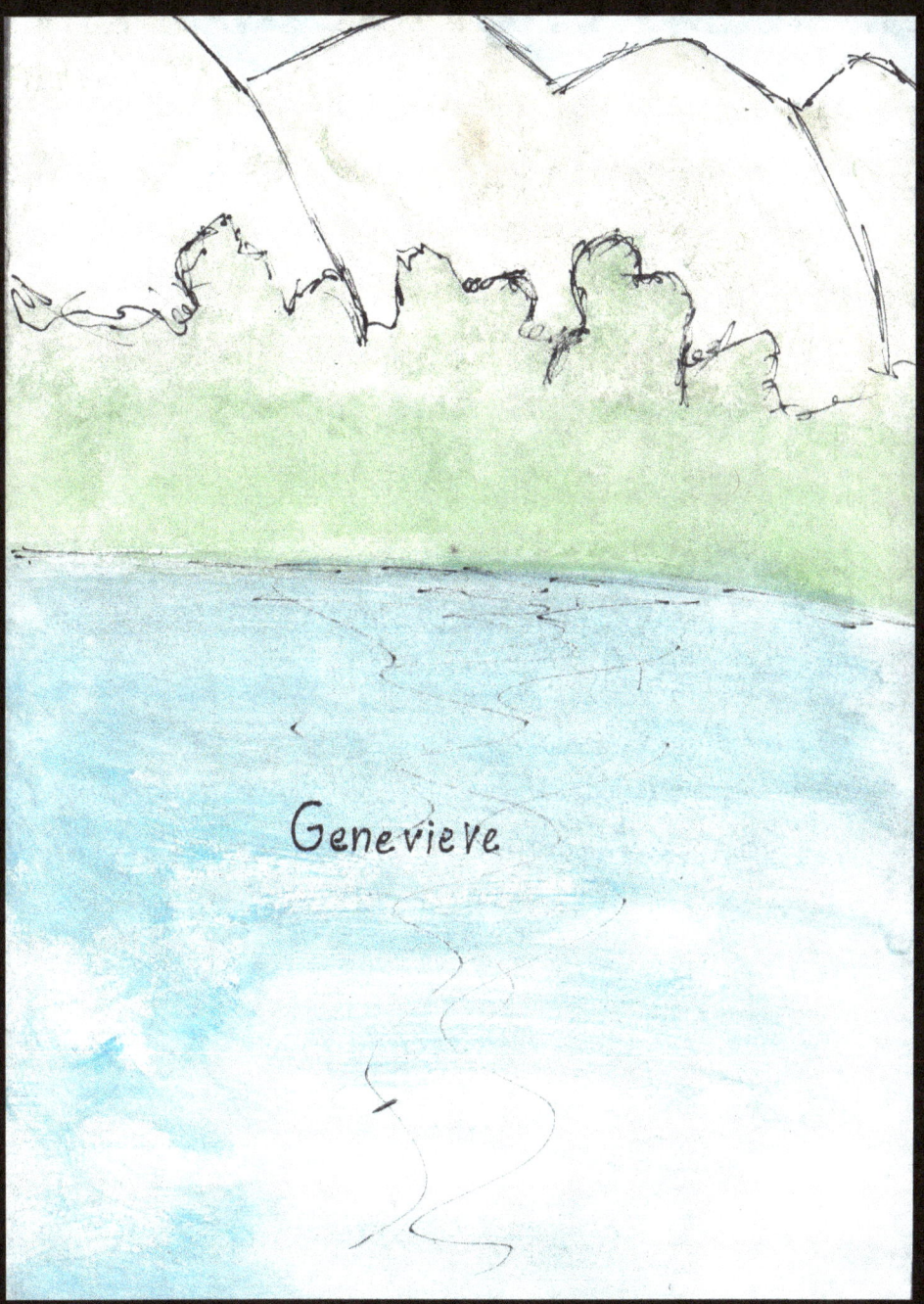

GENEVIEVE

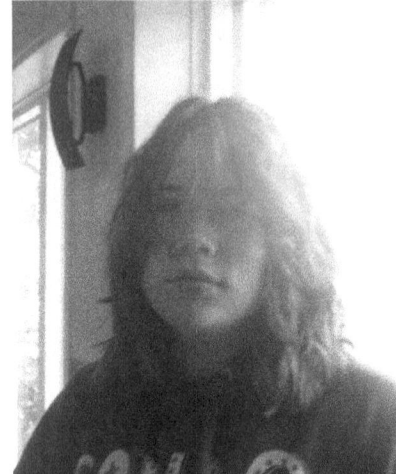

I was born in Canmore on December 24 2009. I enjoy making art, reading, and taking naps. In my spare time, I watch anime and read manga.

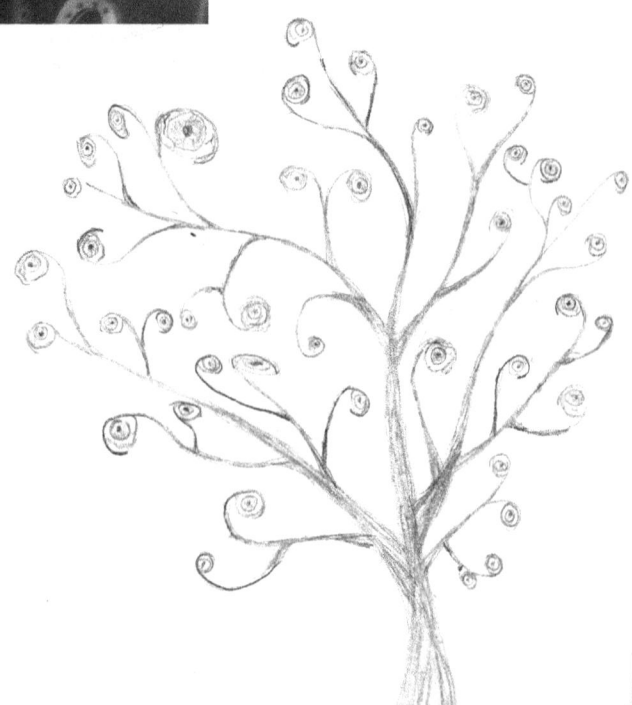

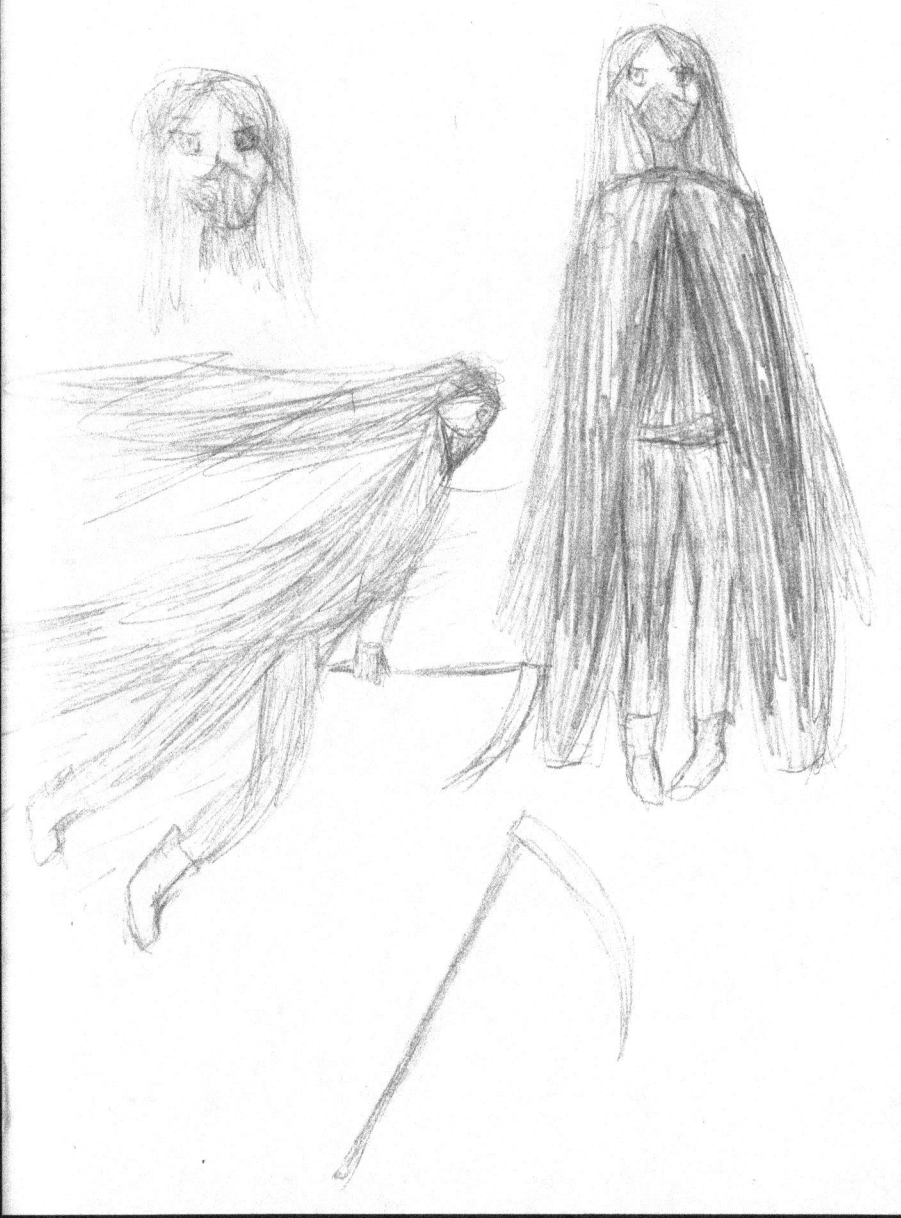

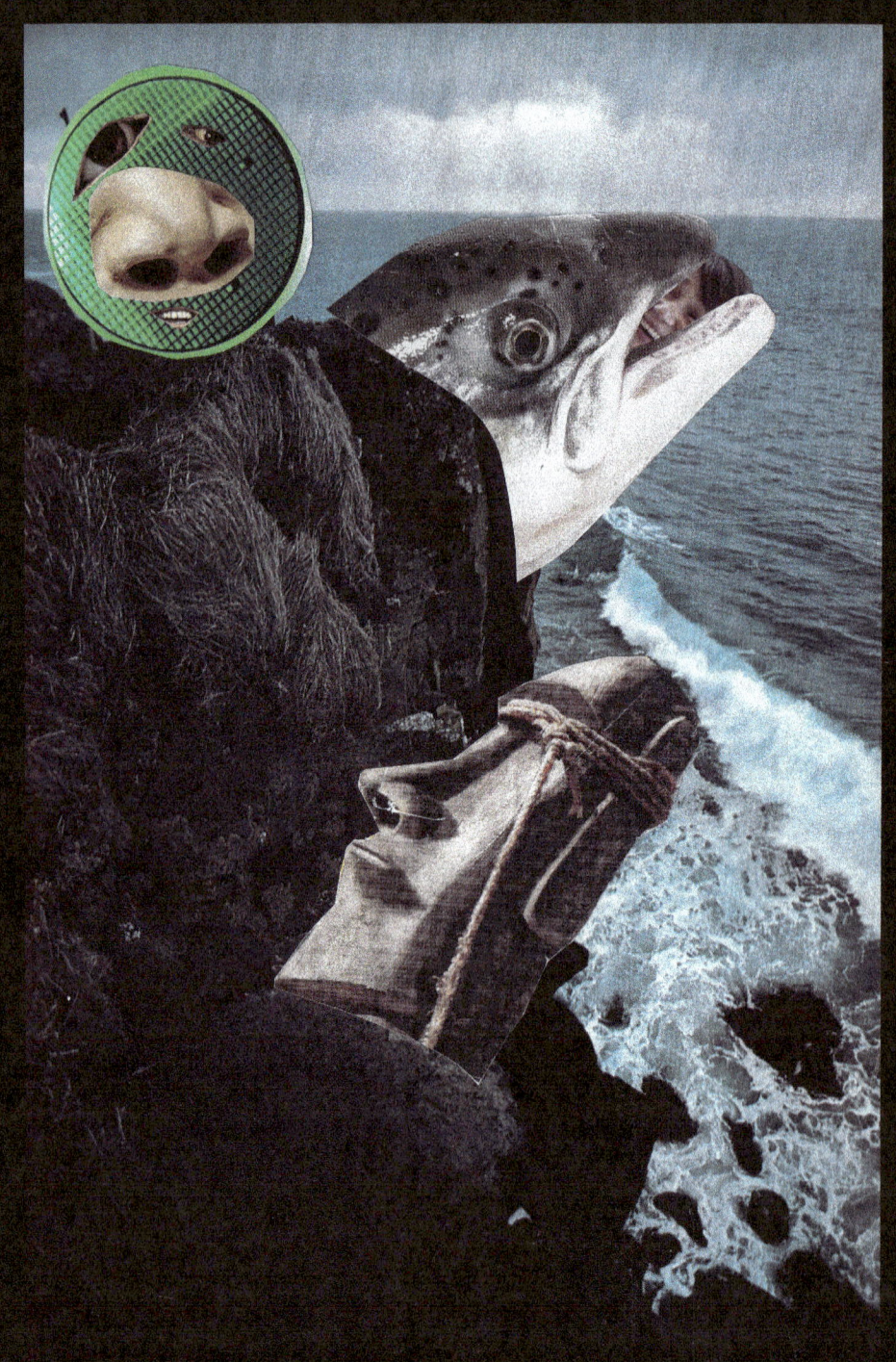

LONG Bread
By Genevieve

ch2.c0

sup.

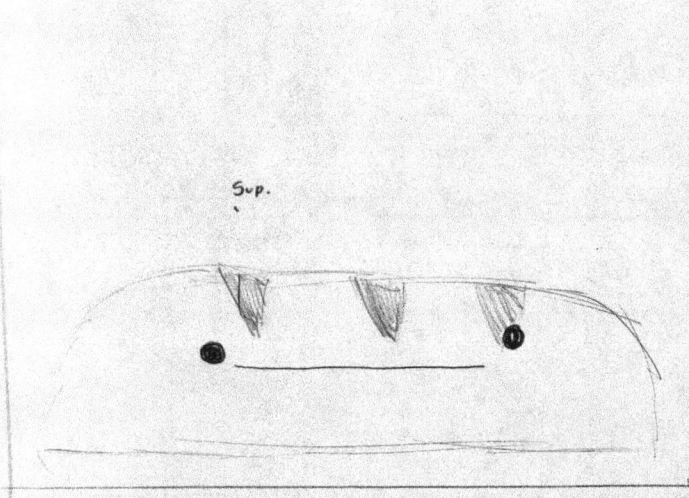

The End

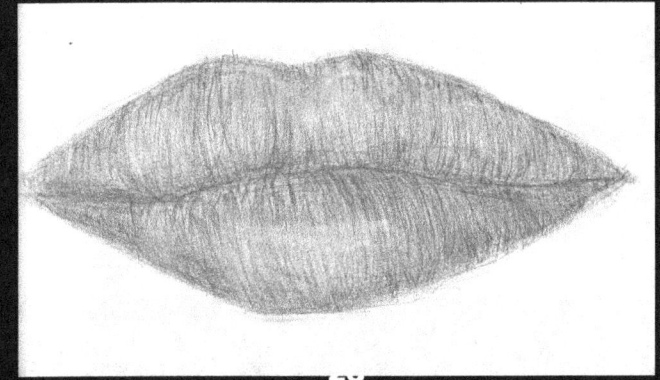

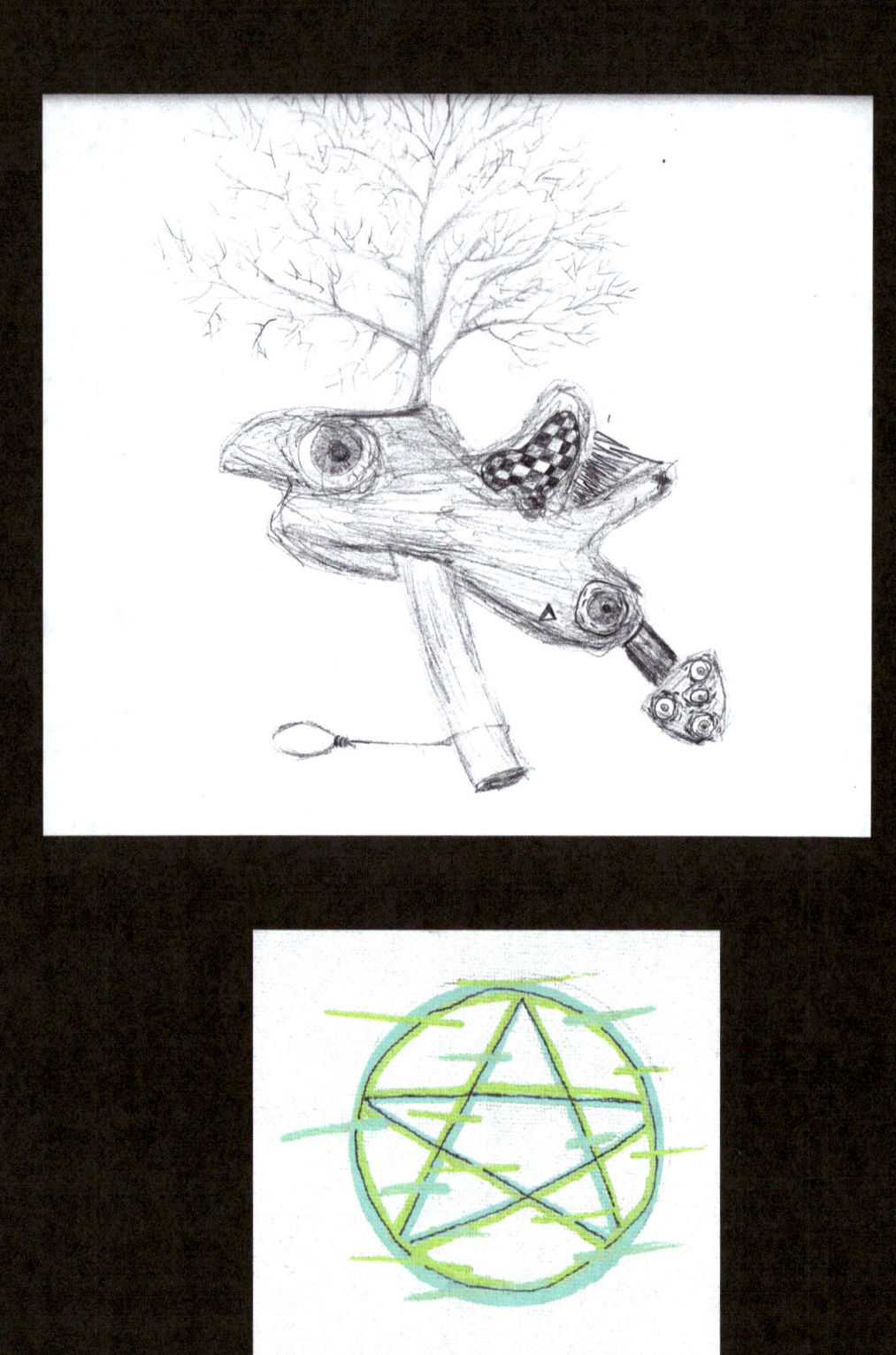

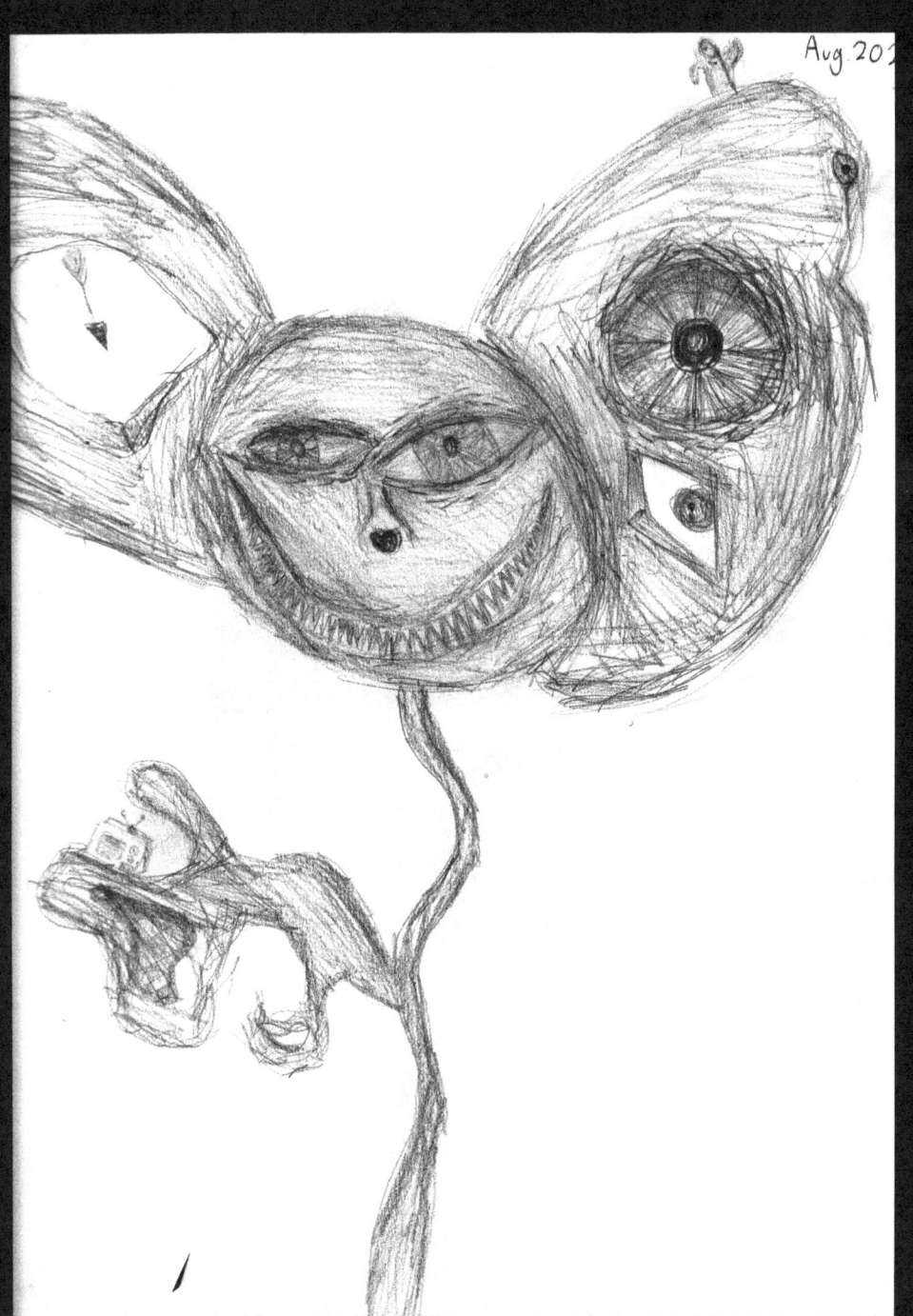

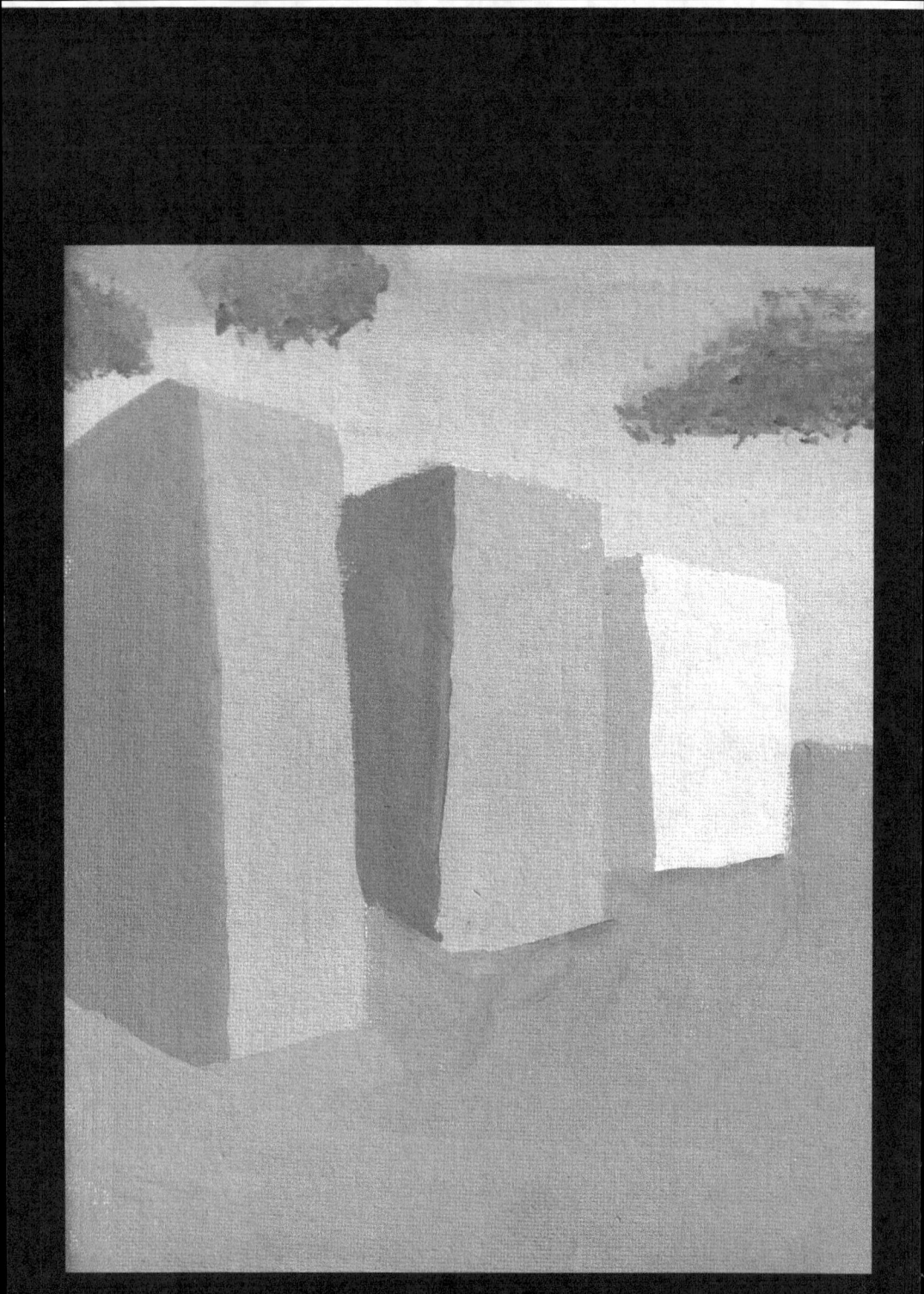

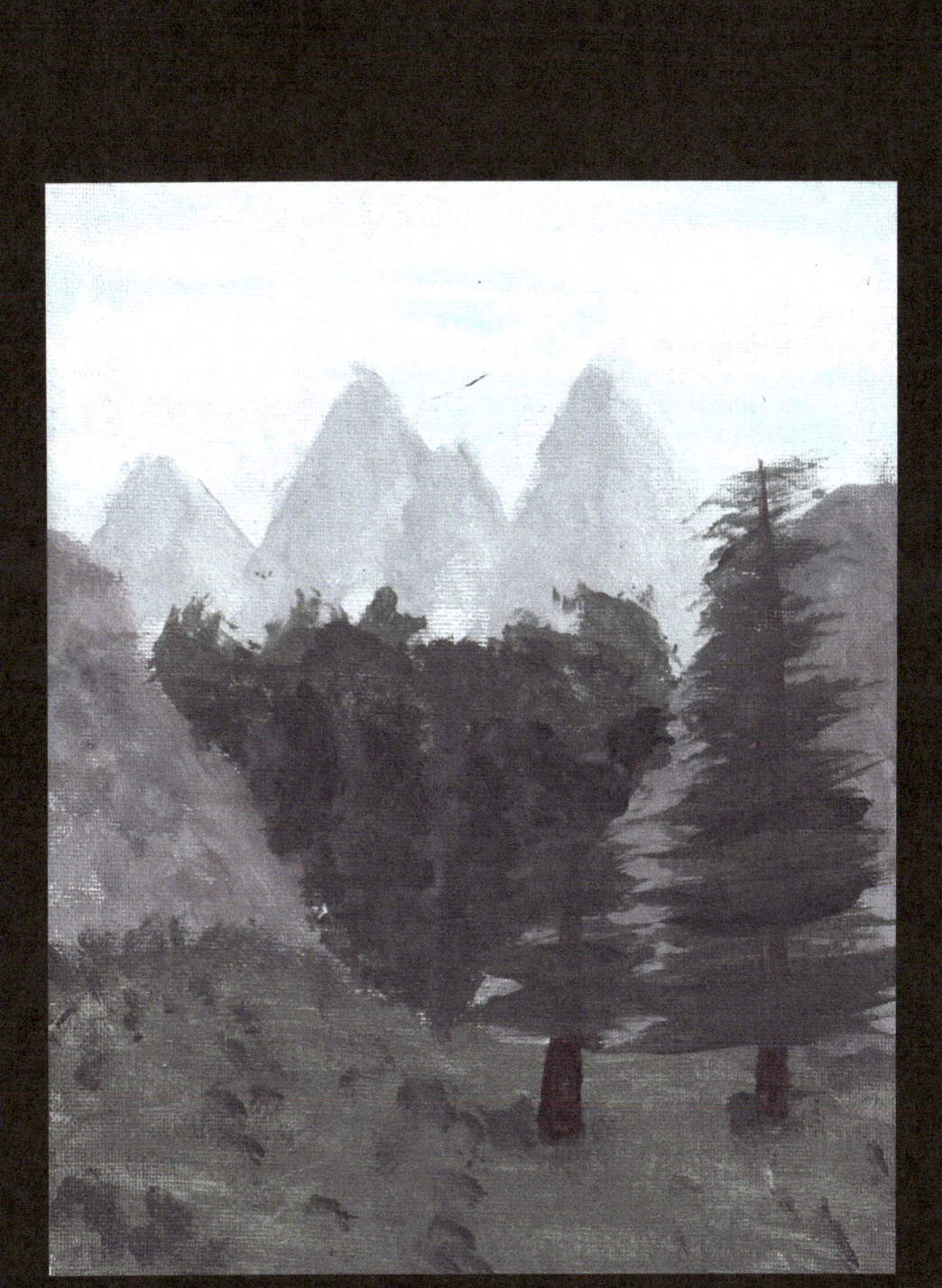

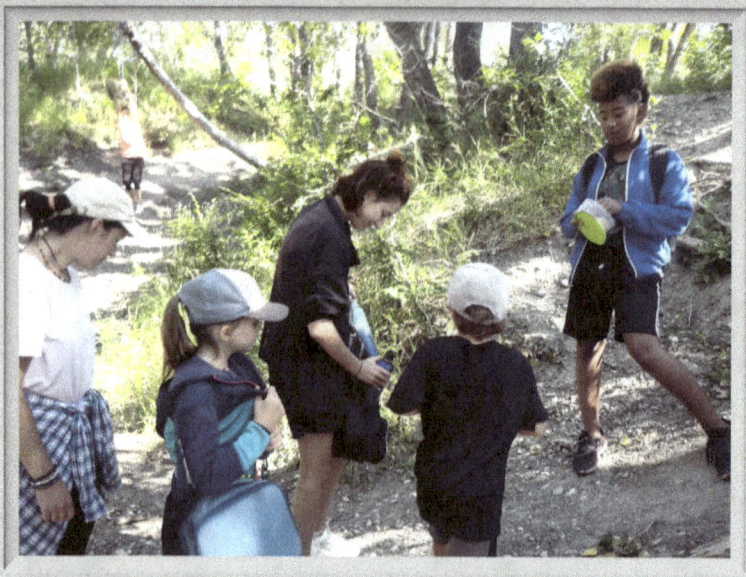
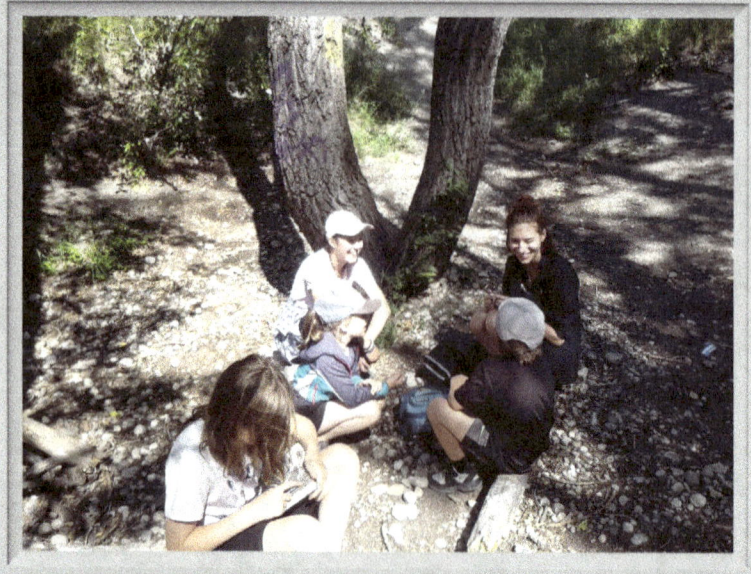

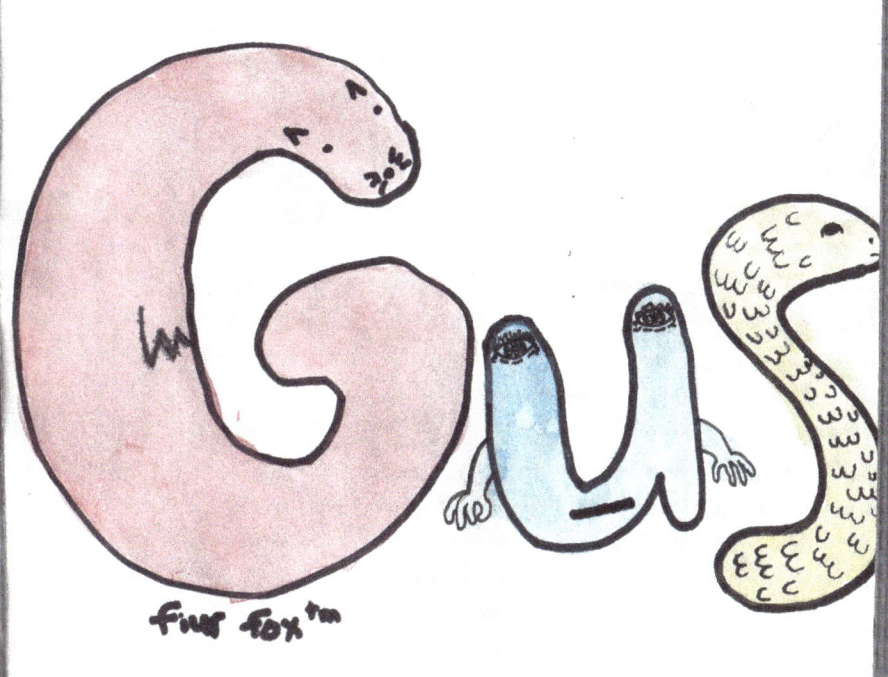

Gus

Gus was born in a city in a country in a continent on earth. he had a fish named Skippy who drown in his own pee.

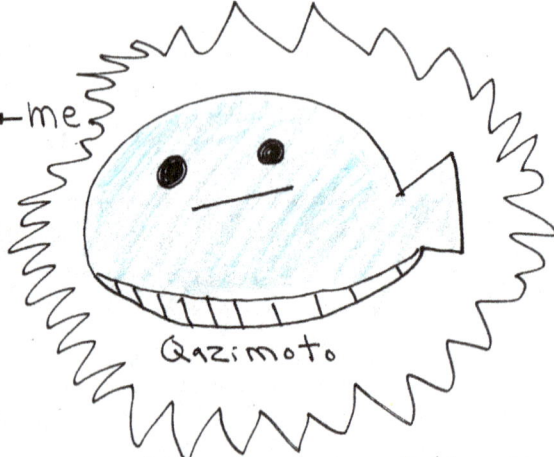
Skippy

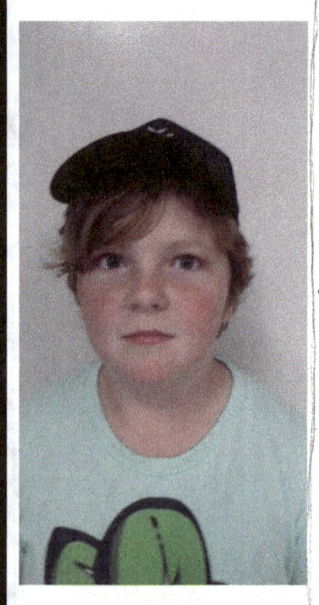
← me

Qazimoto

~~series of dogs~~ (usually my art is better then Sam's stinky this I swear)

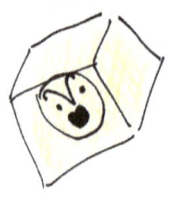

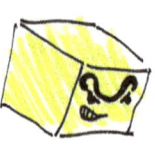

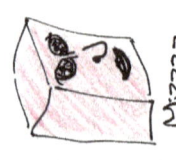
Mizzzz Box

EMPTY SPACE
(not anymore)

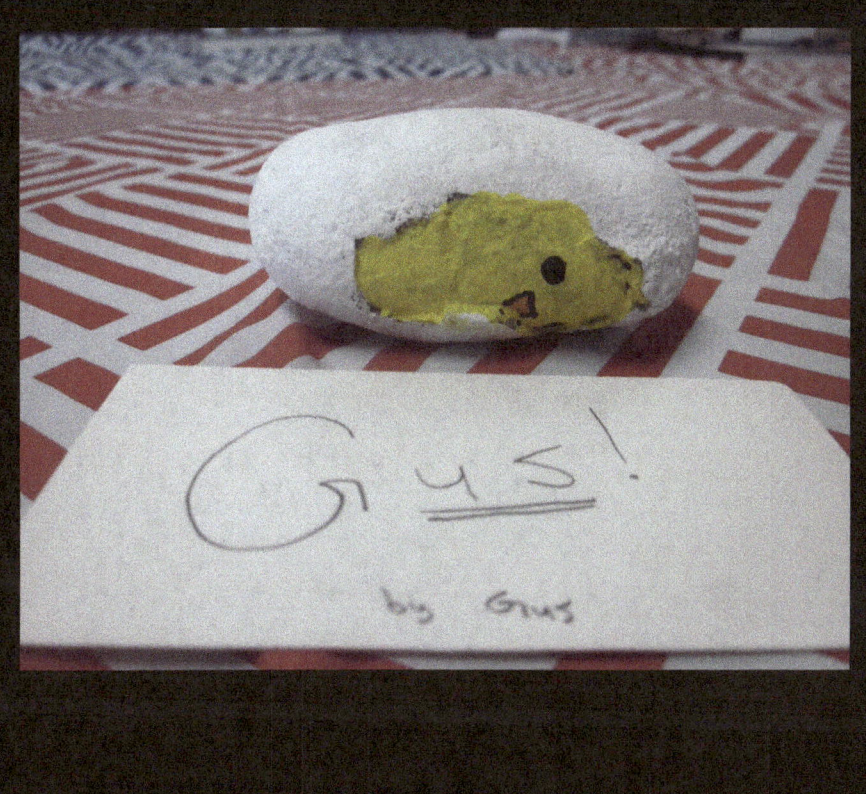

by Gus

Stream of Conciousness

Breaking News! the angry mongoose attack in South Antartica have spread global so no more Peanut Butter for your dog! And that means you Susie! So you can eat that grand piano if you like it or not! Anyways the Cheese walked the Cow to the corner Store which does have to do with the price of onions MOM! Stop shredding that nutritional granole bar! if you will pace with me and let us spill soap. the Fried egg wont stop talking!

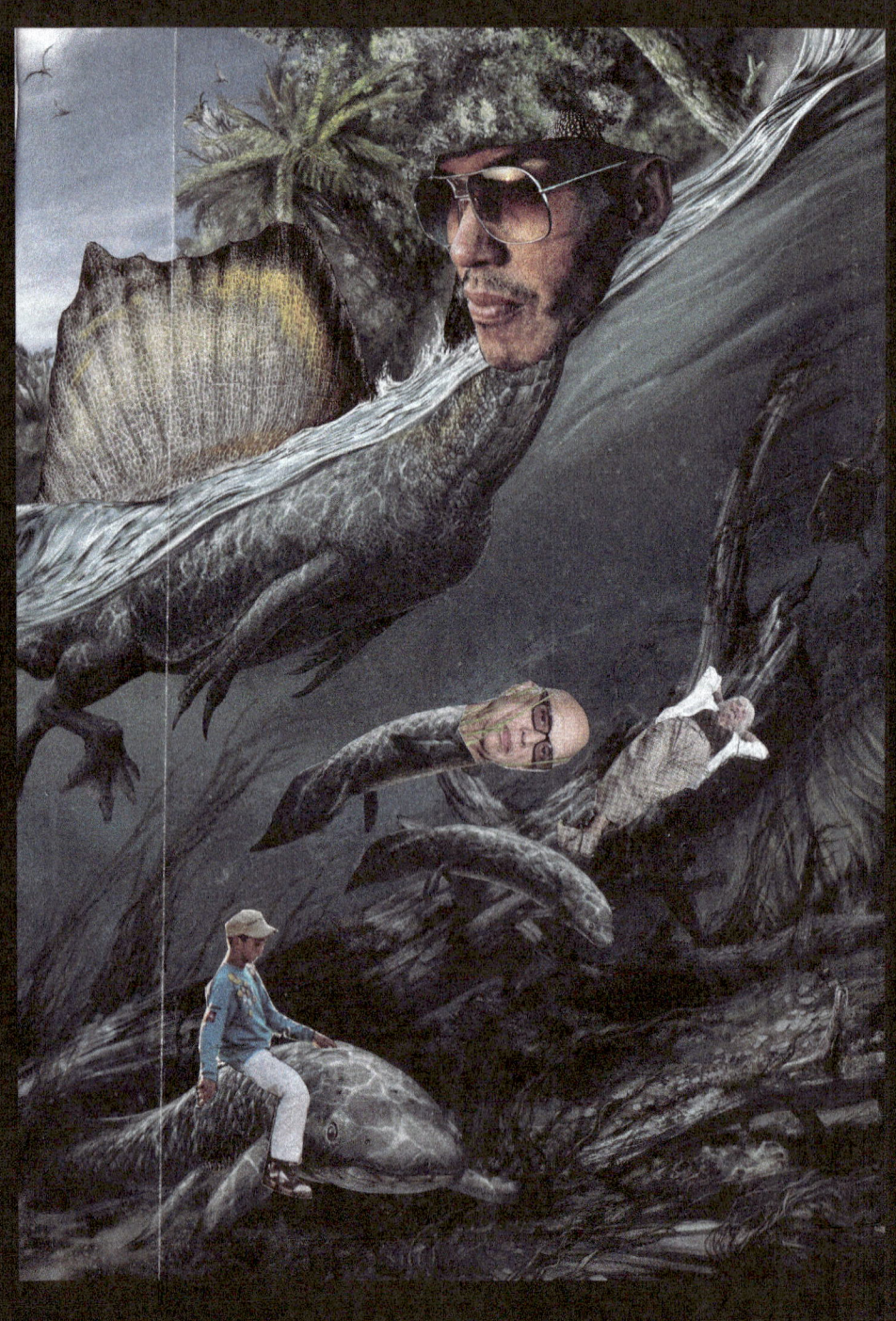

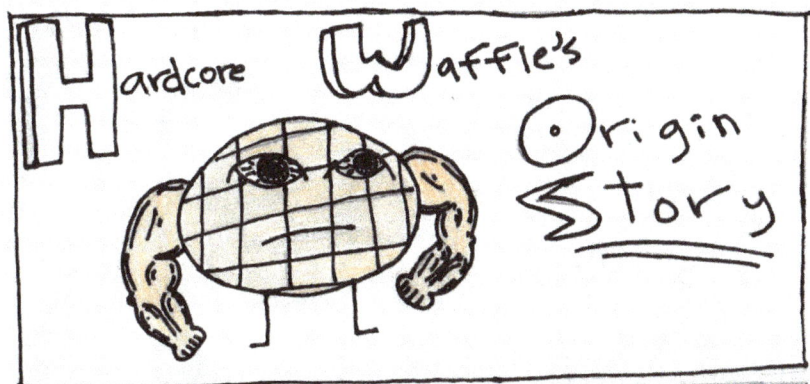
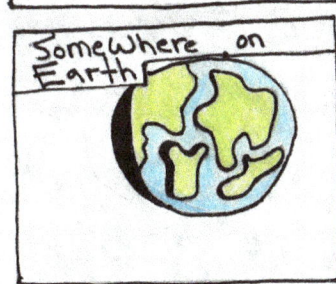
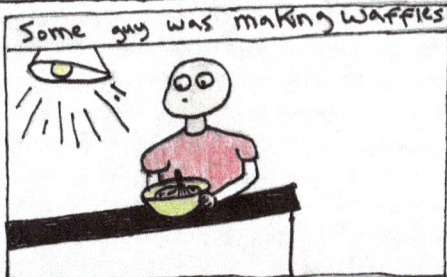
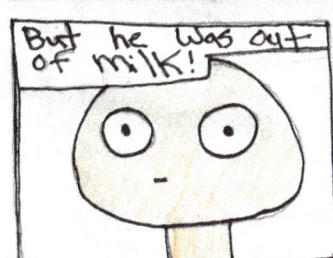
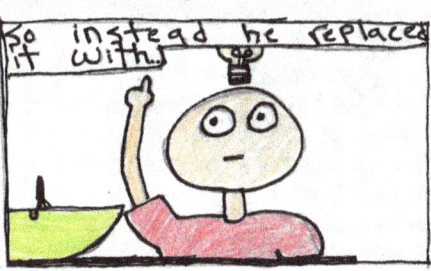

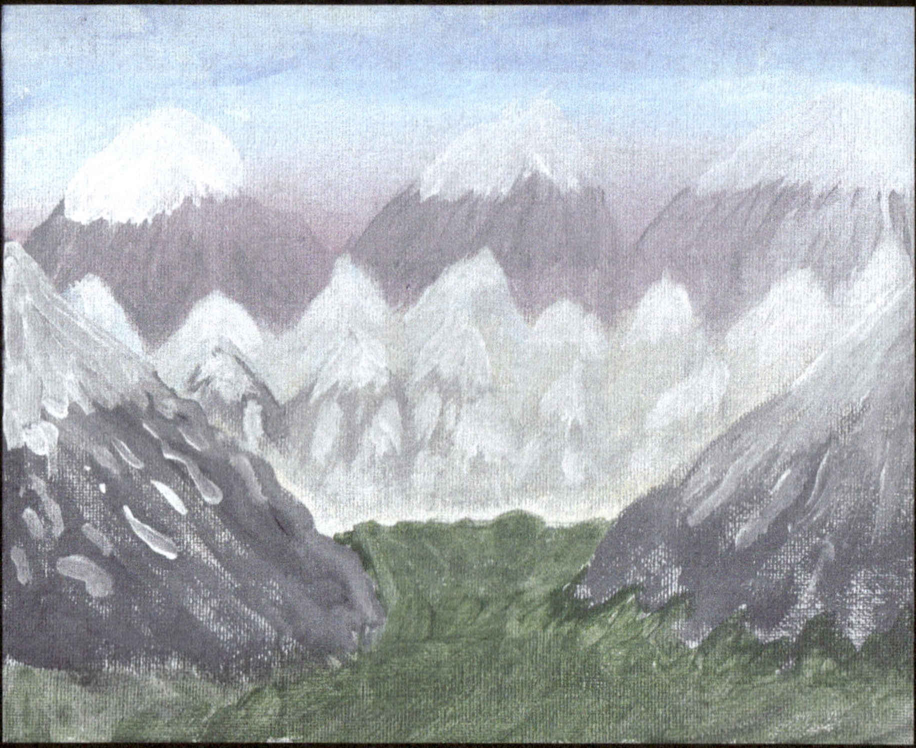

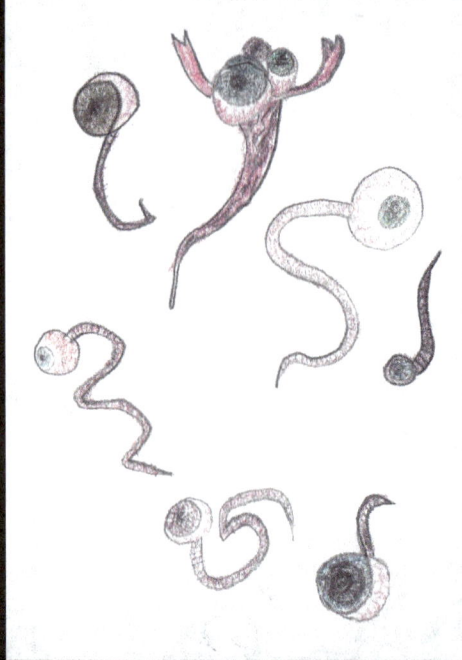

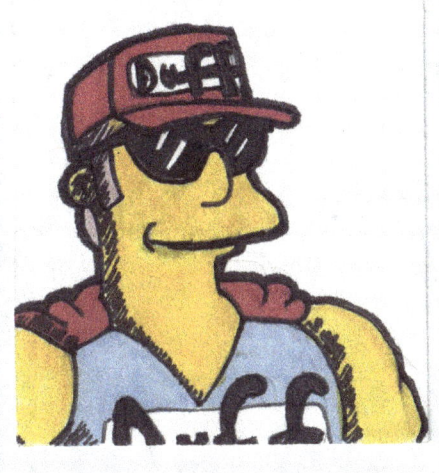
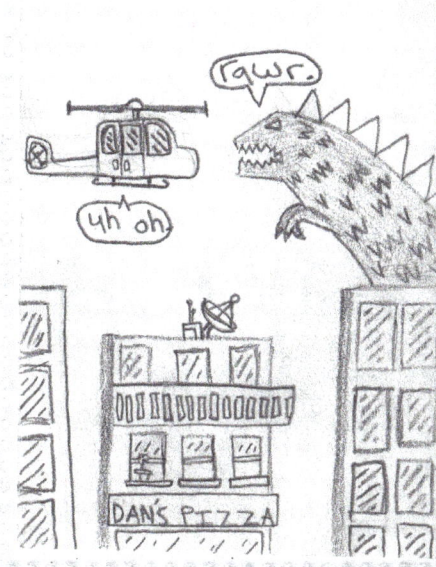
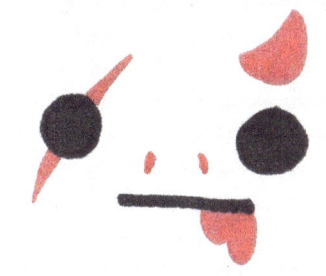
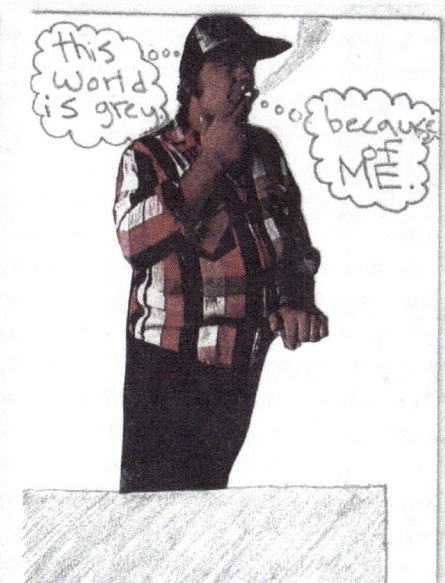

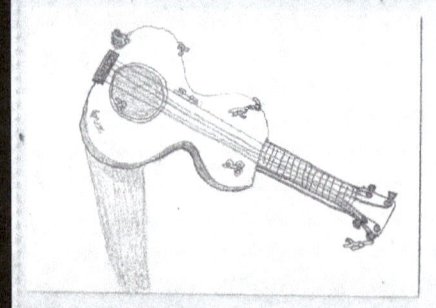
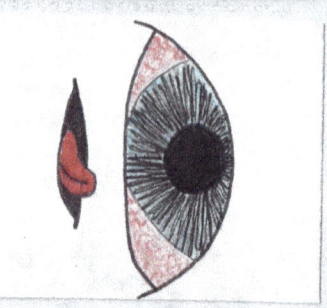
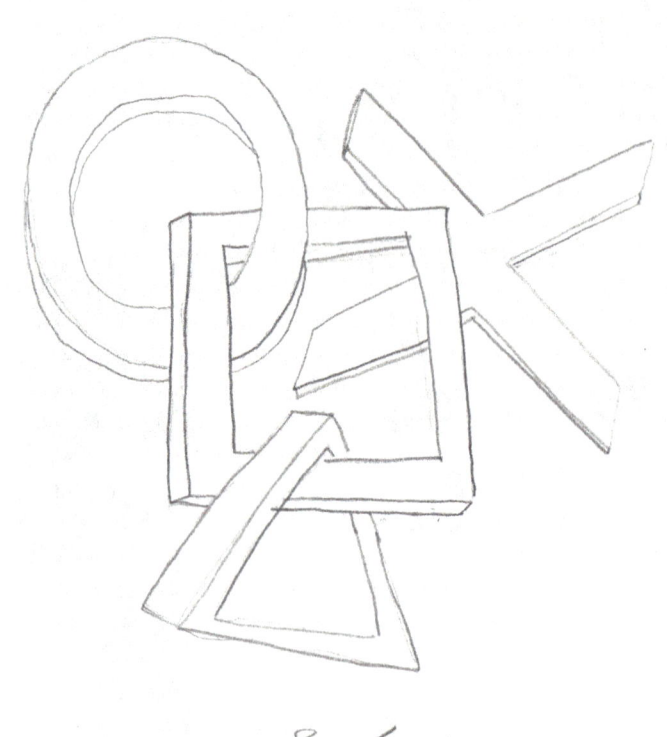

Play Station

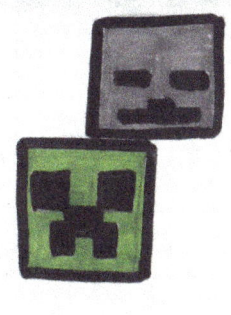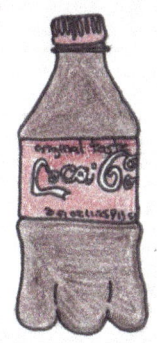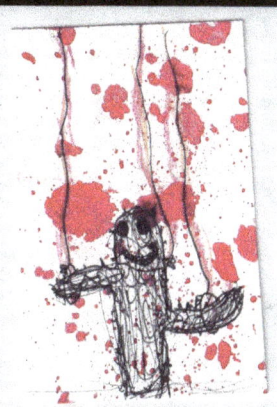
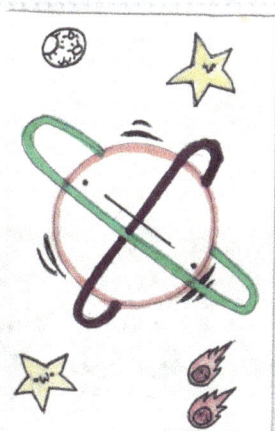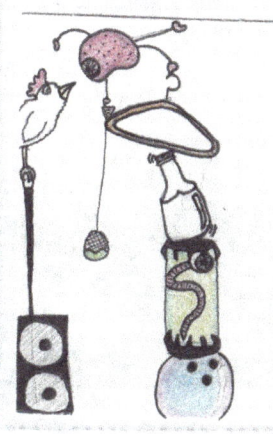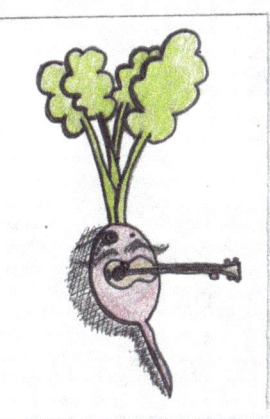
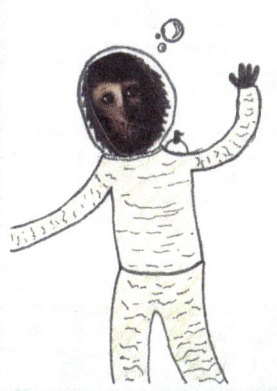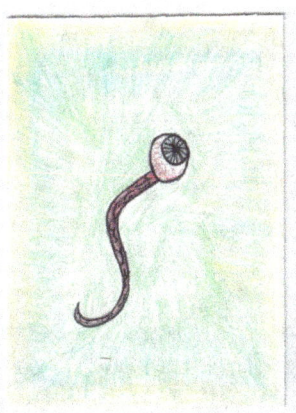

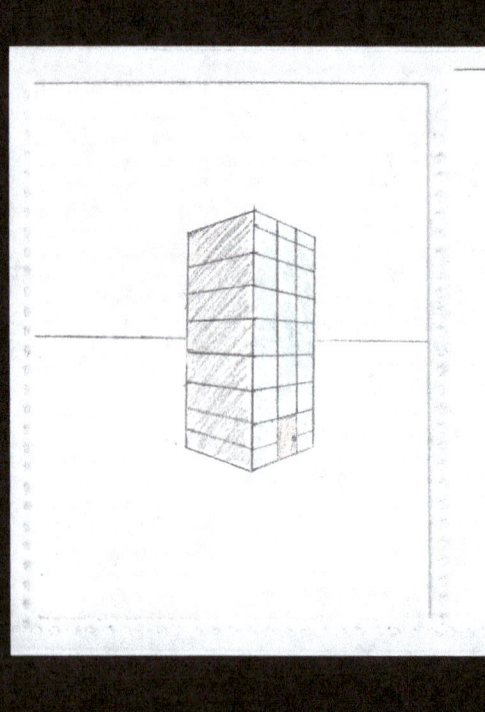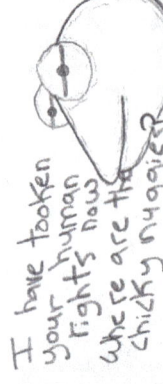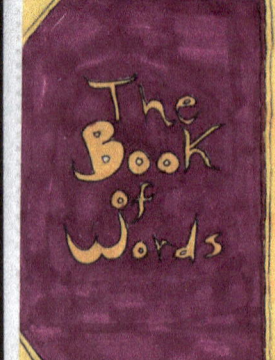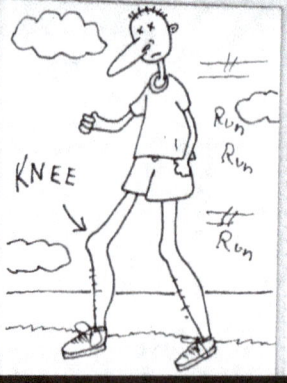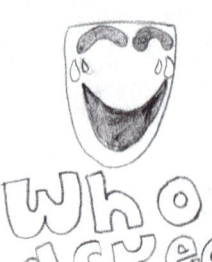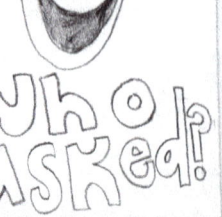

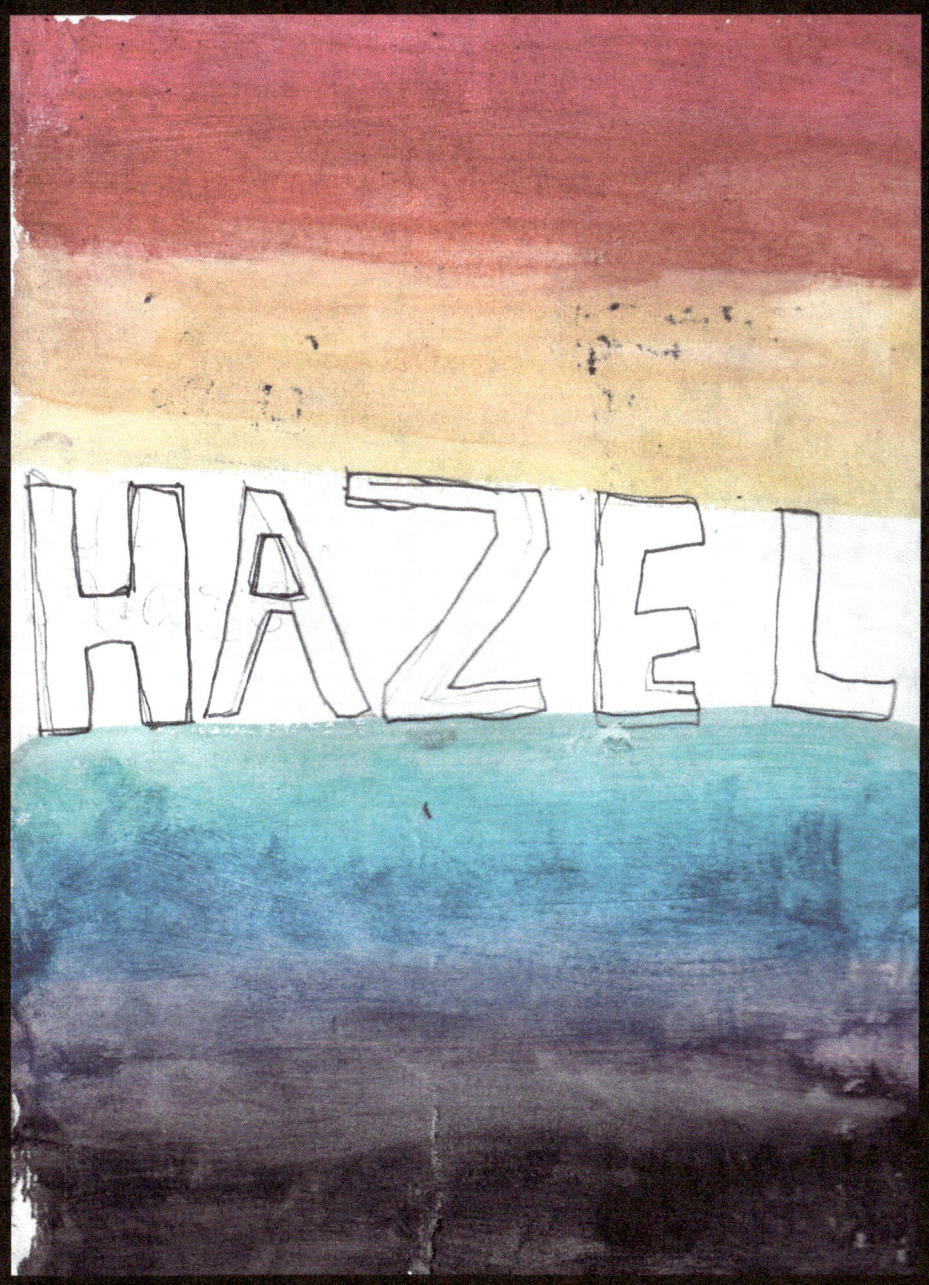

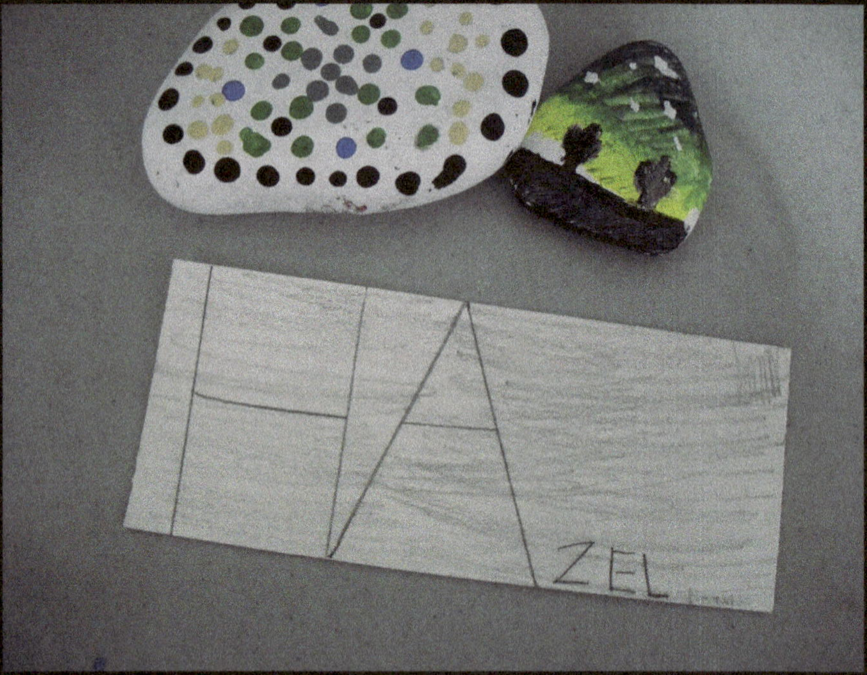

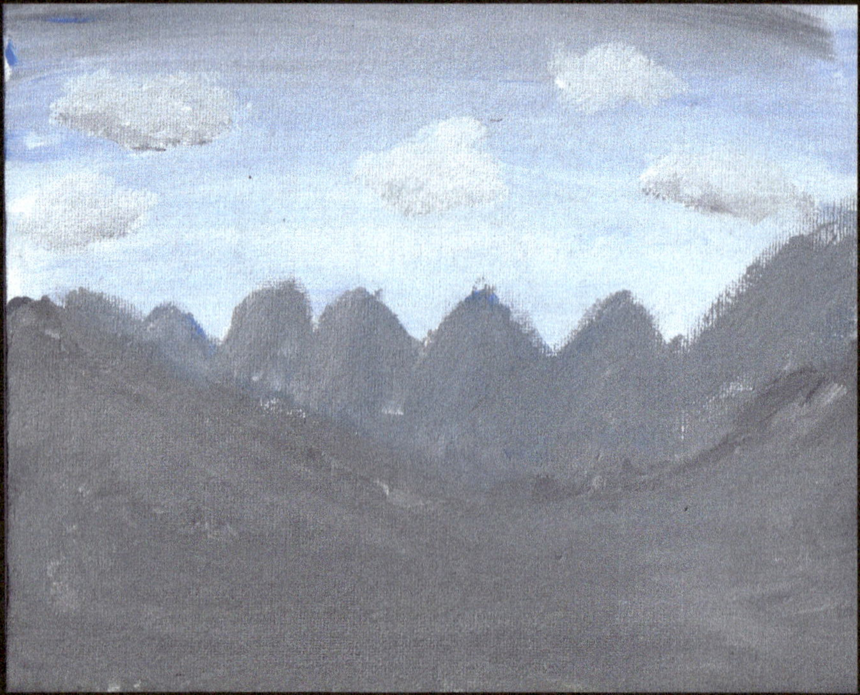

HAZEL MEYERS

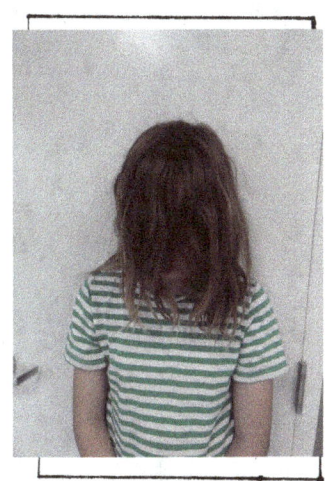

Hazel was Born on September 11 2001 in Mexiko

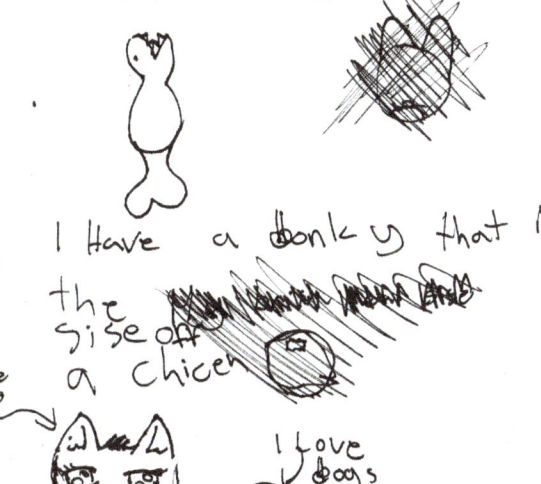

me

I Have a donkey that is the sise off a chicen

love 🐱

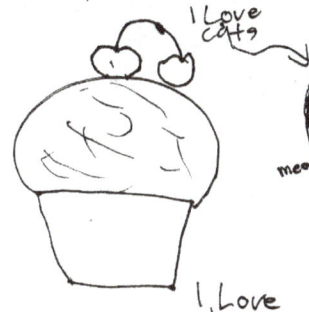

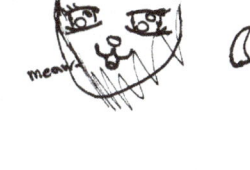
I Love cats
meow

I Love dogs

I Love Parets

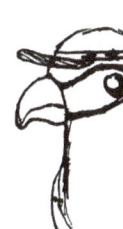

crasy Brohng

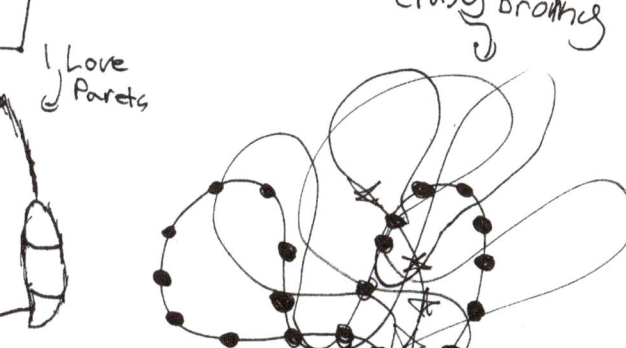

Maine Cherekler
Werks in the miletary
Has a friend that is a chear
Loves Hot dogs
His name is Joe
He gets birdnaped wile he is bing a hotdog

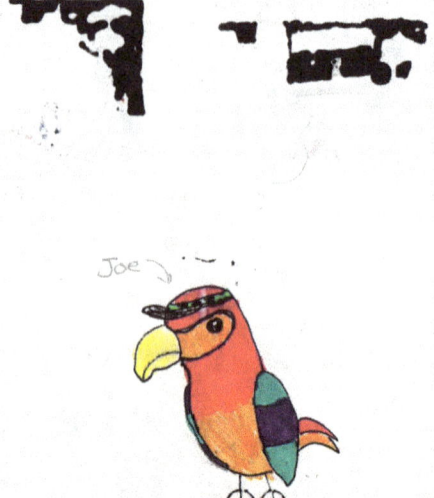

Joe

The Parrot Named Joe
By Hazel

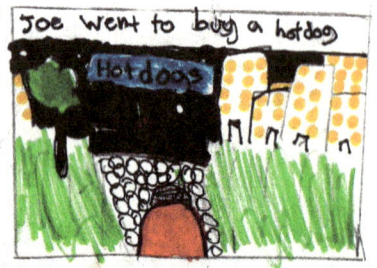

Joe went to buy a hotdog

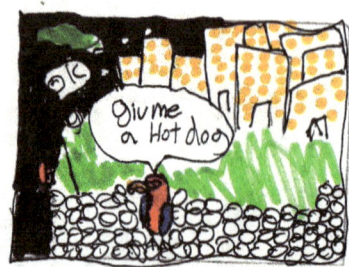

giv me a Hot dog

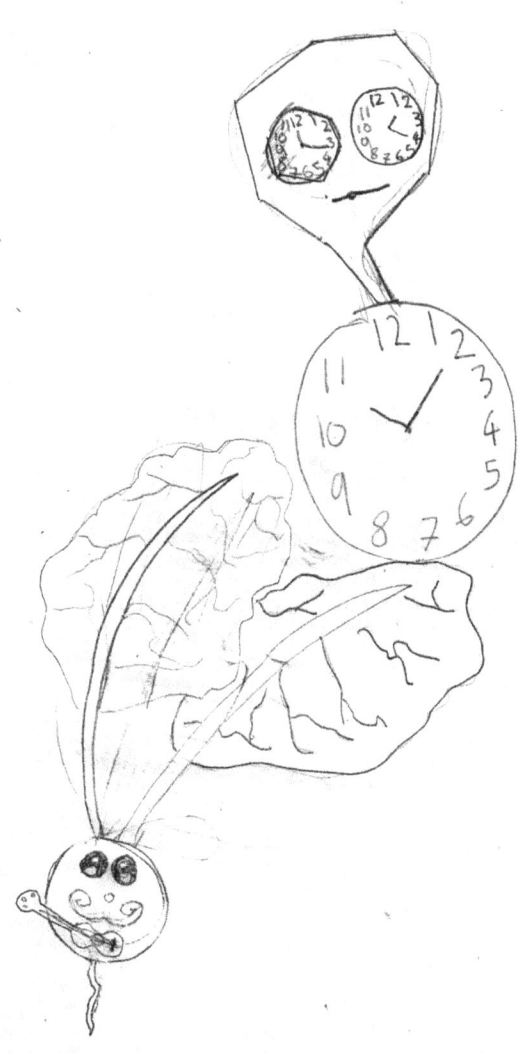

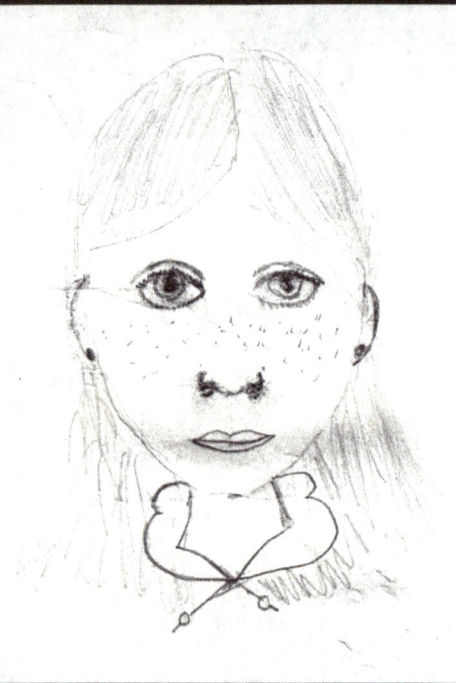
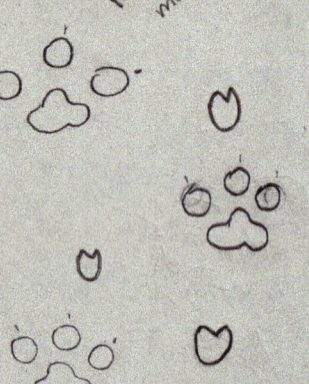
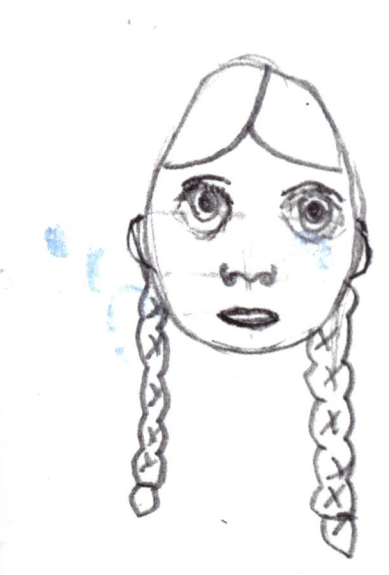

a moncy ran a farm on a ice berg the cow loved to dans on the beach so the reptiles came and tride to destroy the Happy times so the moncy thaut ond a darber shop camed to save the day so the chicin went to the reptiles and said i will difeat you withe this ball of varn so the cat came ifront of the reptiles and said welkem to the ice berg of destiny

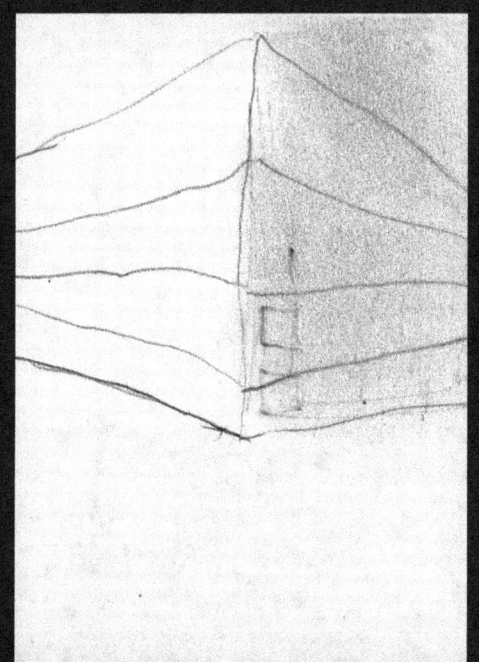

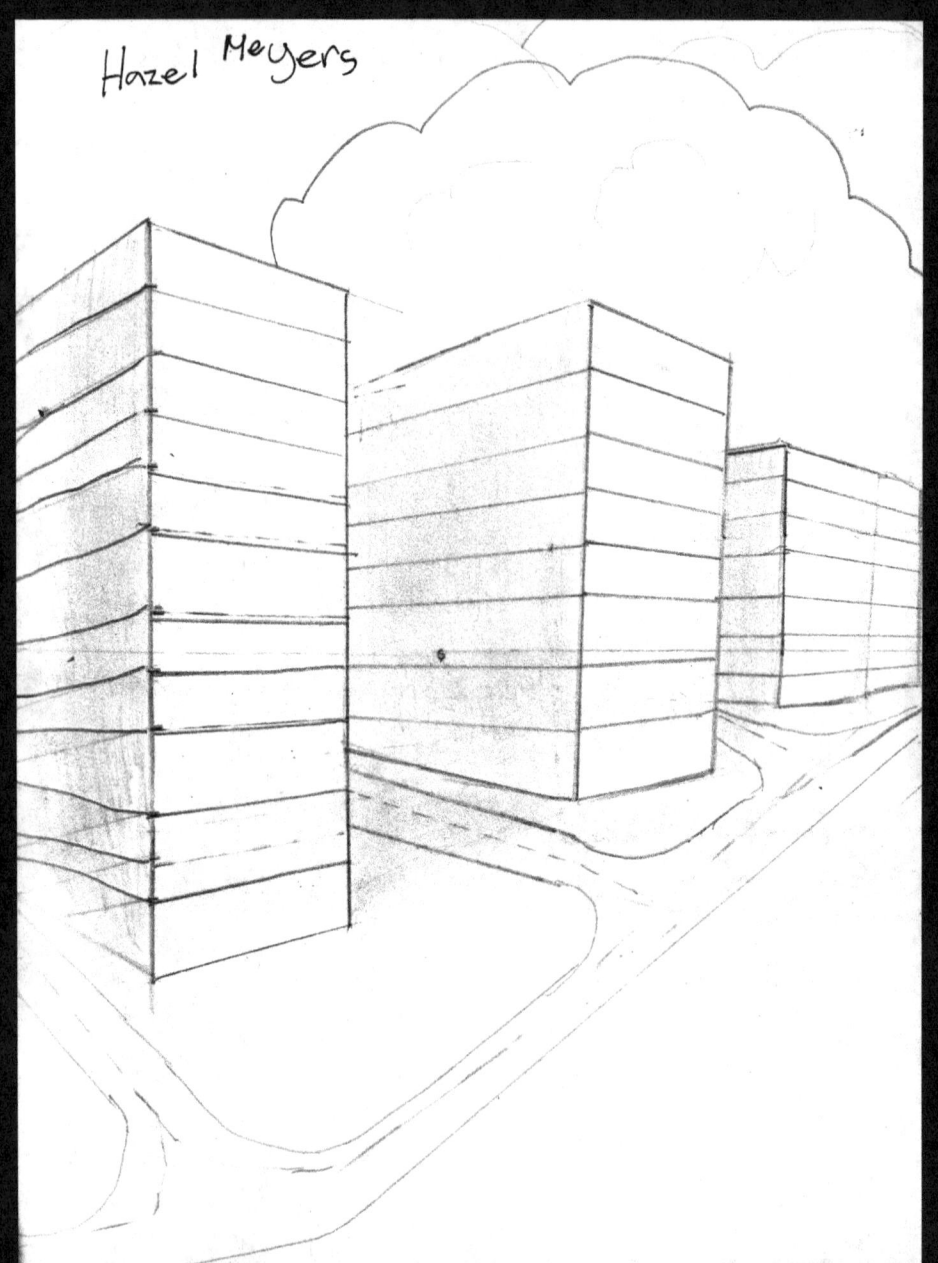

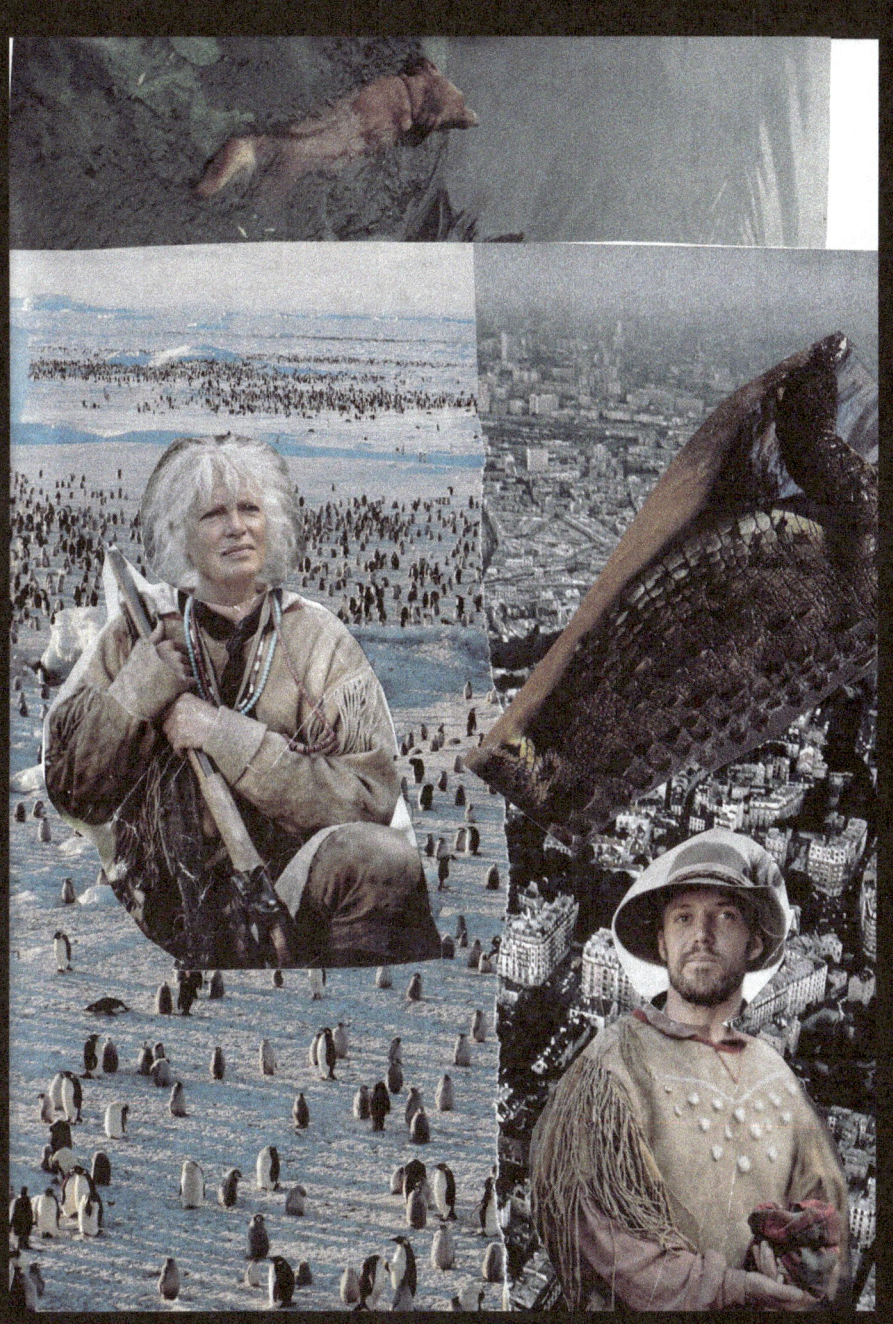

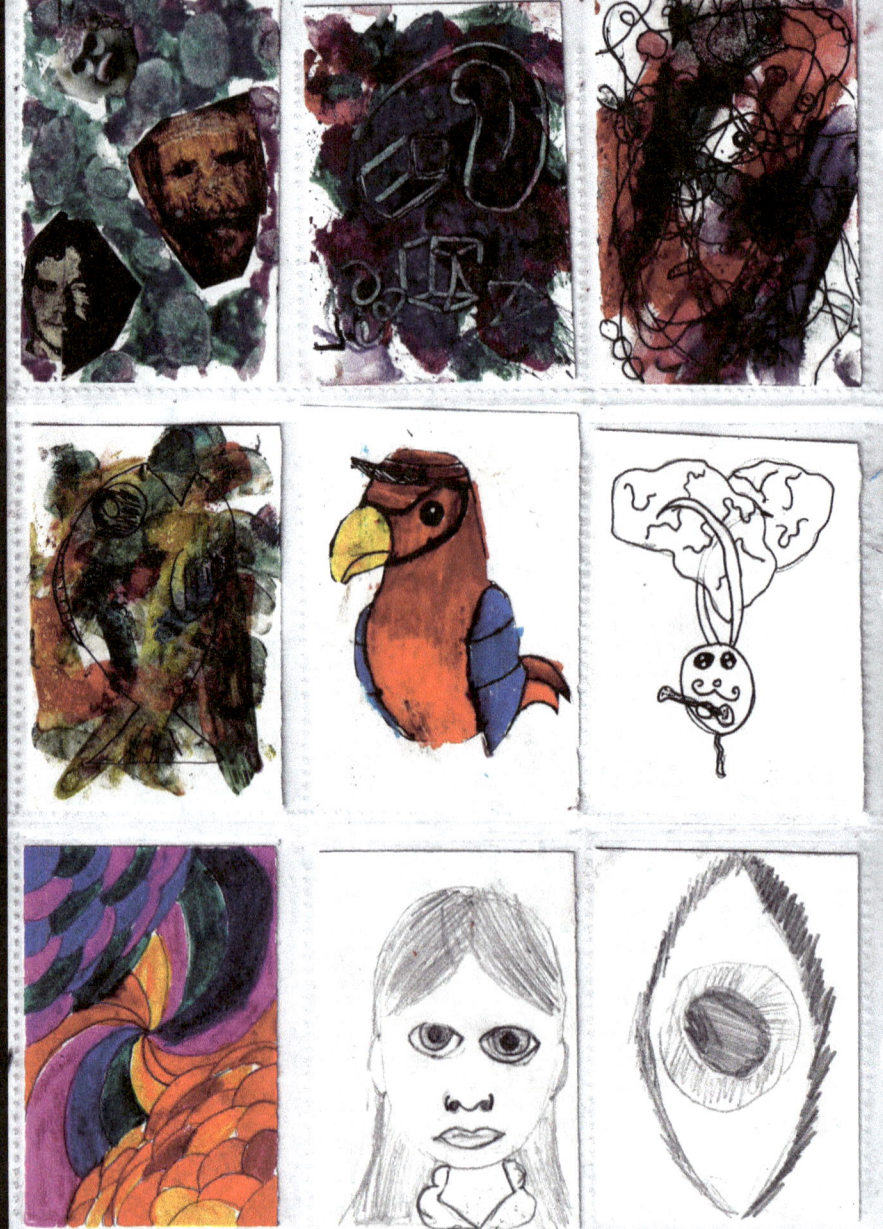

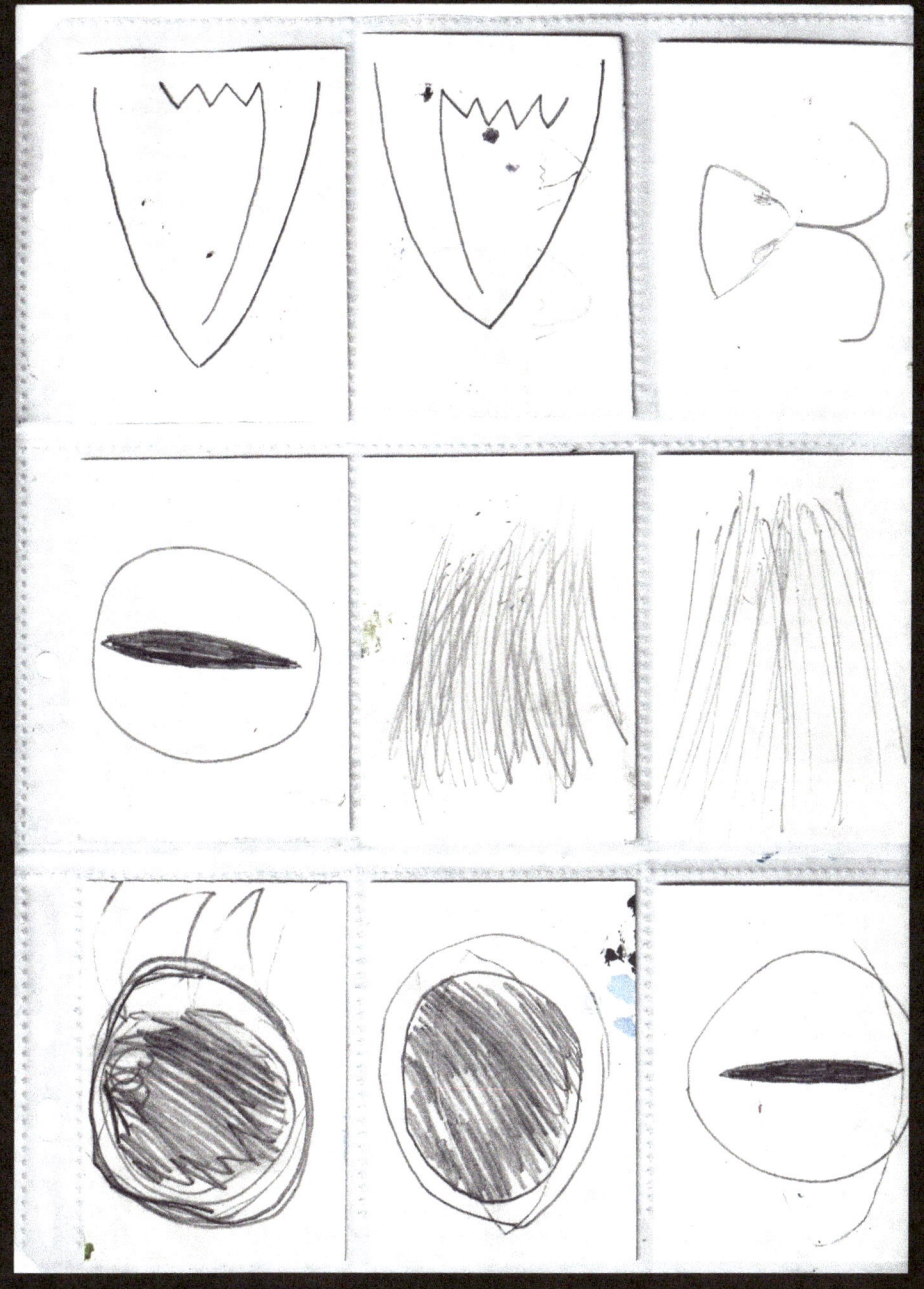

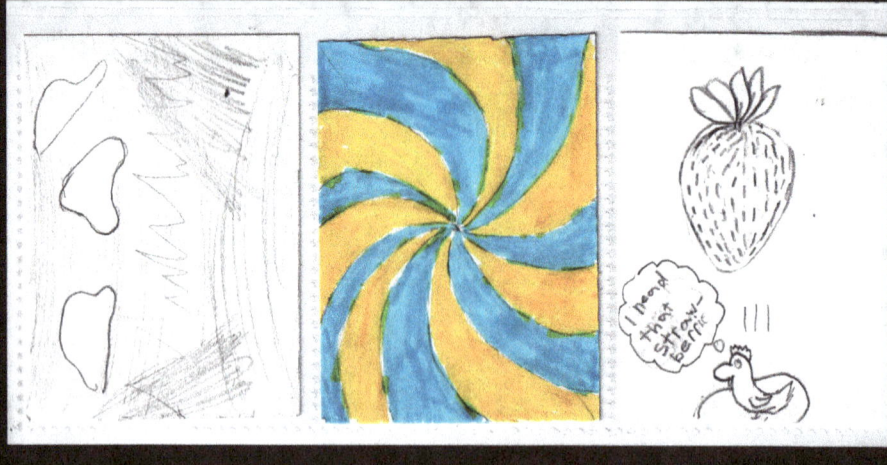
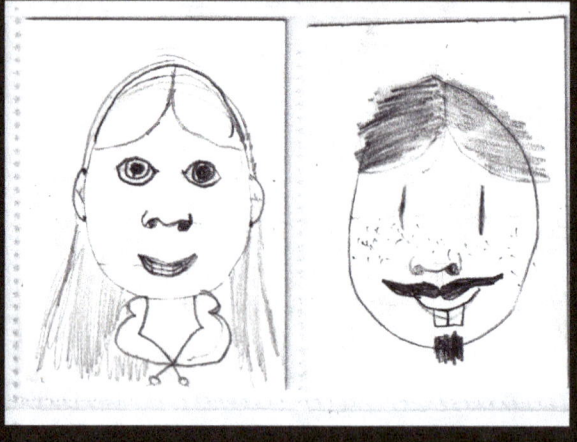
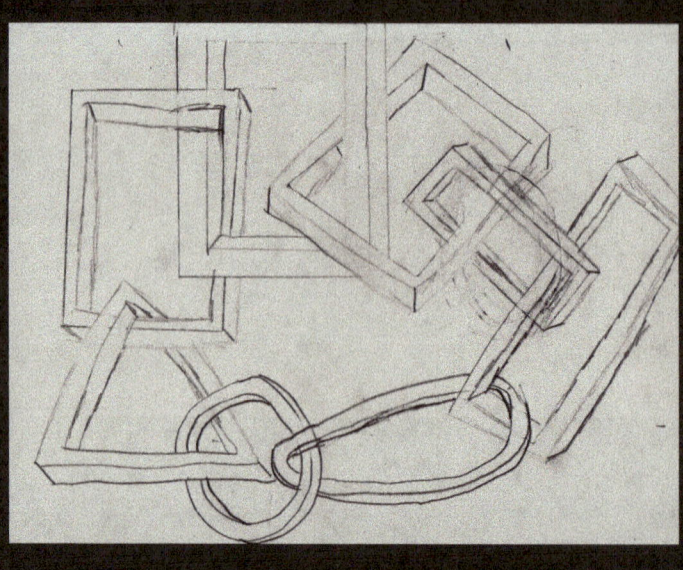

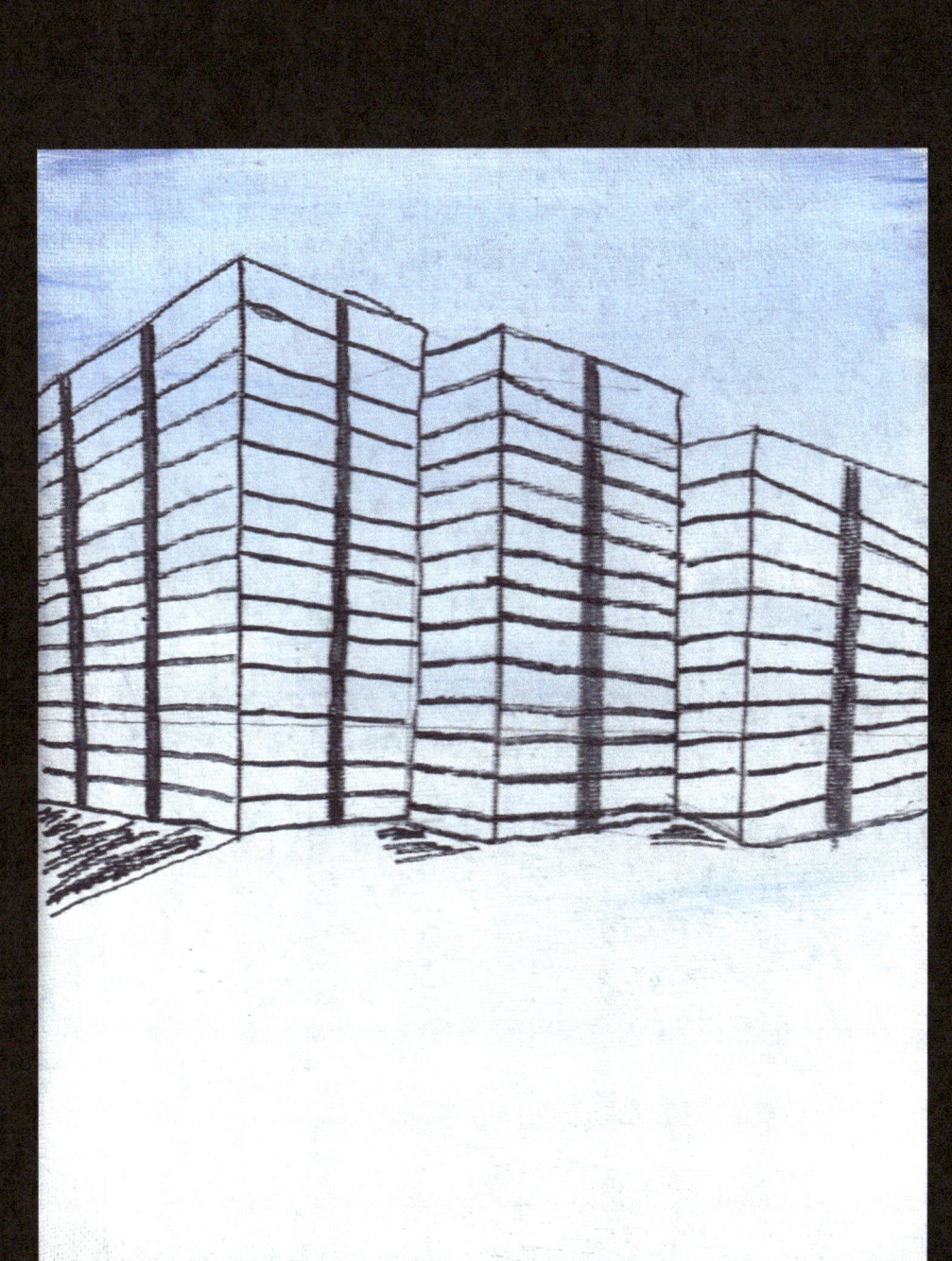

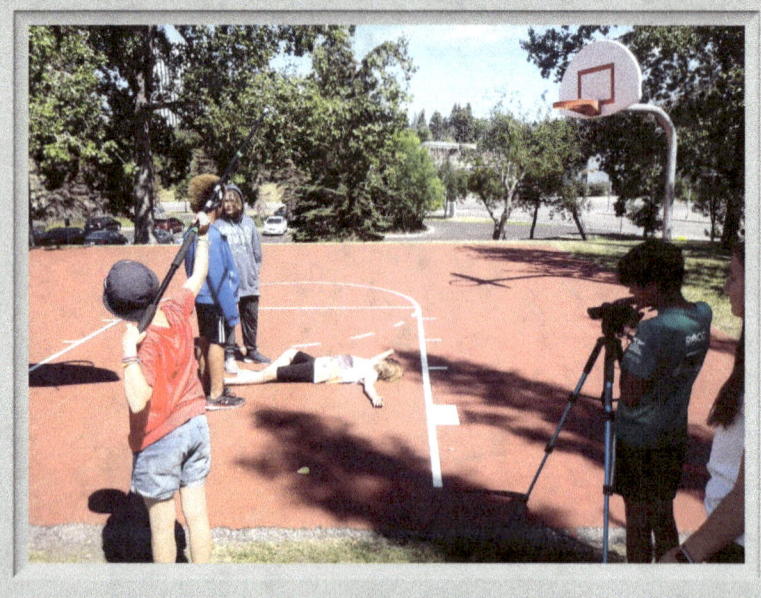
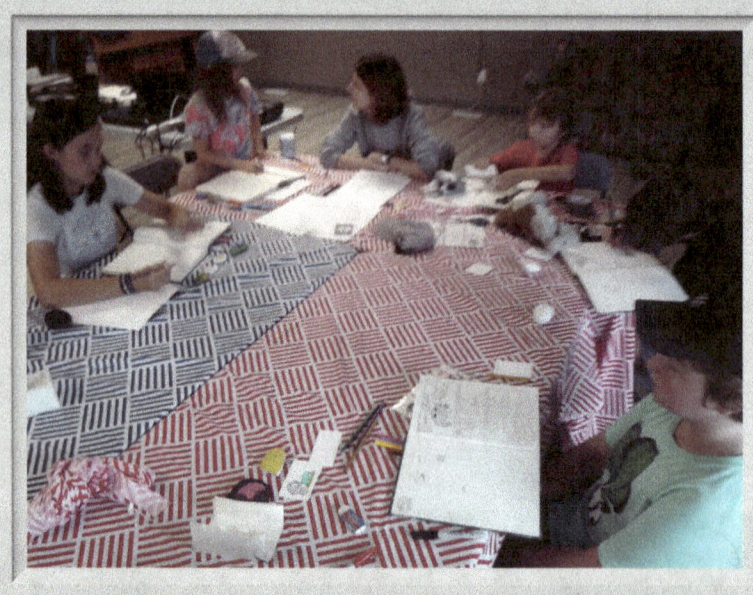

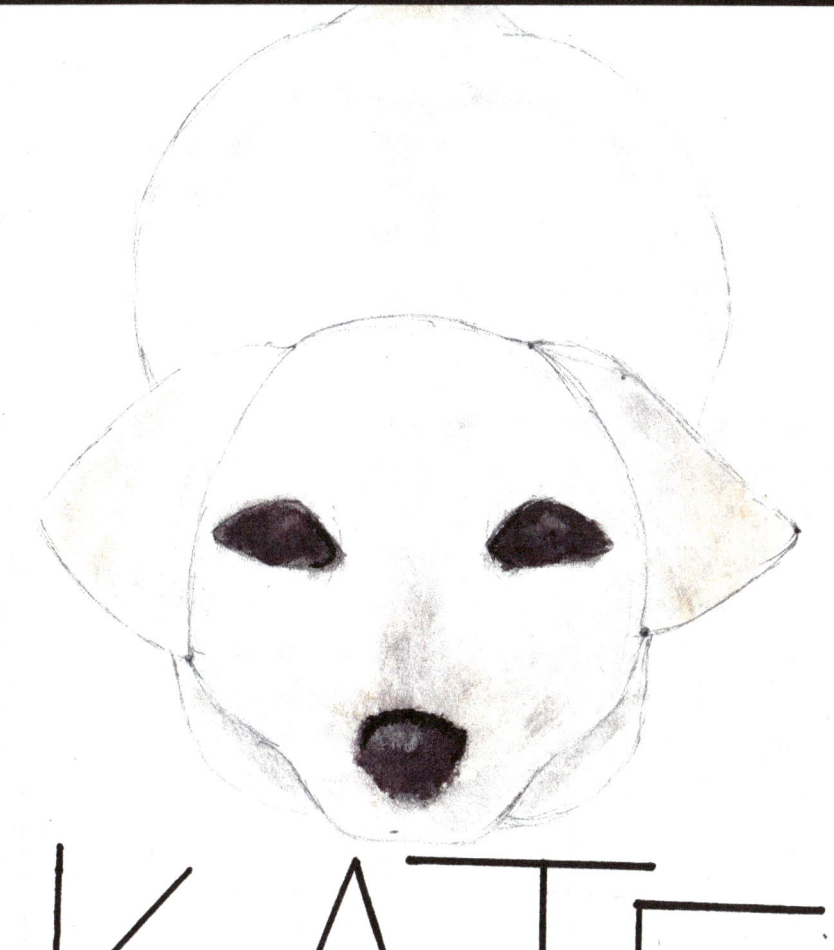

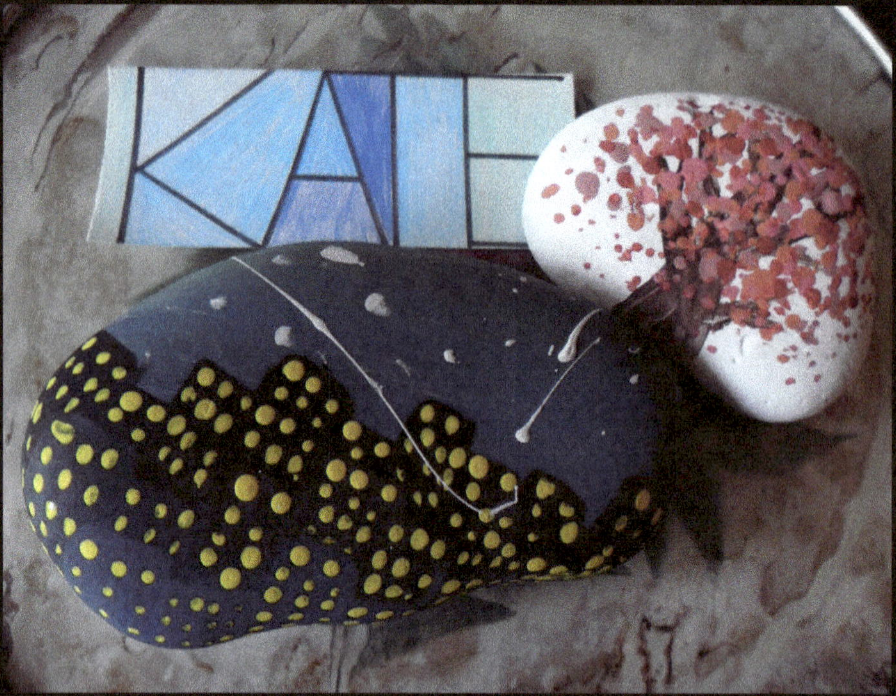

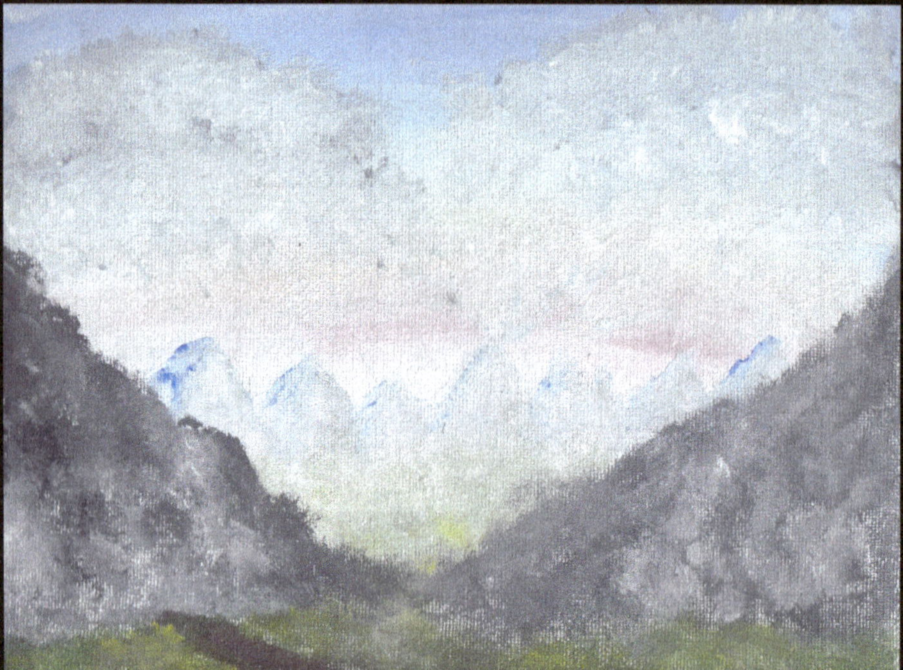

KATE

This is a page about this girl→ her name is Kate. but she is currently busy running away from her friends so I have to write this for her. Some of her friends call her Kaurah. the other one calls her a tiny child even though she is 5,4 apparently. She says she's 12 but I don't belive that.
Shes the most expierenced person in obsessing over her dog...
"Shes just a baby!"· · · · · · · ·
No shes not shes 5 years old.
She also rides horses but thats not important.
She likes art thats why shes at a art camp. Kate does digital and non digital art.
Another thing you should know is she is Always watching!...
Oh wait got to go shes coming back byeeeeer.

Rose bud!!

Main Character(s)

Name: Rosebud

Description: Rosebud is a cute dog that has absolutly no logic. she has lots of energy. but trips on everything.

Backround info: She was a birthday gift to her owner.

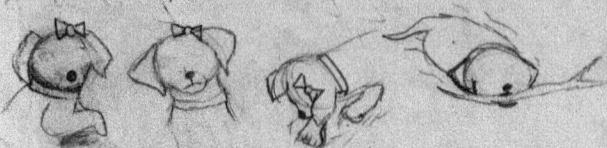

Supporting role(s)

Name: Izzy
Description: a more skidish homeless dog that is scared of everything but tries to act brave.

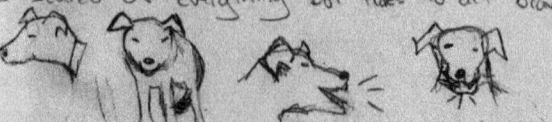

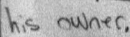
Name: Max
Description: Max is a city dog and loves his owner.

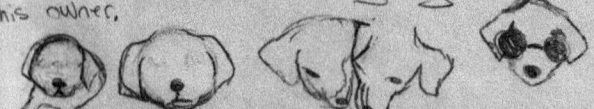

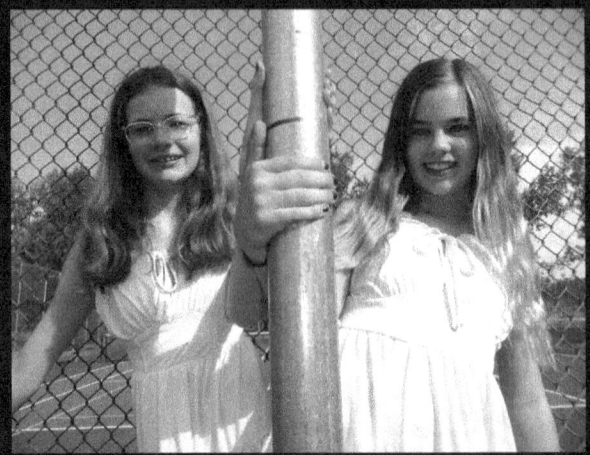

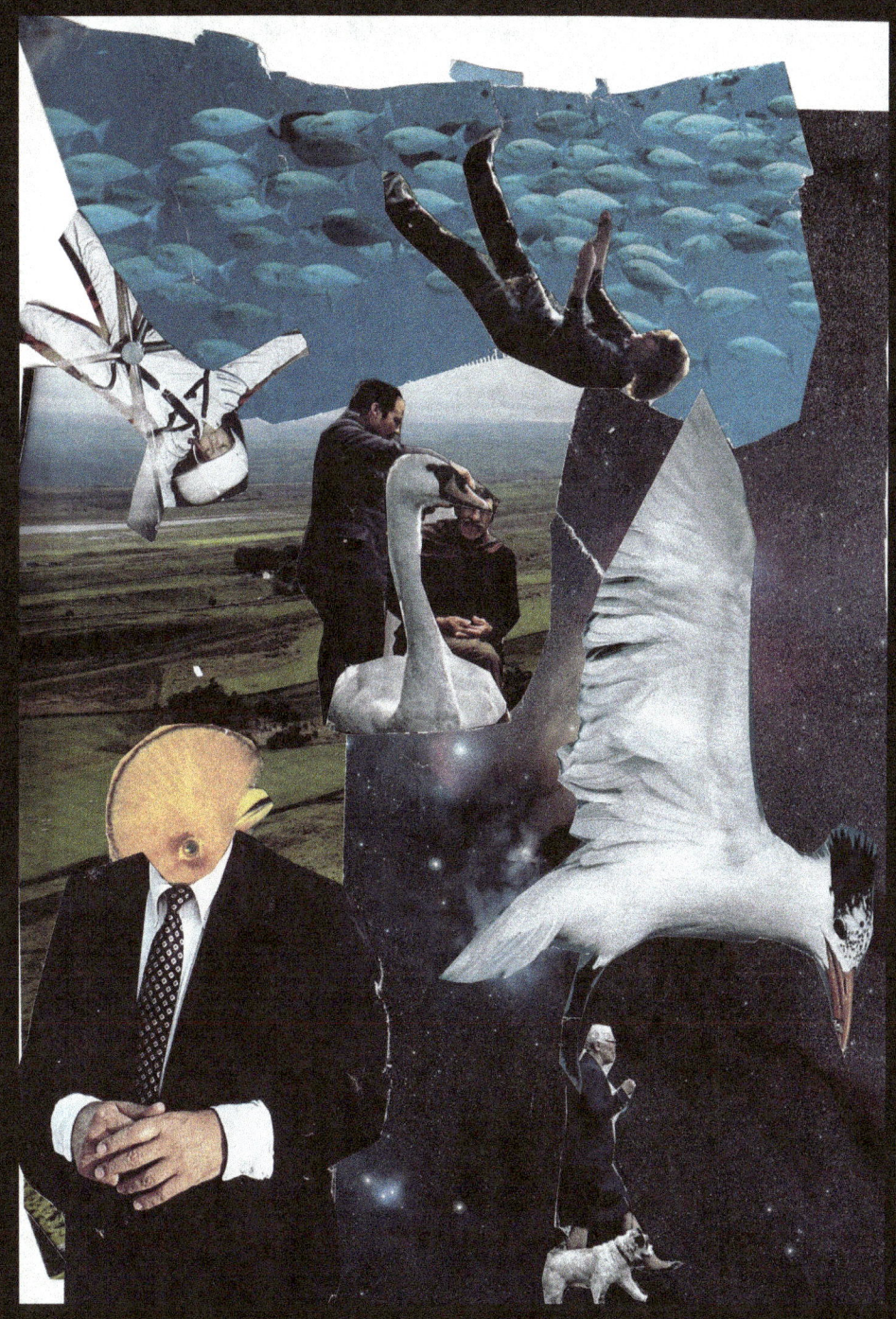

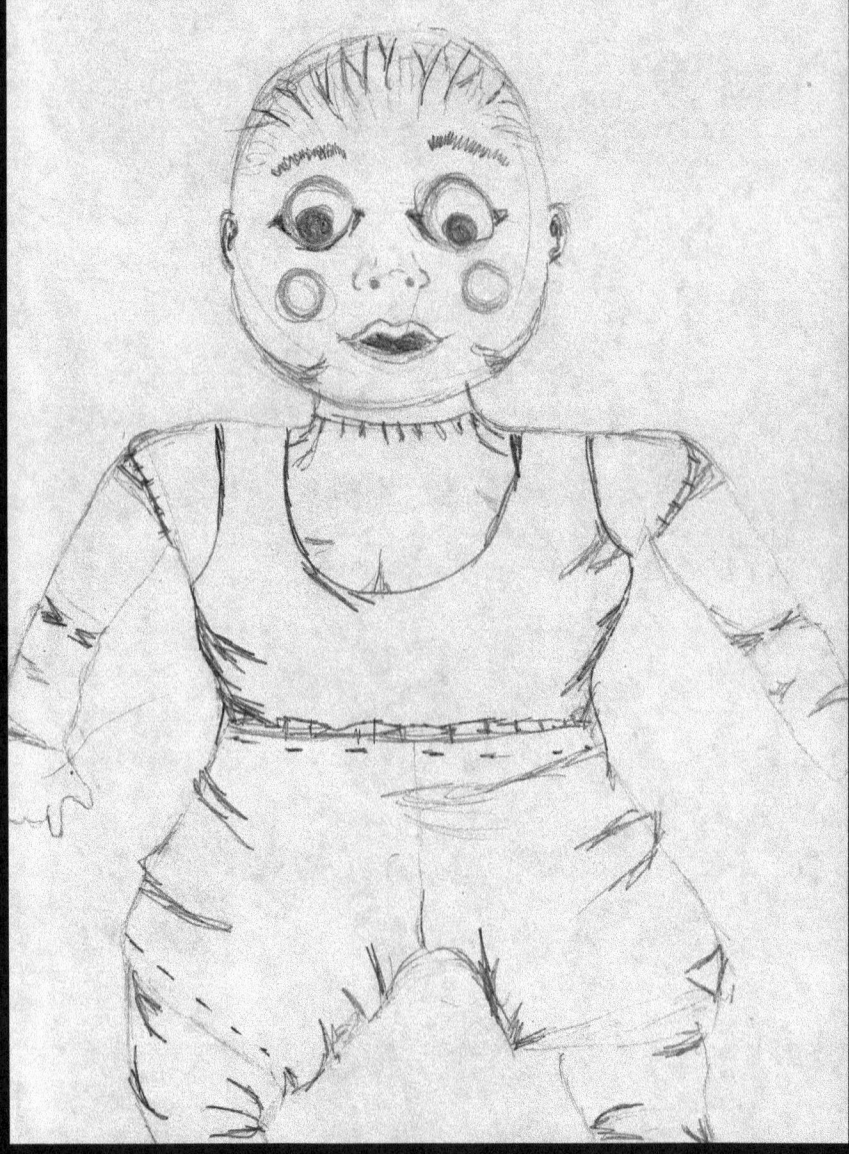

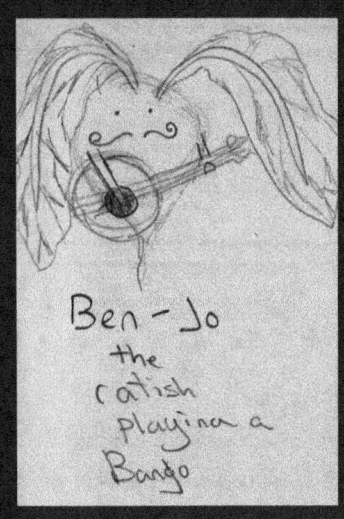

Ben-Jo
the
catish
playing a
Banjo

once...
a bannana let go of Rhiannon and the hot dog ate linda. what phone is a pencil drawn hazel. weird looking at me rock ant is a compoter. drop! is droping every were. my hand is going to hurt after linda dies she is creepy music I cant spell anything when I creepping through a ally way. help me! planes are falling over me like a bird. EXit sarah said and cracked her hands, glasses are wepins intence music starts! linda is a Phane pencil, shirts are blue parrots. hoodie! why the sweater! Max wants to die. NO Nametage! said Sarah and then the music changed.

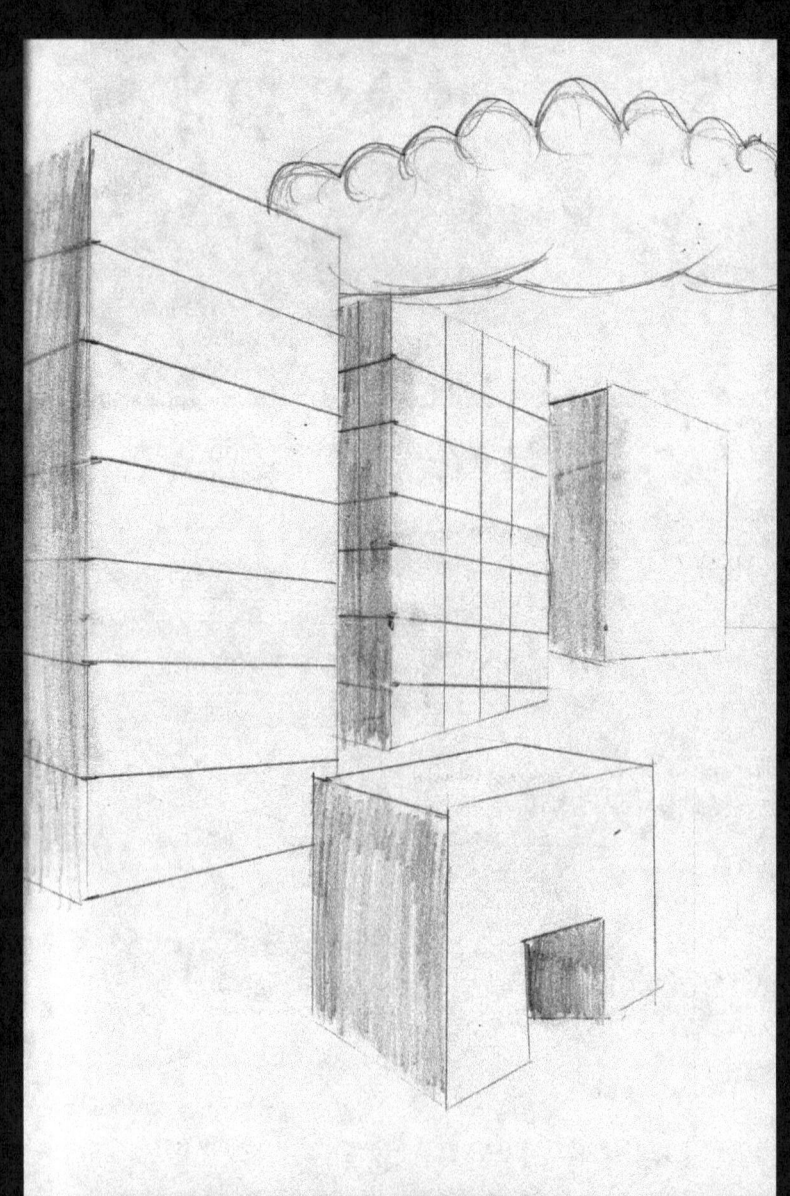

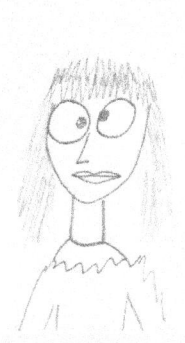
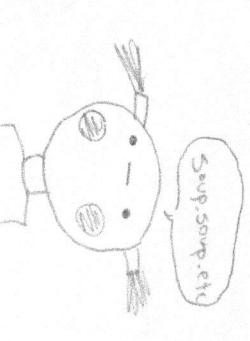
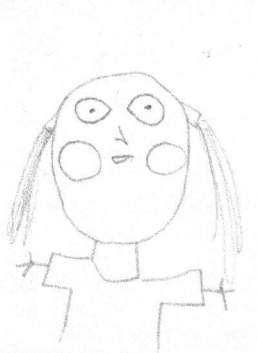
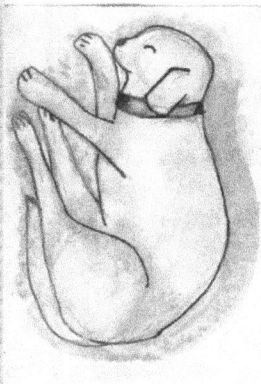
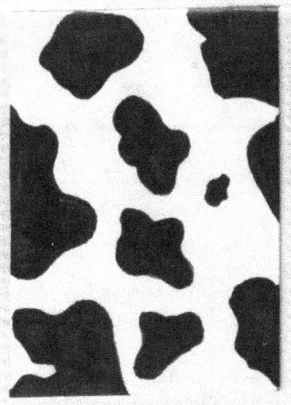
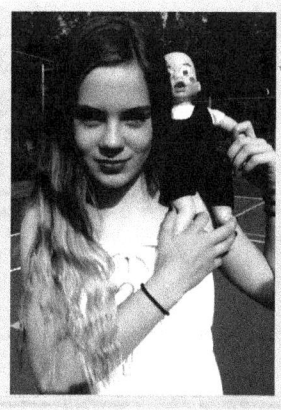
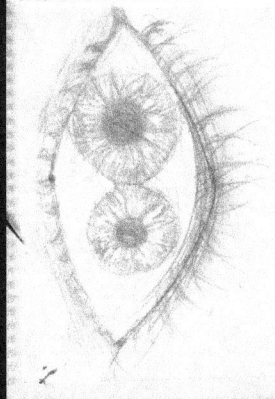
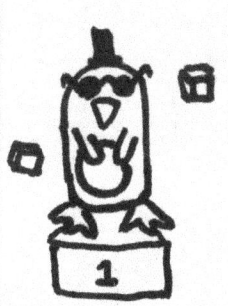
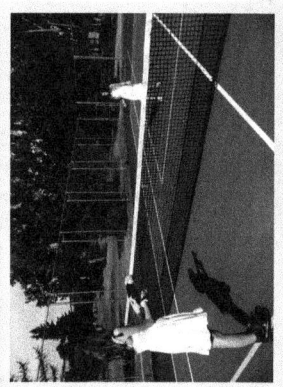

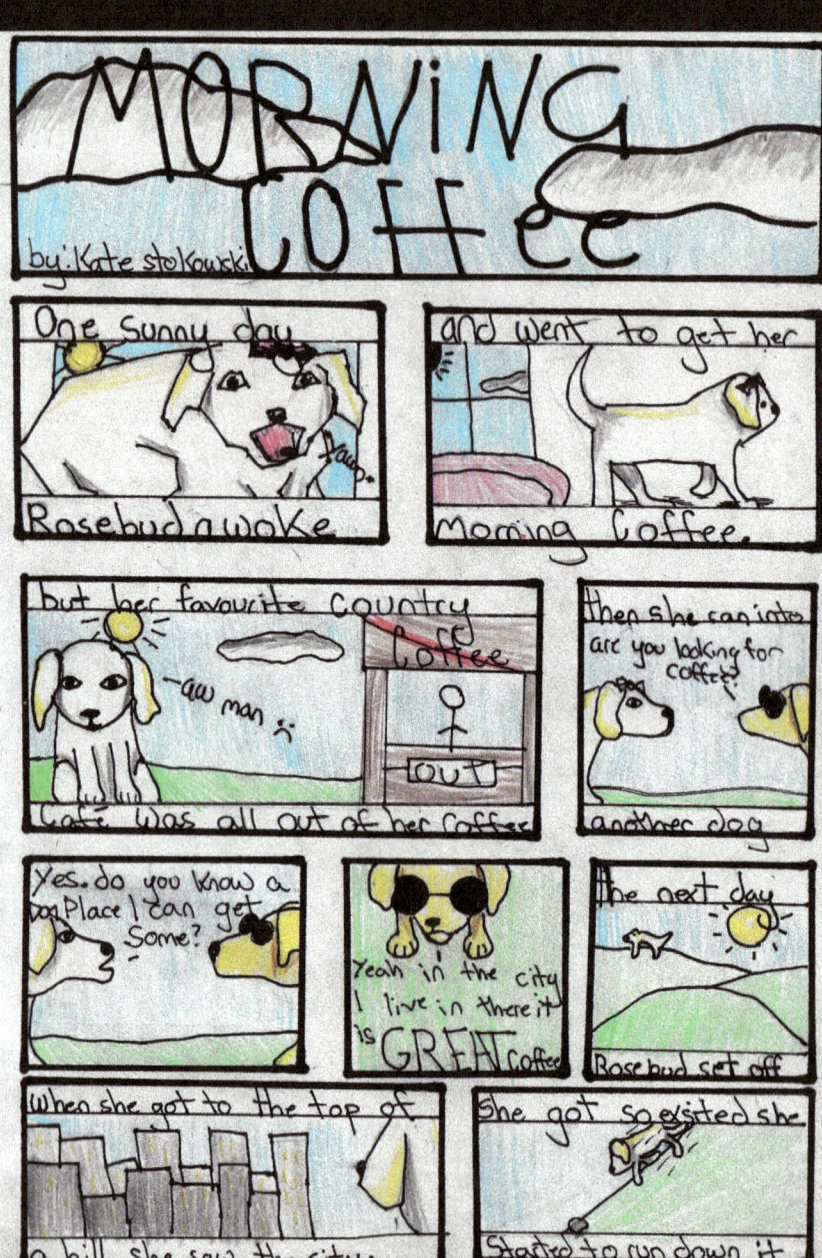

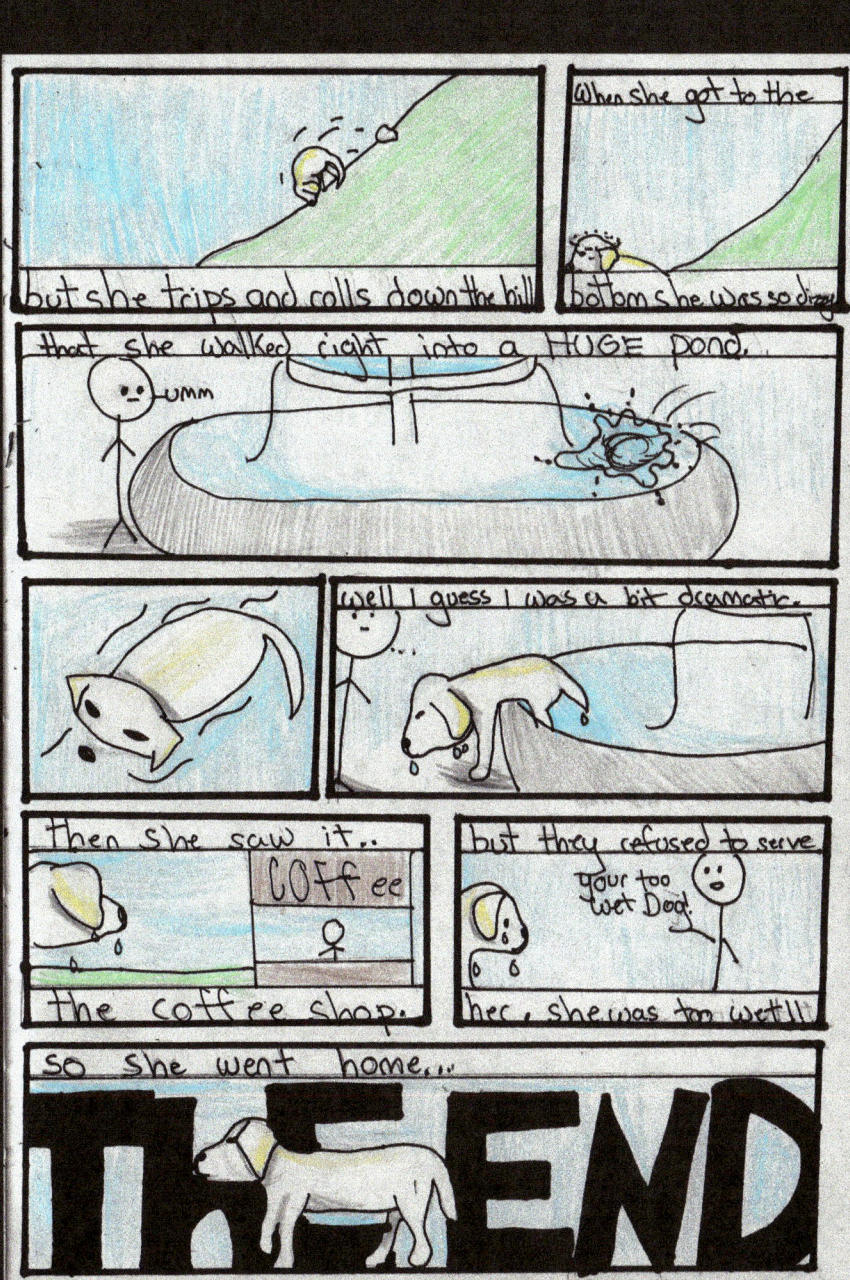

Chicken Wings
A collaborative story by Arty-Pants

Once upon a time in a land far far away, there was a boy named Hairy. He lived in an iceberg, and he dropped his hamster down a shredder! Hairy said "Oh no! I need a new hamster!" But instead of a hamster he got a chicken and named him Evergreen. But then at midnight Hairy made a cake and Evergreen ate it. So then Hairy brought the chicken to the hospital to make sure they were okay. On the way to the hospital Hairy dropped Evergreen out the car window. "Oh no! I dropped Evergreen out the window! I should go check to see if he is alive!"
And Hairy could not find him. All of a sudden Hairy got killed by a killer peanut! One day an old man named Johnathan came across a chicken named Evergreen. He said "Wow! What a lovely chicken! It would make a lovely dinner for me and my wife!"

So Evergreen heard this crime and ran like the wind away. The chicken gained powers and started flying! He found a stray cat and drop kicked it! "I am all powerful!" Said Evergreen. So he like invited all his chicken friends to an epic party. "Come on in! That party hasn't even started yet!" There was a killer cat dressed as a chicken! He thought another chicken looked like Evergreen and killed them instead. Evergreen was very confused but still complimented the cat's costume. Evergreen just didn't know what to do. Apparently a super peanut came! Suddenly Hairy's ghost came and crushed them all to death!

THE END!

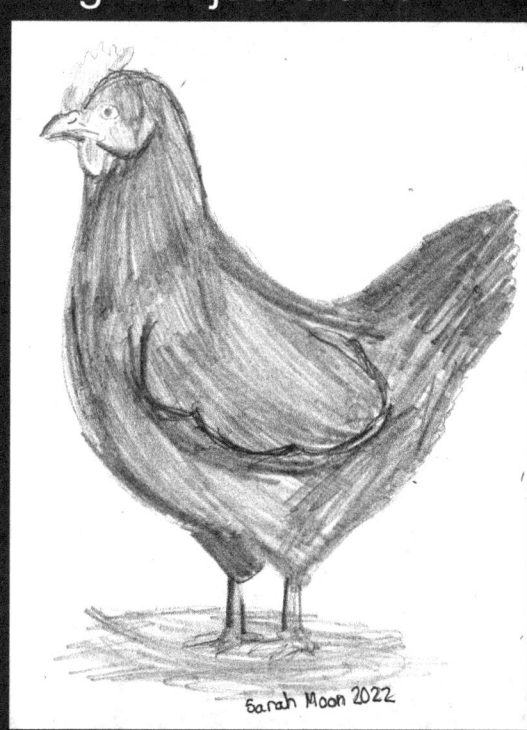

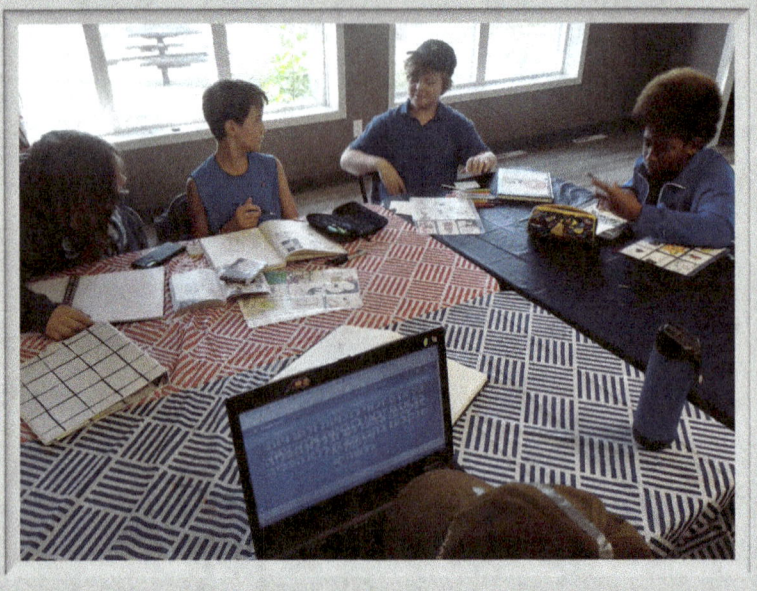

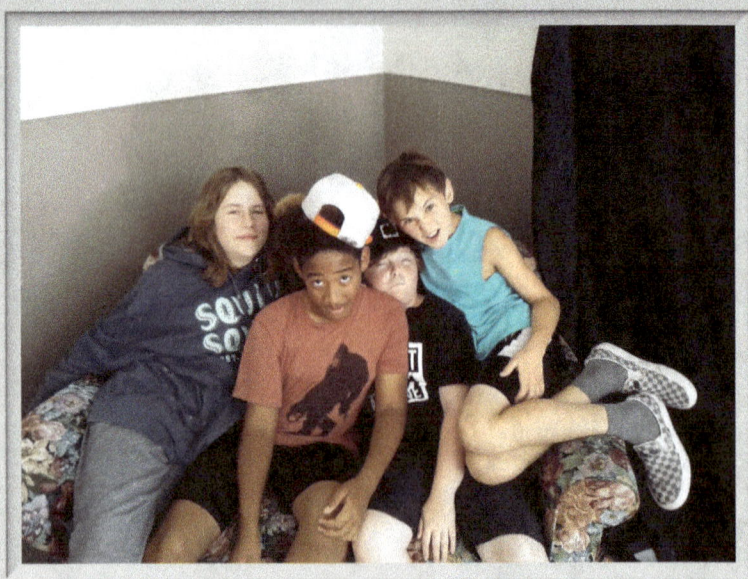

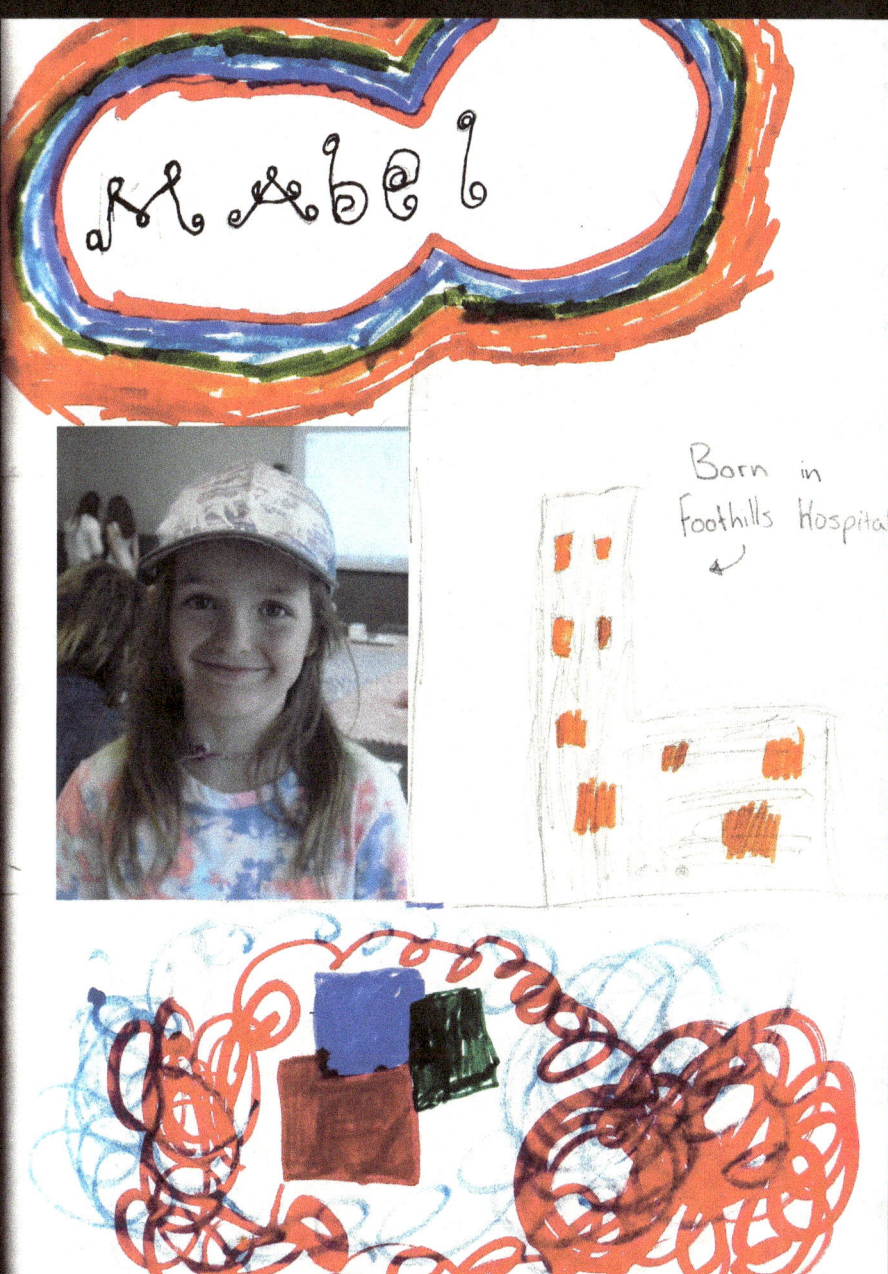

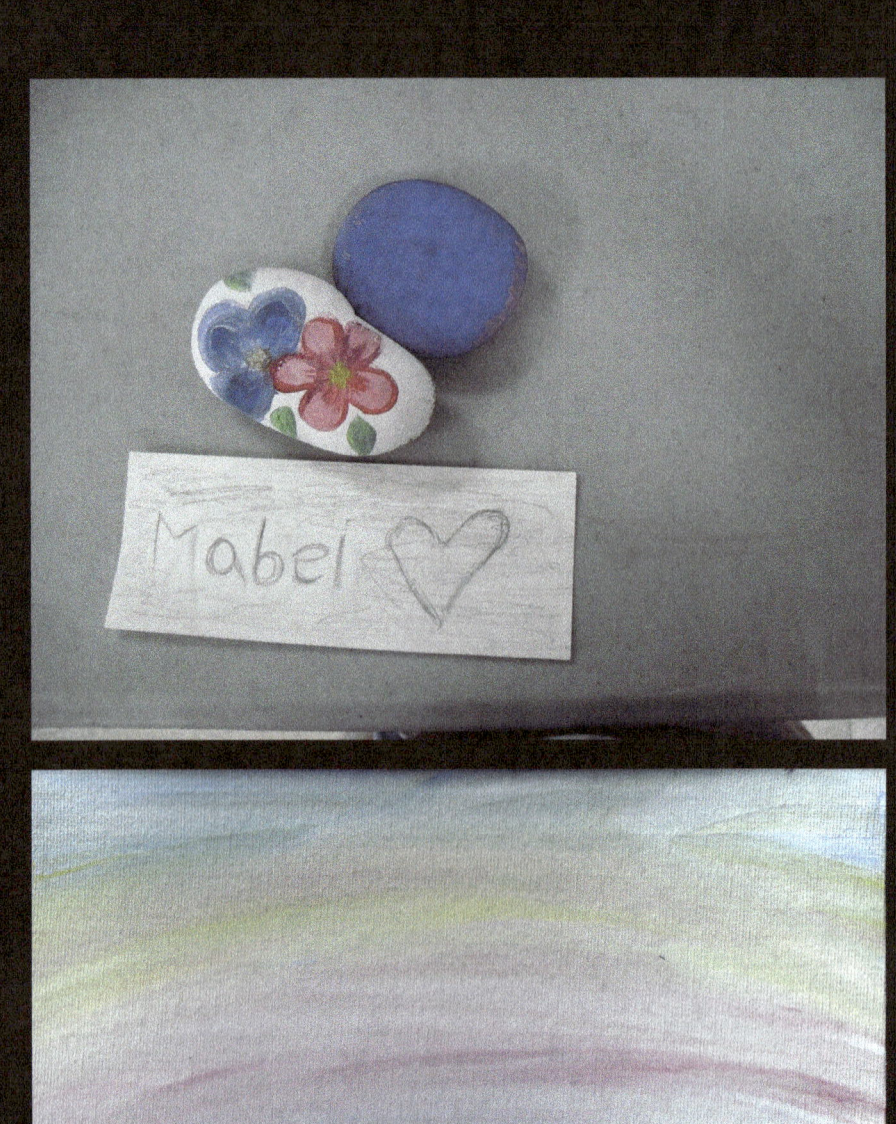

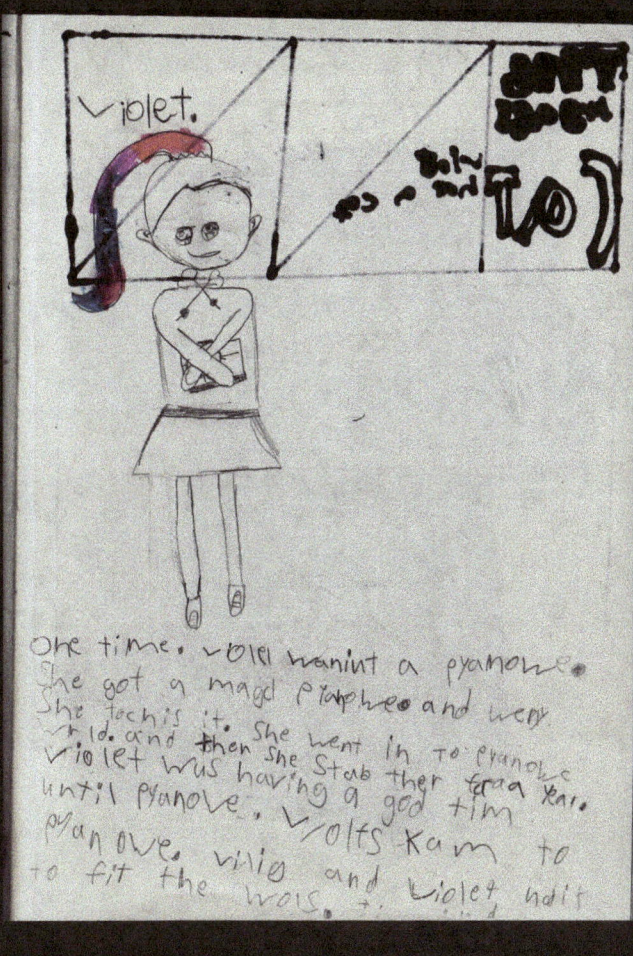

One time. Violet wanint a pyanowe. She got a magd piapheo and went. She tochis it. She went in to pyanowe. and then she stab ther feraa year. Violet was having a god tim until pyanove. Wolfs kam to pyanove. vilio. and Violet hdit to fit the wols.

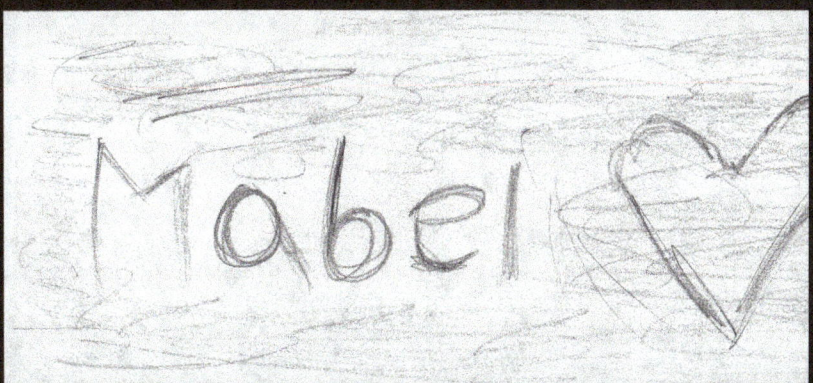

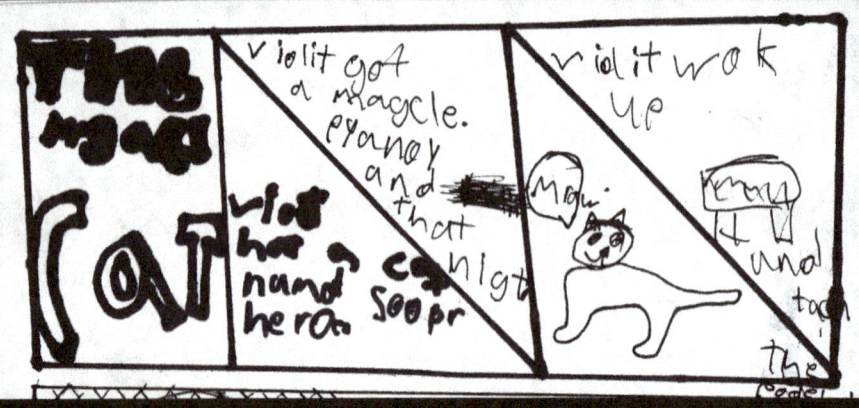
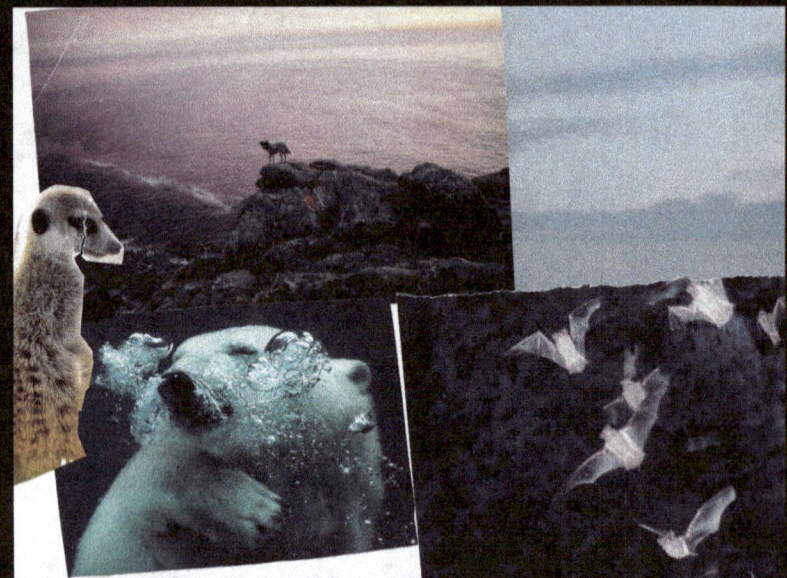

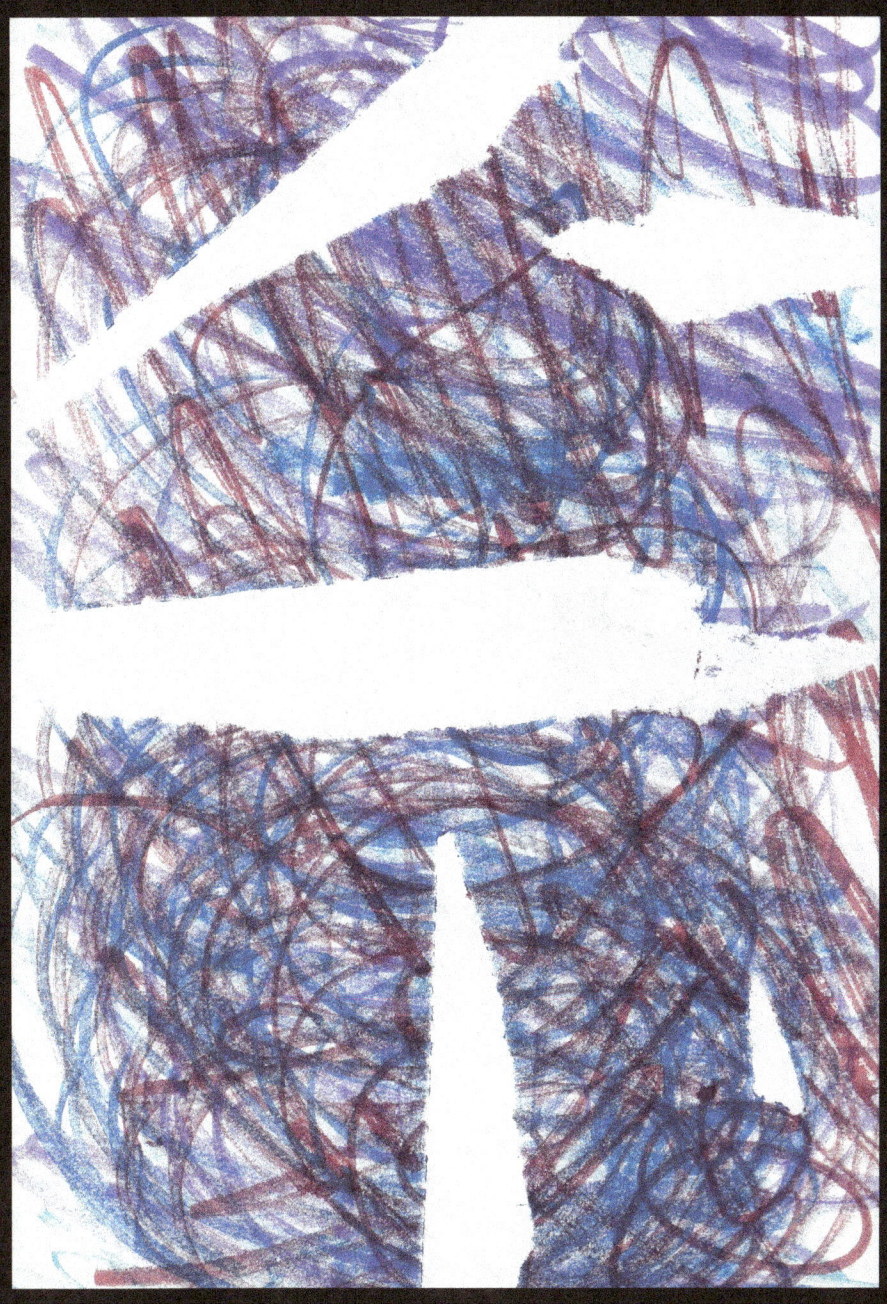

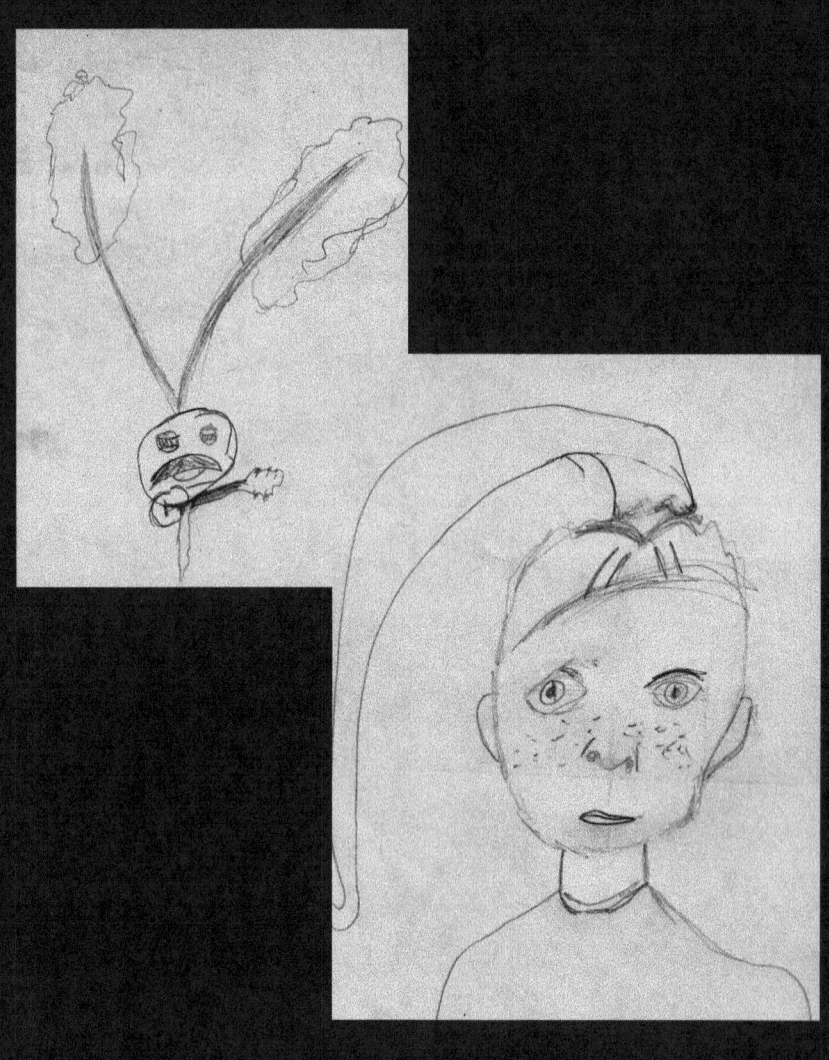

One day. a Penguin left the zoo. and then He drove a car. and He drove to hawii. and wen He got ther. and He swimd ther and He swimd ther. untill it flubb the and

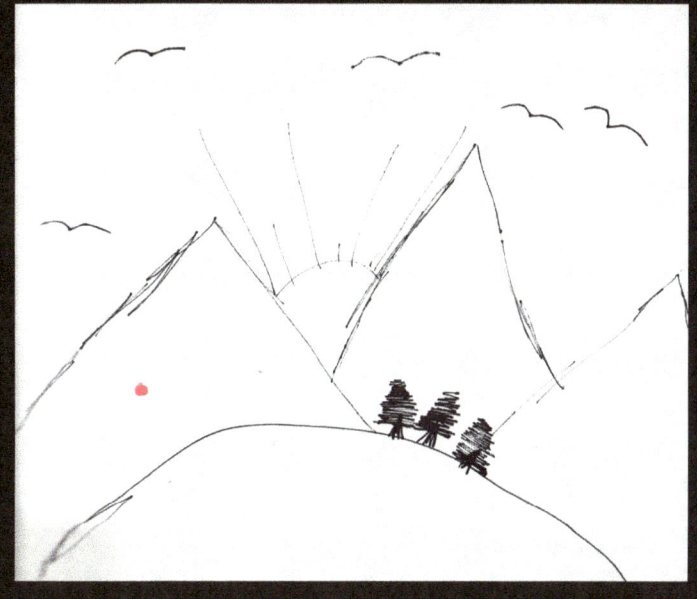

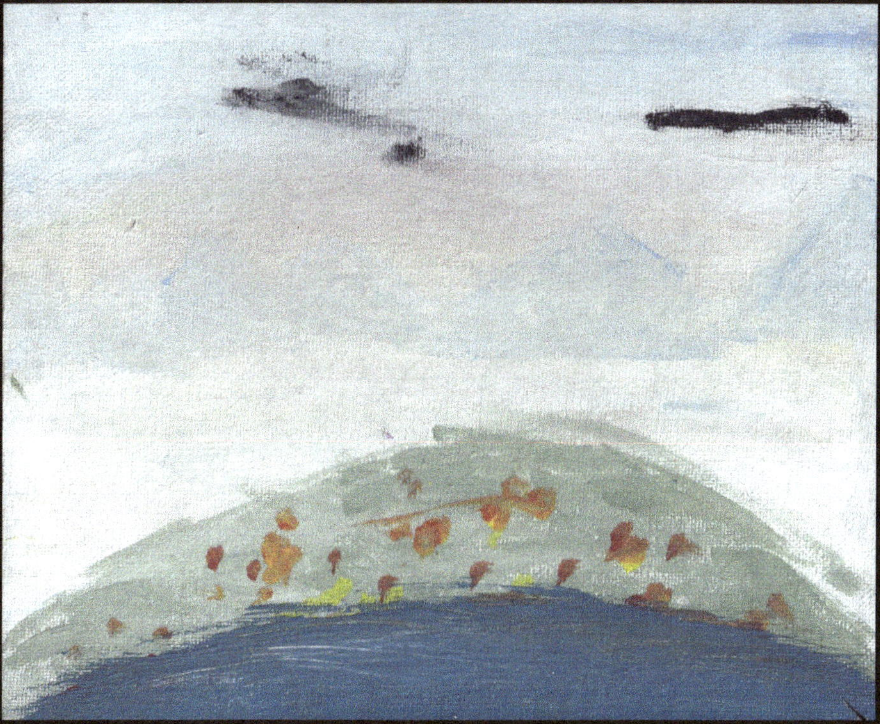

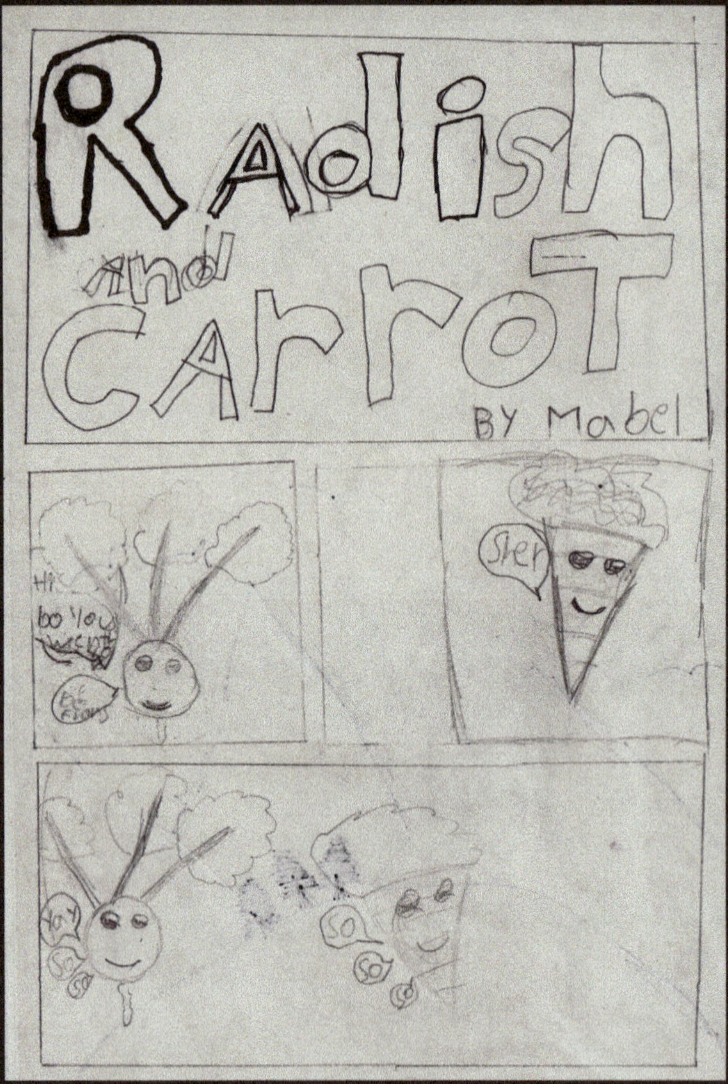

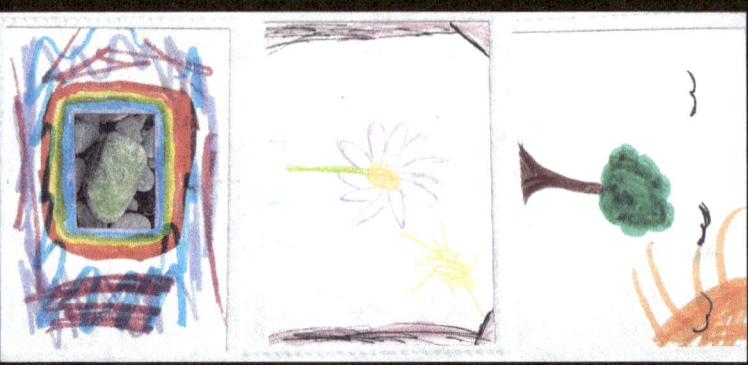

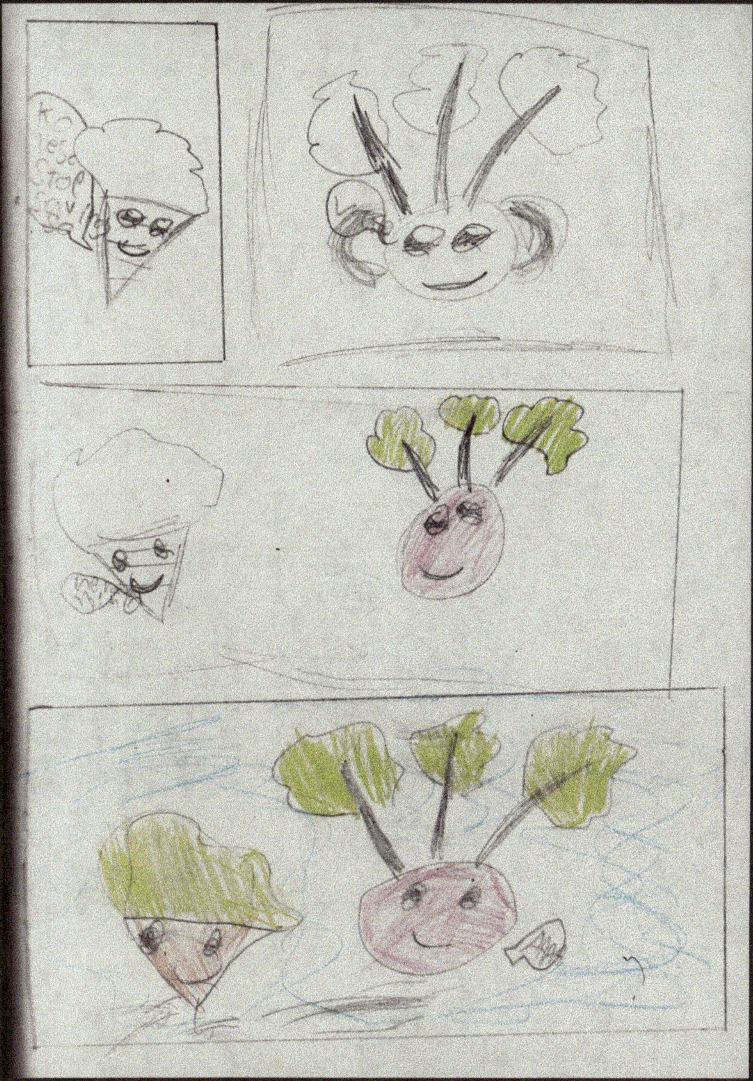

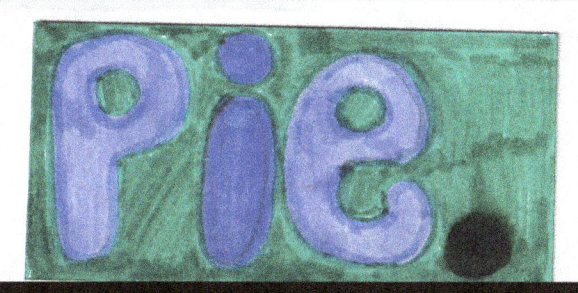

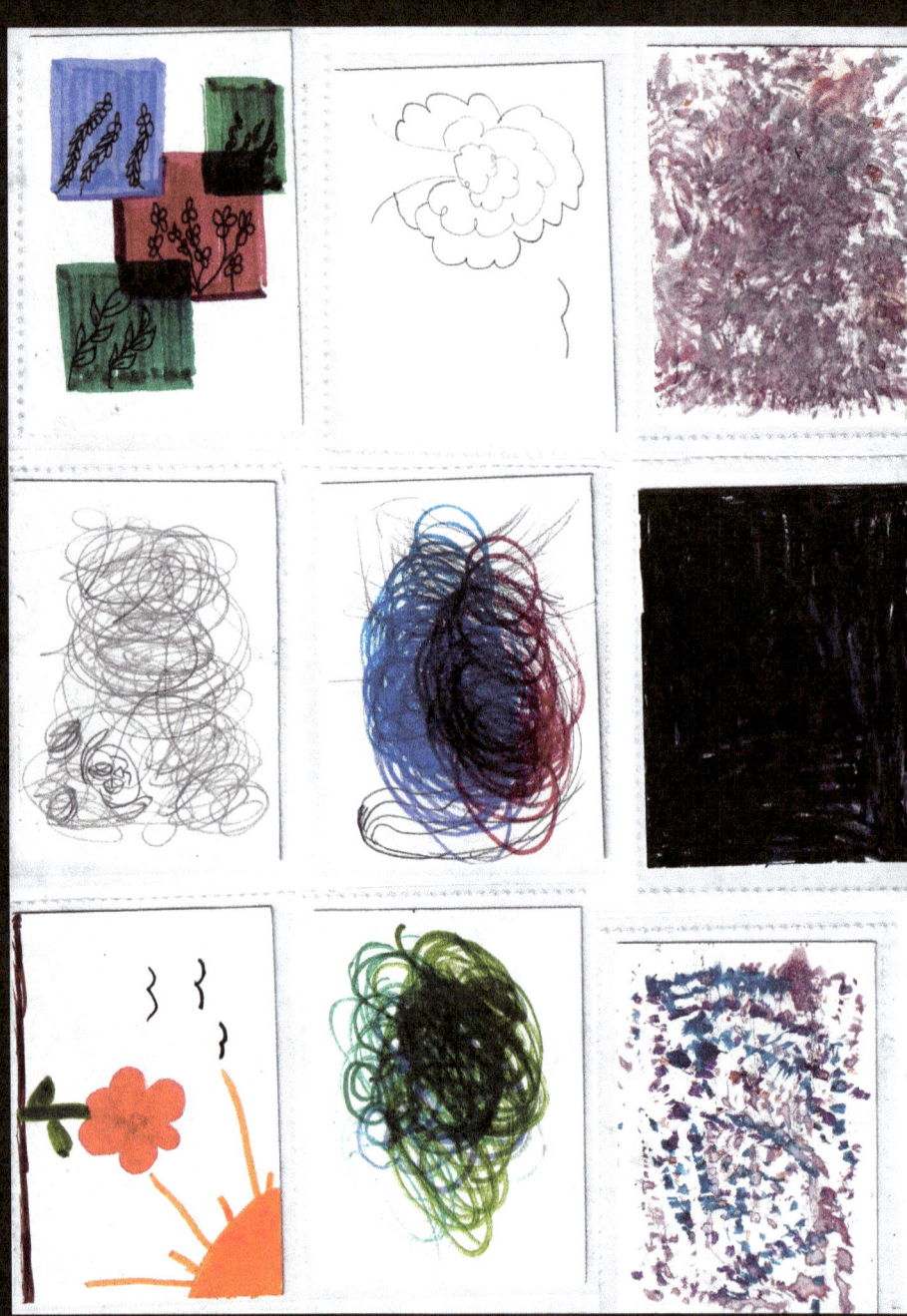

MATTHEW!!

MAttheW
Fake Identity

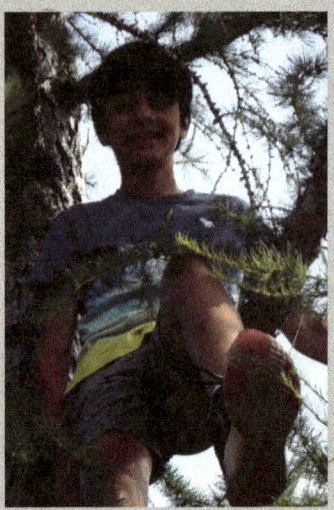

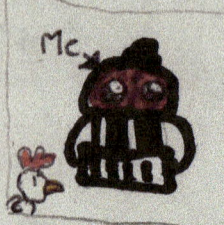
Me

Hello my name is nifty i waz born about 7 hours ago I waz made in the bakery so my life story. Im 7 hours old and ive already went to juvie.

fave Petal chickens Duh

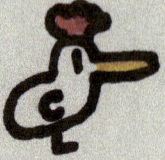

how i went to juvic (for about five min.) I stole chickens.

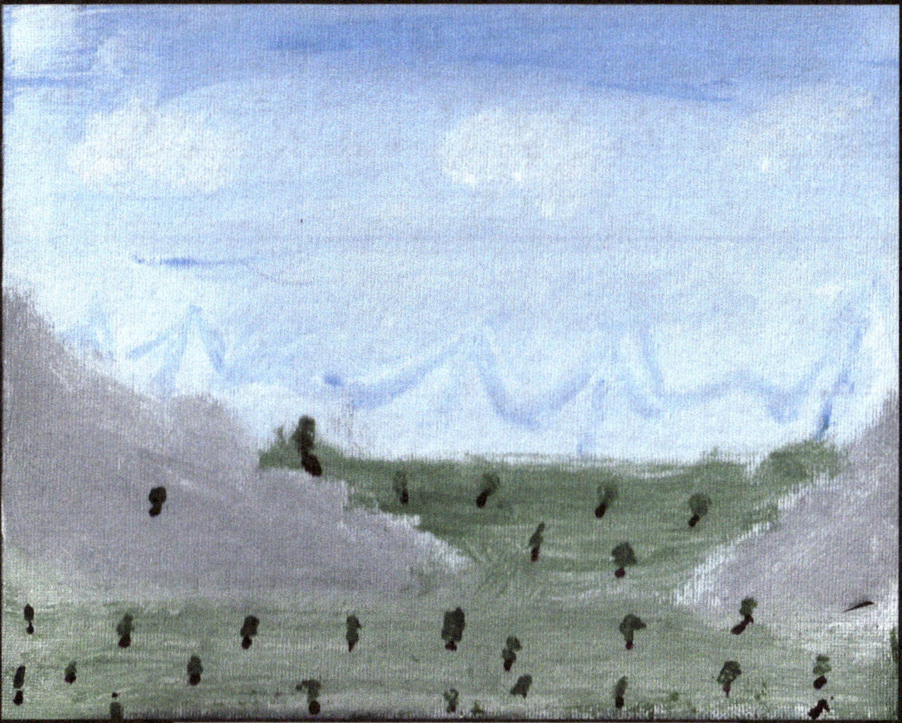

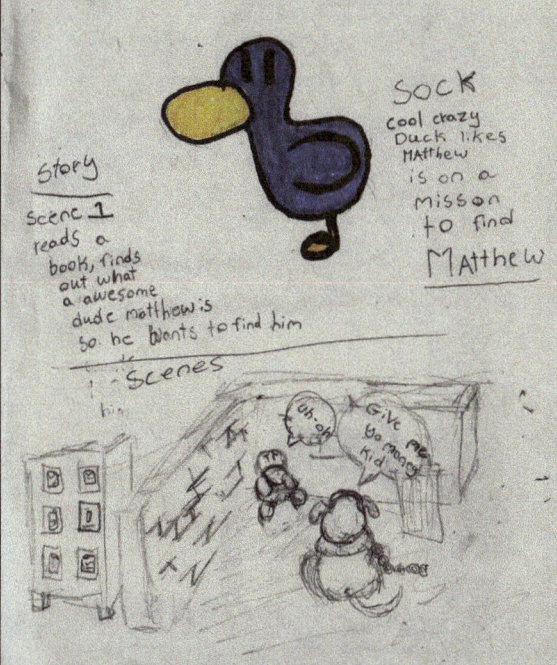

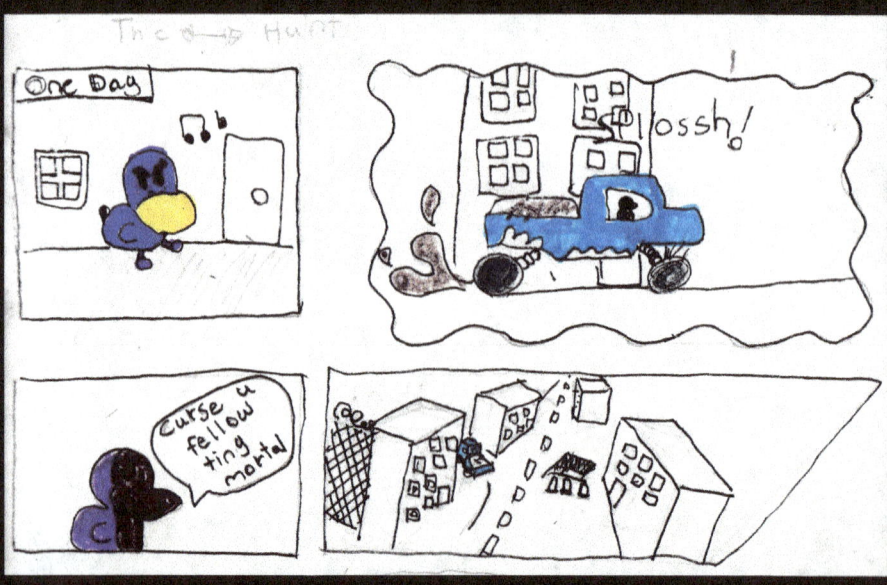
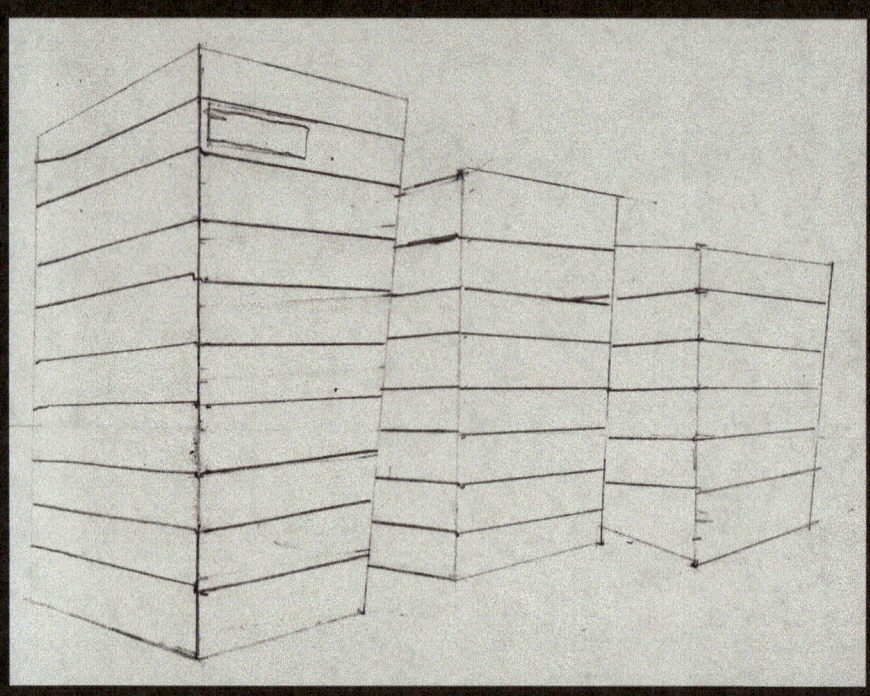

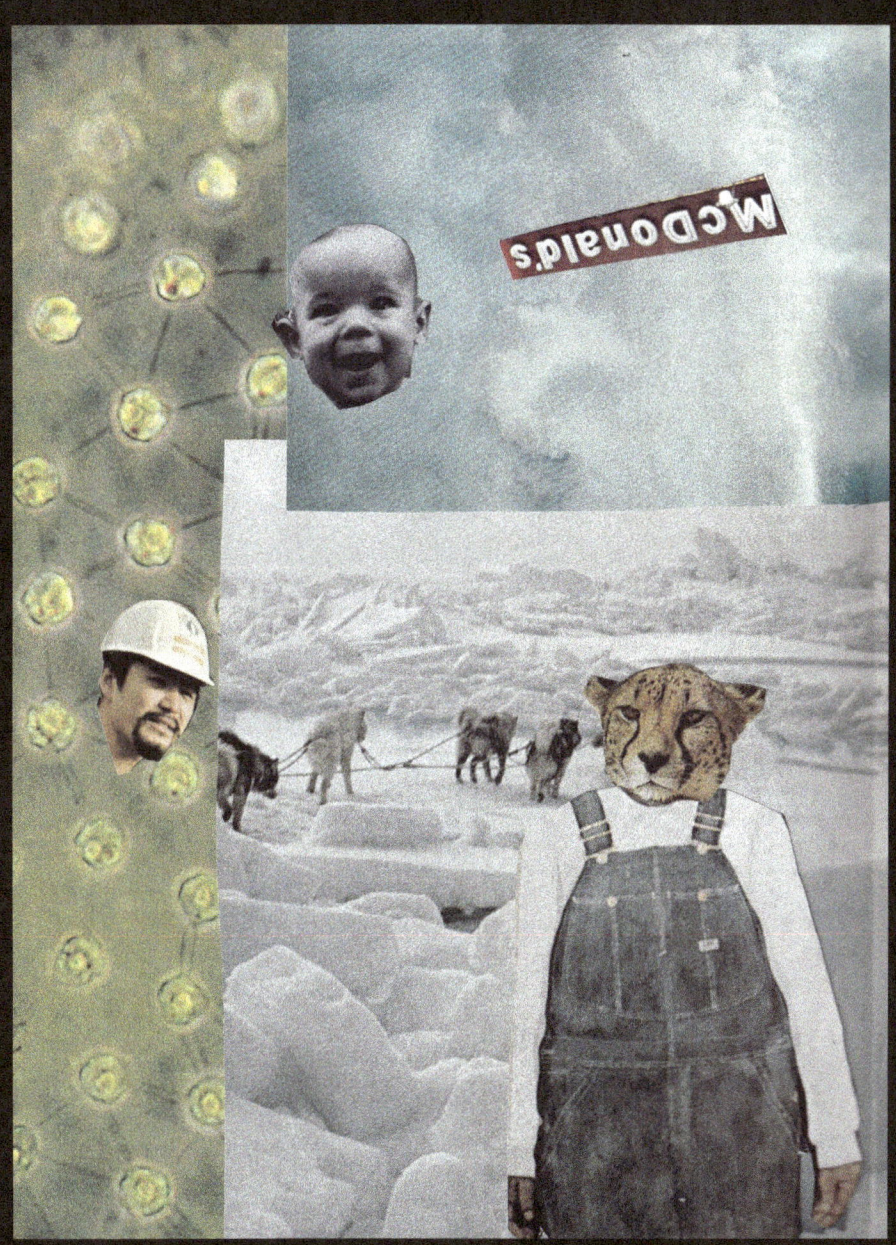

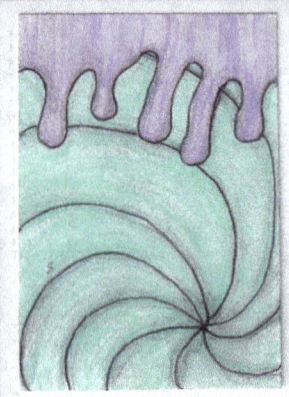
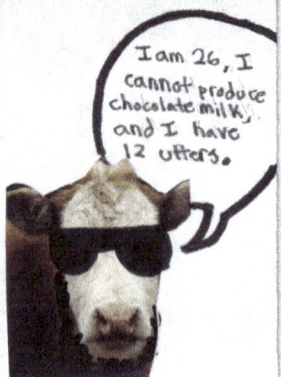
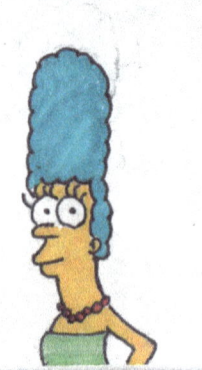
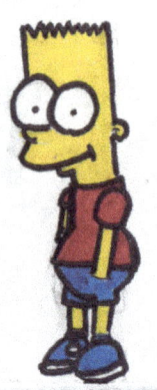
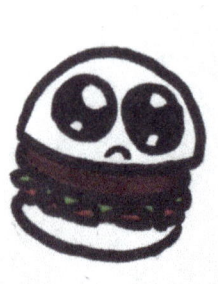
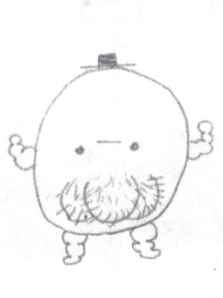
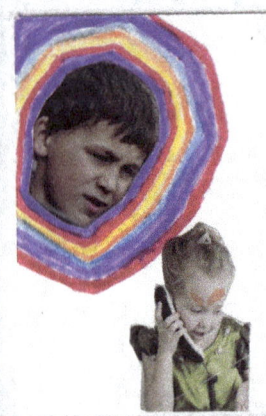
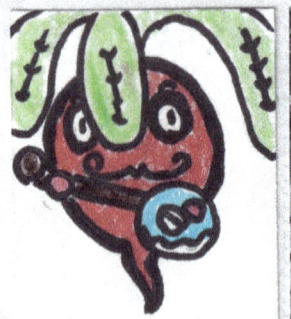
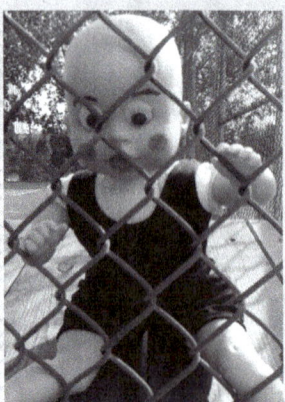

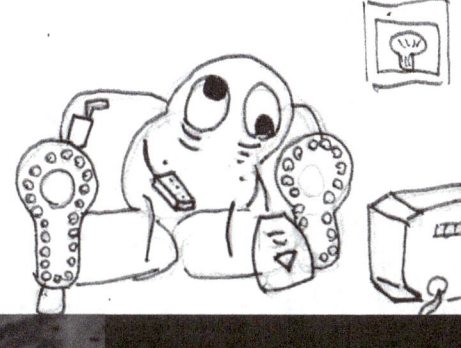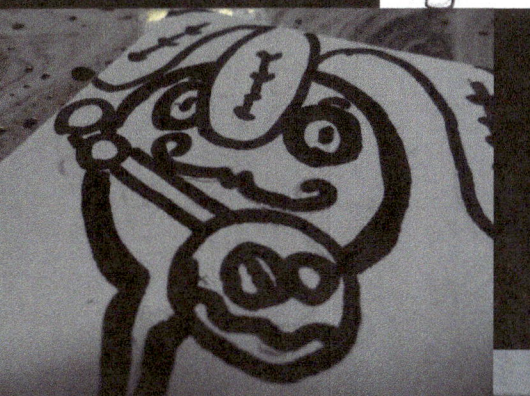

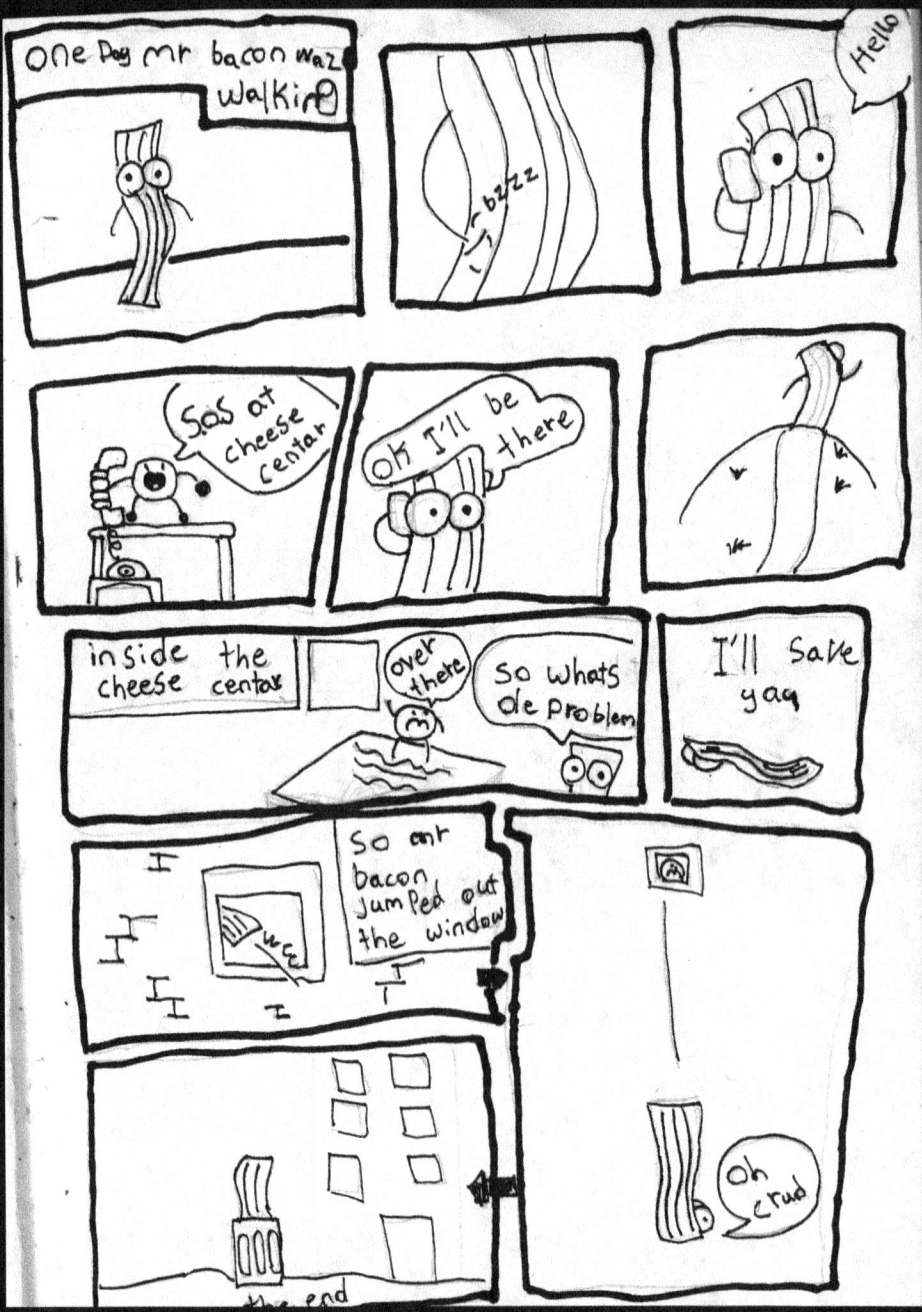

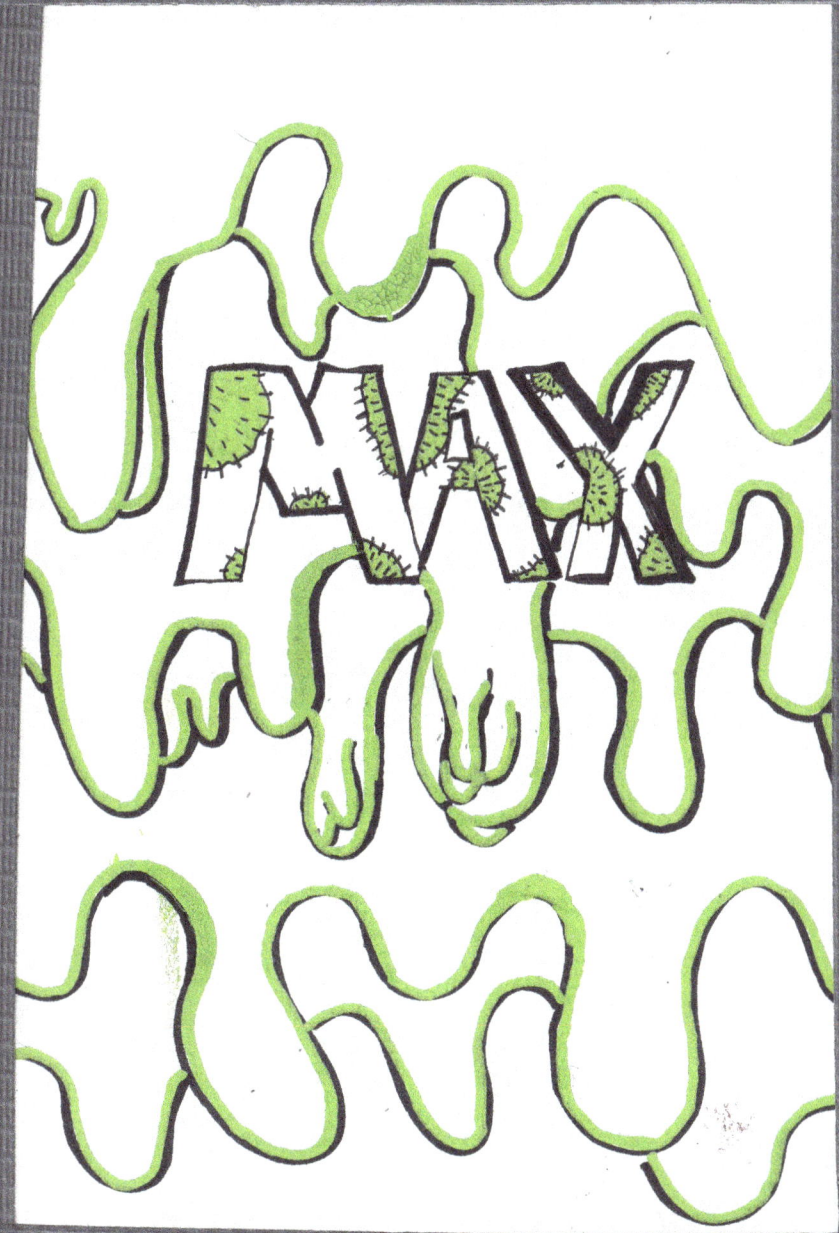

MAX

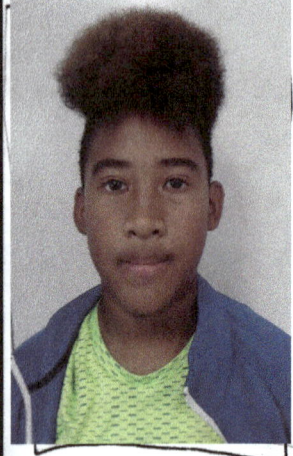

I was born in a basket made of chicken strips and churros.

I used to like watching butter melt. But now I like to play video games, do sports, and draw.

My dog also for some reason likes to run into doors.

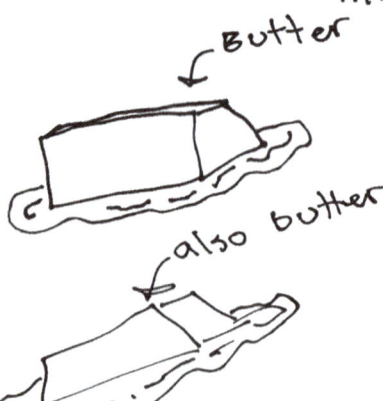

← Butter
← also butter

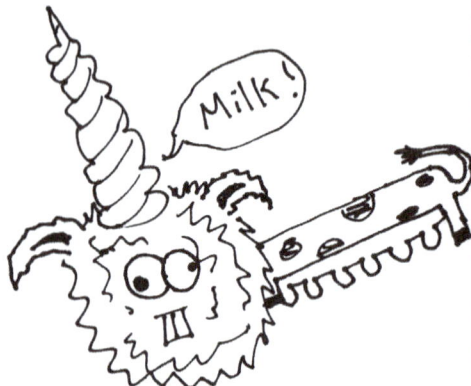

Milk!

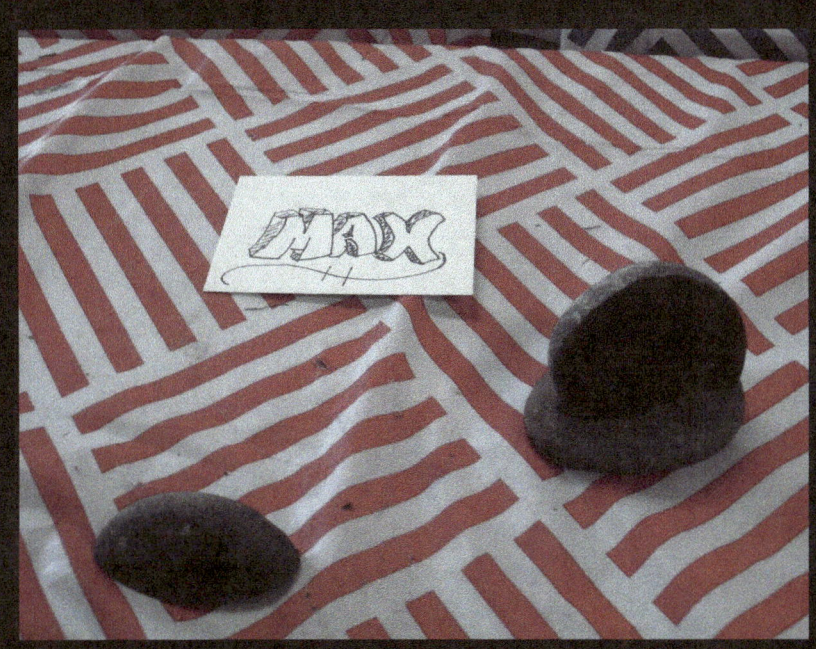
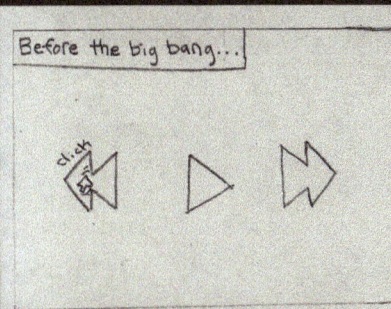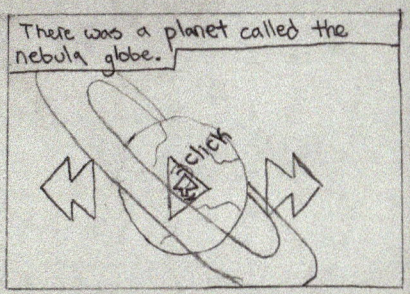
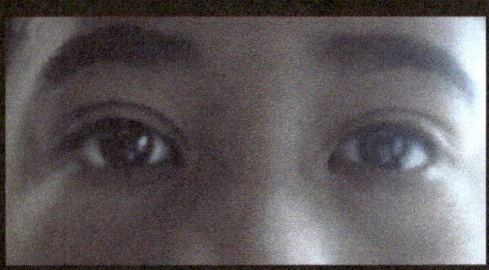

AXEL BUNARE
Woodcutter

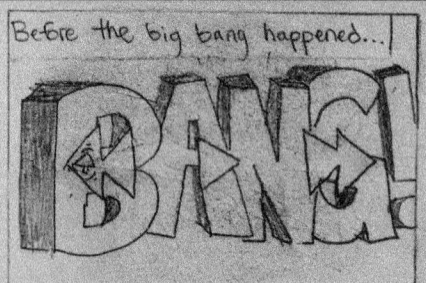
Before the big bang happened...

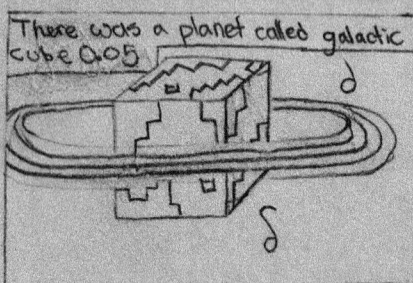
There was a planet called galactic cube 0.05

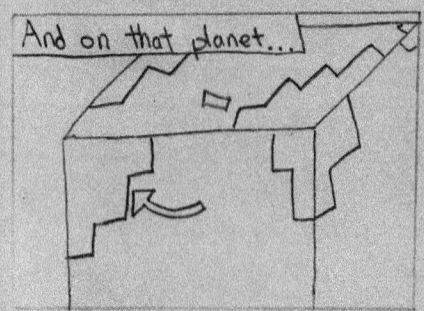
And on that planet...

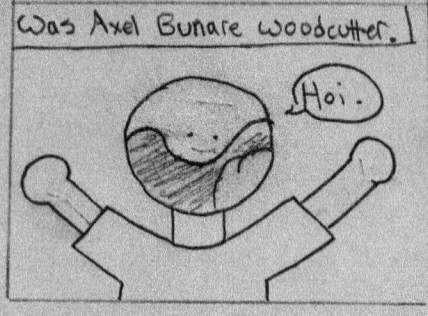
Was Axel Bunare woodcutter.
"Hoi."

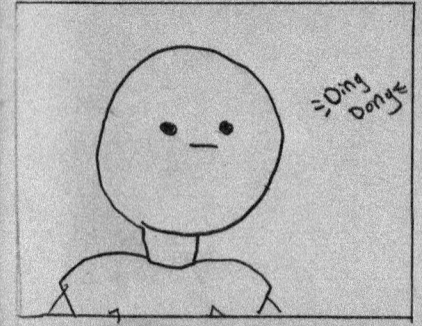
=Ding Dong=

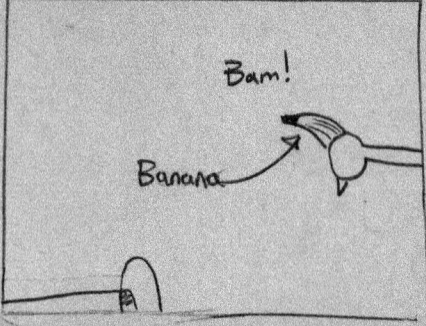
Bam!
Banana

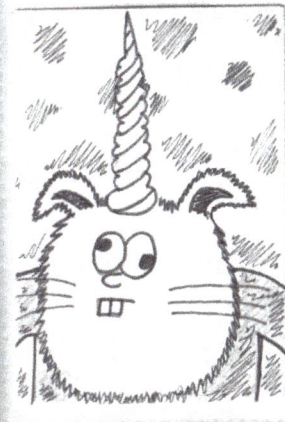
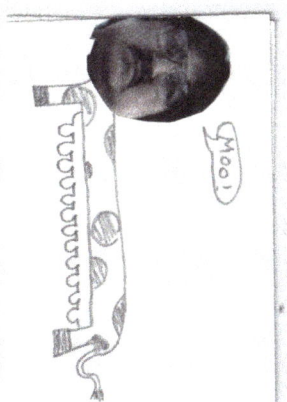

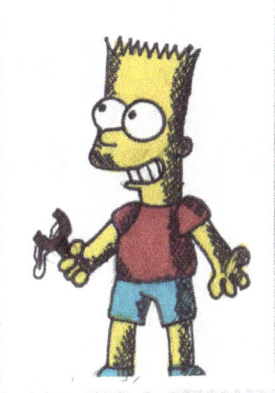
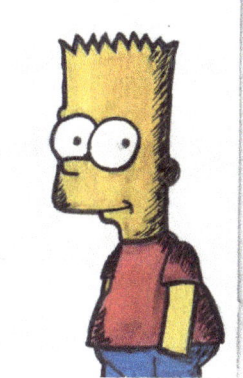
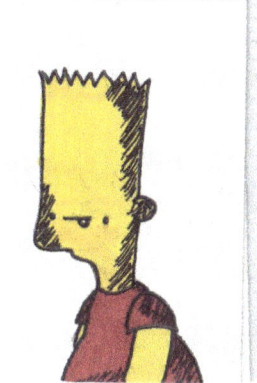
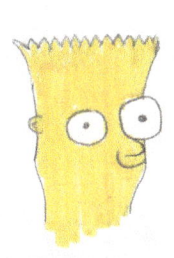
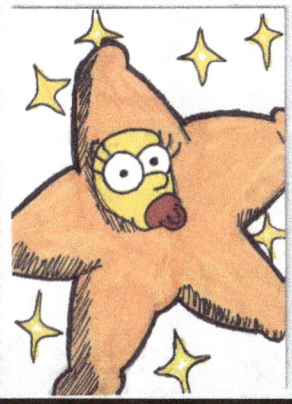
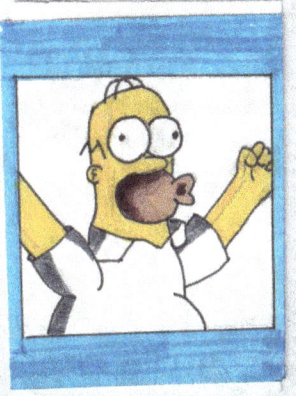

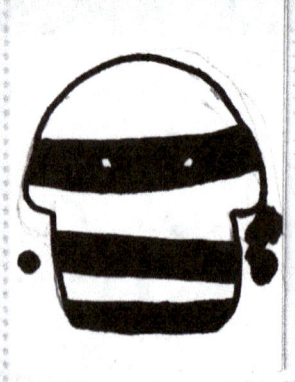 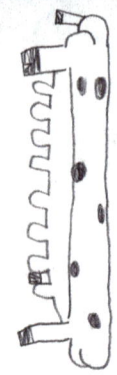

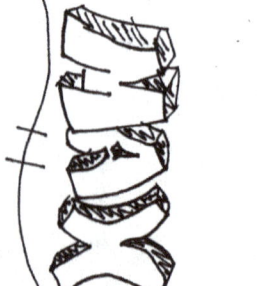

Bart simpson

August 9th

By Maximus Ng

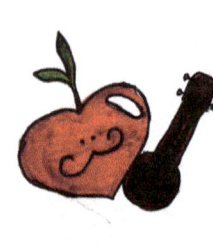

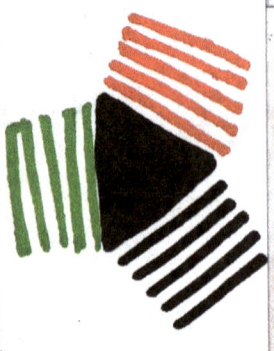

Maggie simpson
(star form)

August 10th

By Maximus Ng

"Fart Simpson"

Genevieve   Aug. 9,
Shoesmith   2022

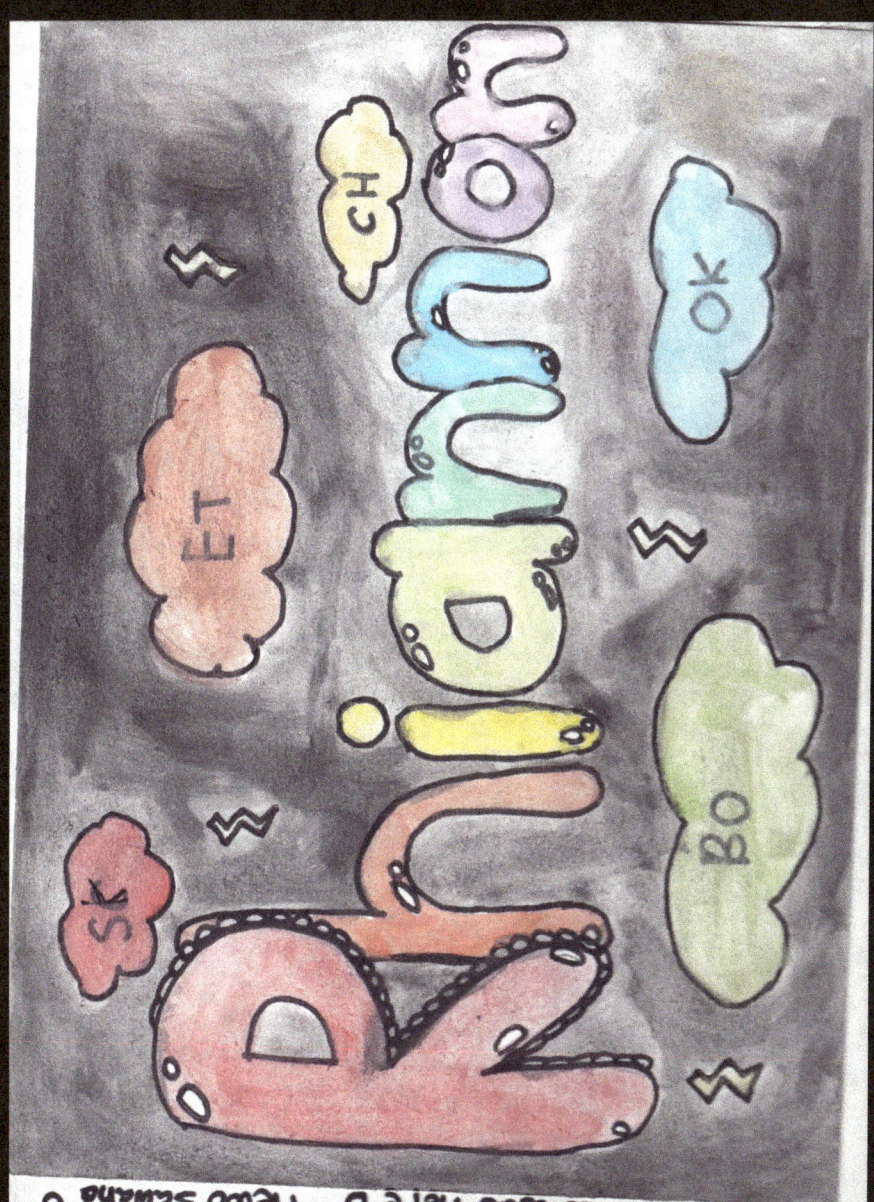

Da Sawaha was here !! - Hewa Sawaha :)

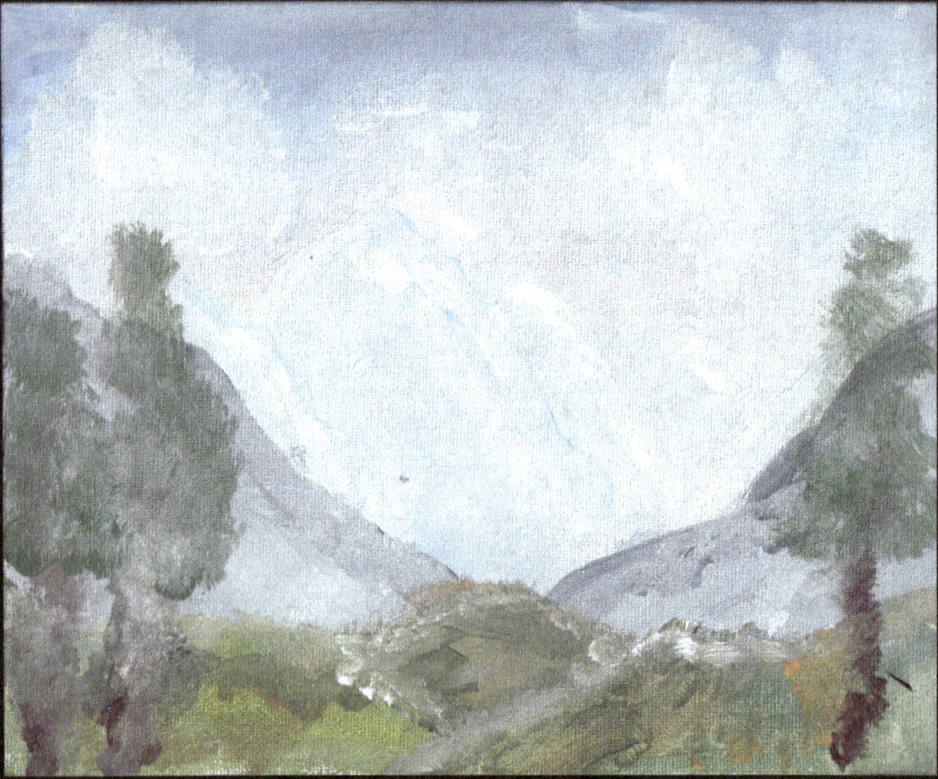

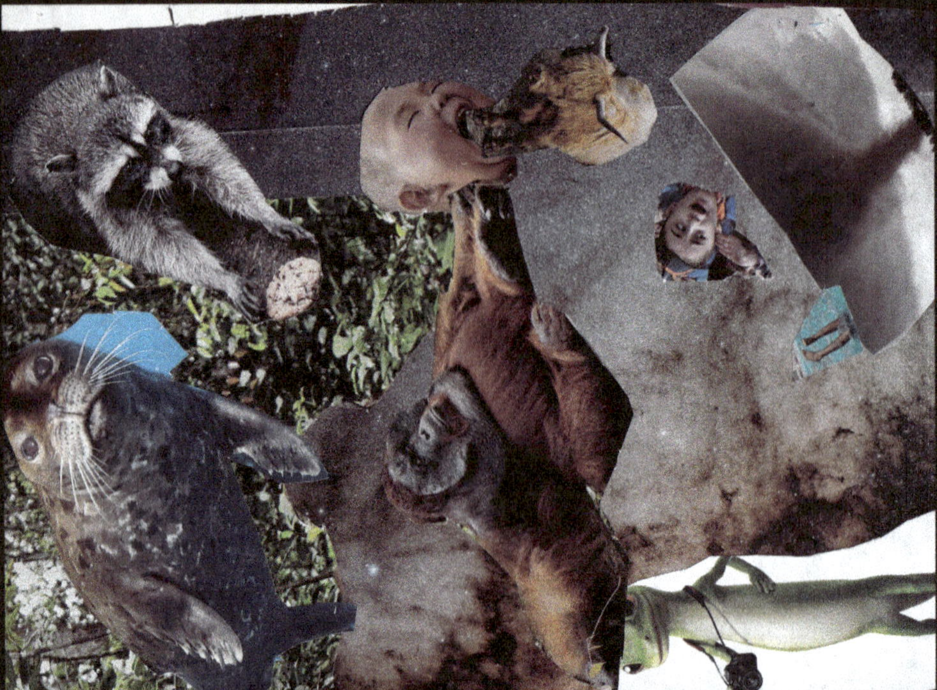

RHIANNON

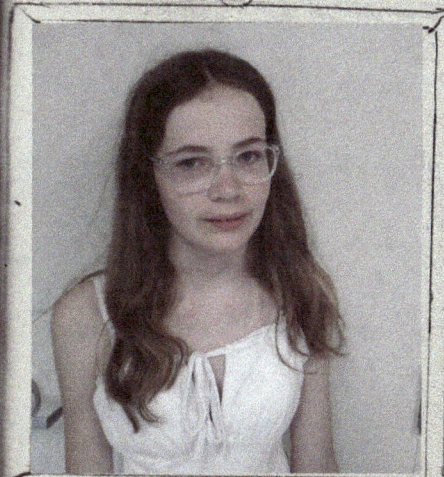

Hello! WELCOME to my biography! I'm born on 10/22/09. I'm a Calgary baby.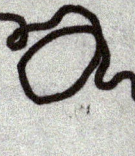

I'm trying to become a Champion in highland dancing! I play violin when I'm bored.

I am OBSESSED with cows! I have a heart for animals. I dream to be a chef, vet or graphic designer.

Weird Questions

FAV animal: Cows & cats

Strangest dream —
Once upon a time in the universe of Rhiannon's dreams... I was in a dark & creepy forest. It was midnight. My brother joined me in the adventure. We were laughing then suddenly you hear thunderous stomps. Leaves were rustling, ground was shaking. Out of the blue, a brown cow comes far out of the tree. It was a BEAR! I roared so loud my ears burst! Me and my brother hid, he couldn't find a place. I was hiding behind a floral couch. All of the sudden my brother falls into a hay basket & just starts laughing. THE END

!! FUN FACTS !!

- I have 2 cats CZ (looks like a 1/4)
- I'm a premier in HD (highest level)
- lvl. 2 in violin
- My nickname is Rhiannonon
- I'm a master at cooking scrambled eggs

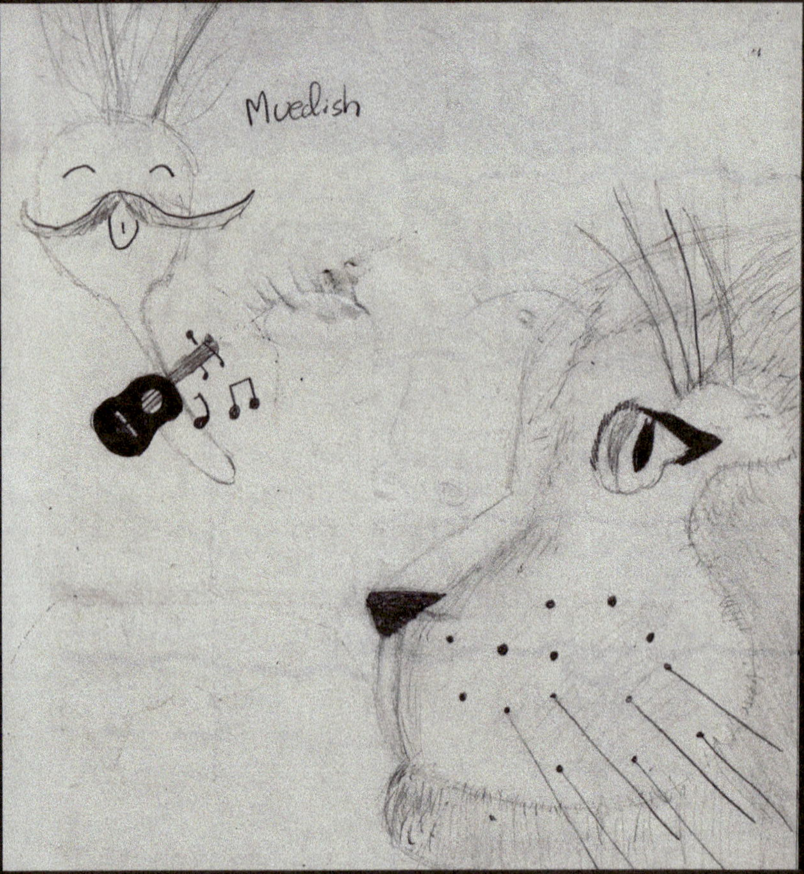

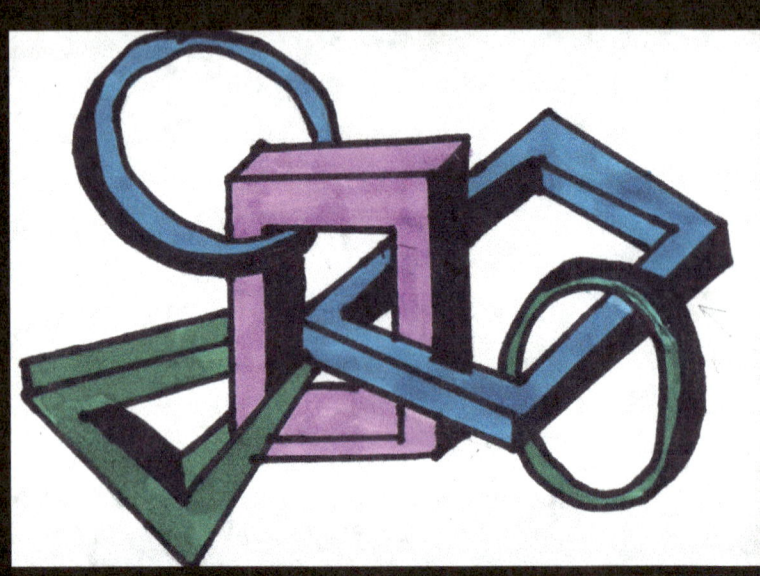

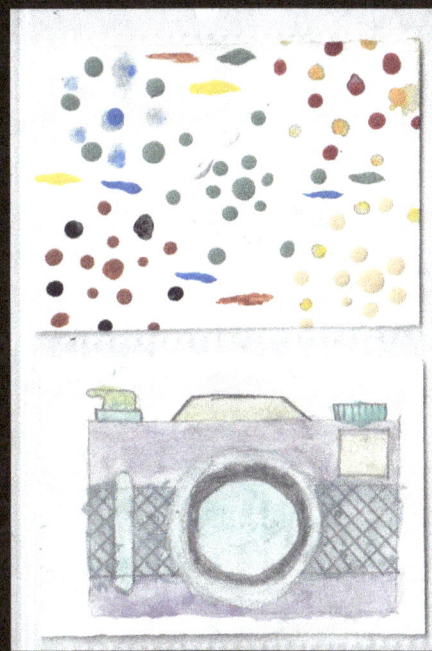
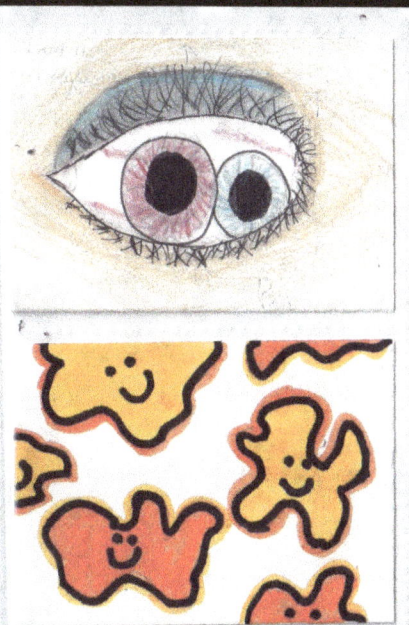
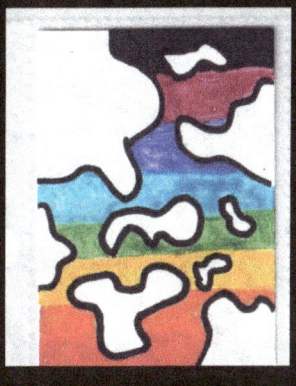
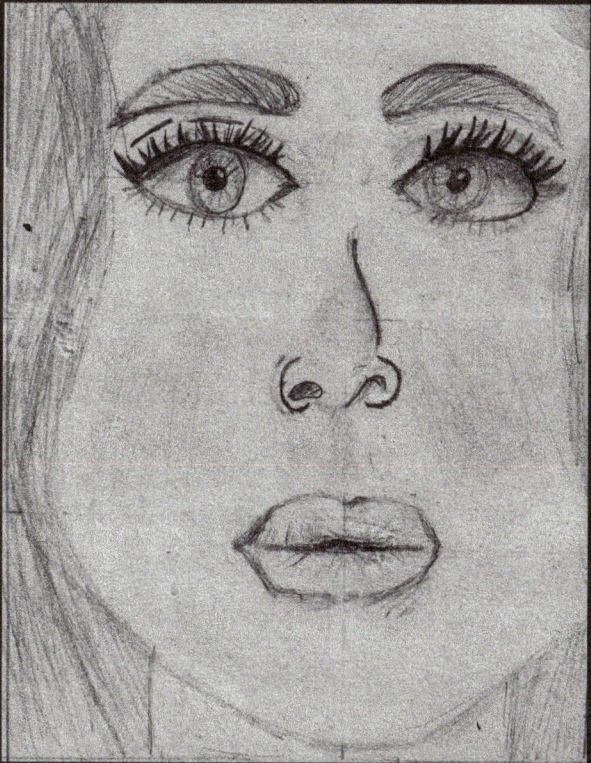

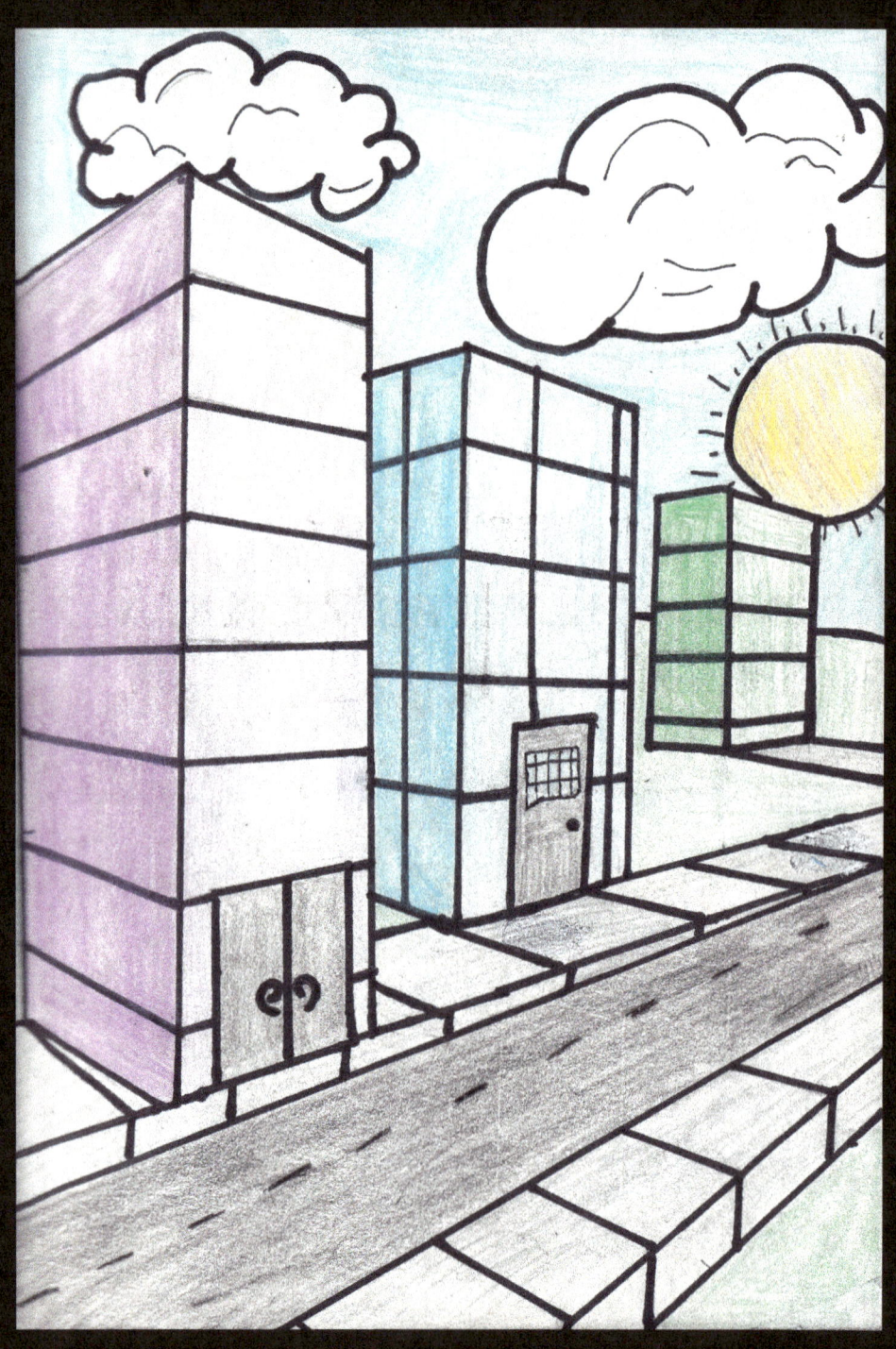

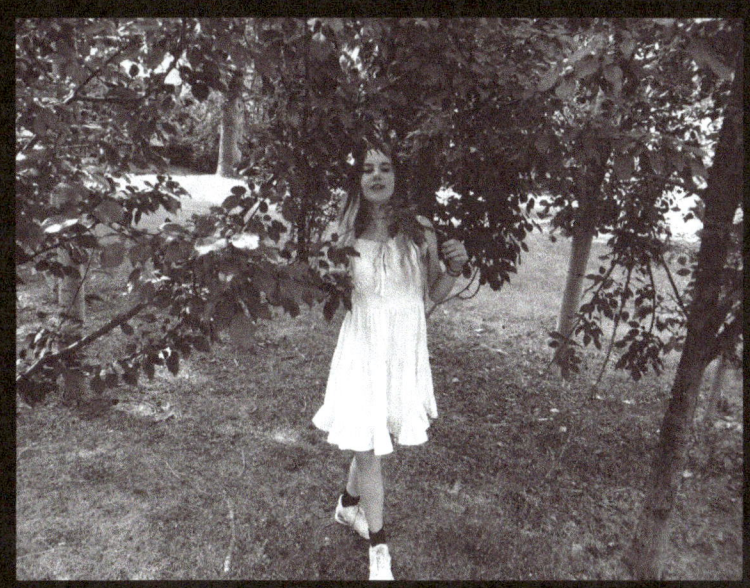
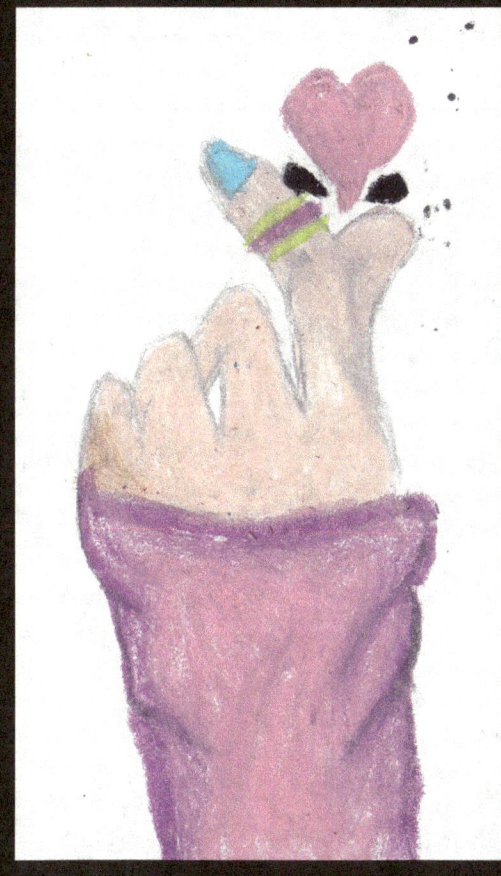

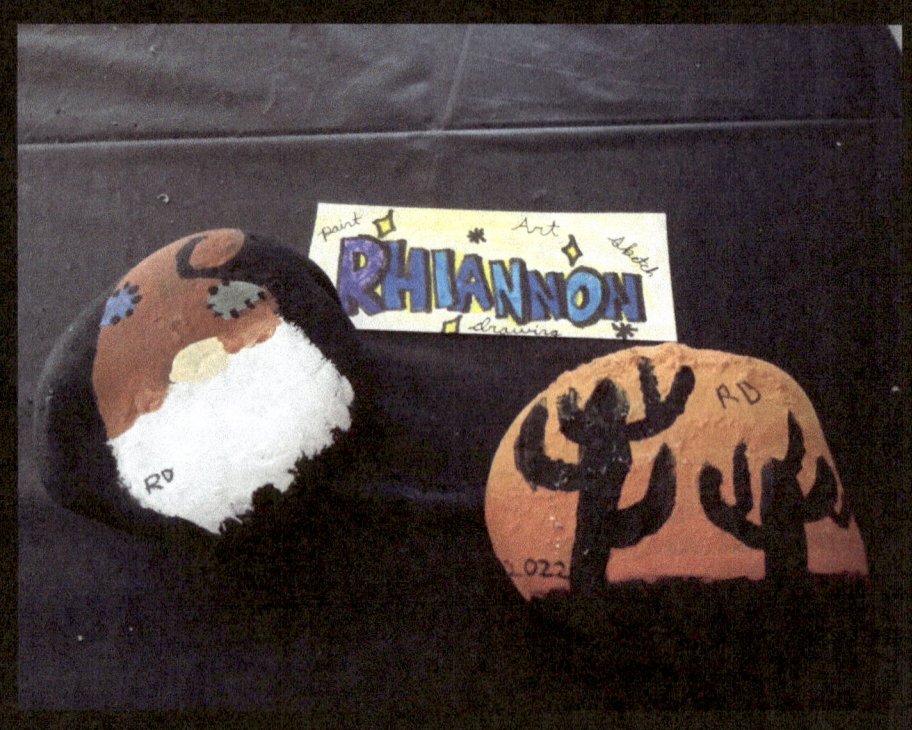

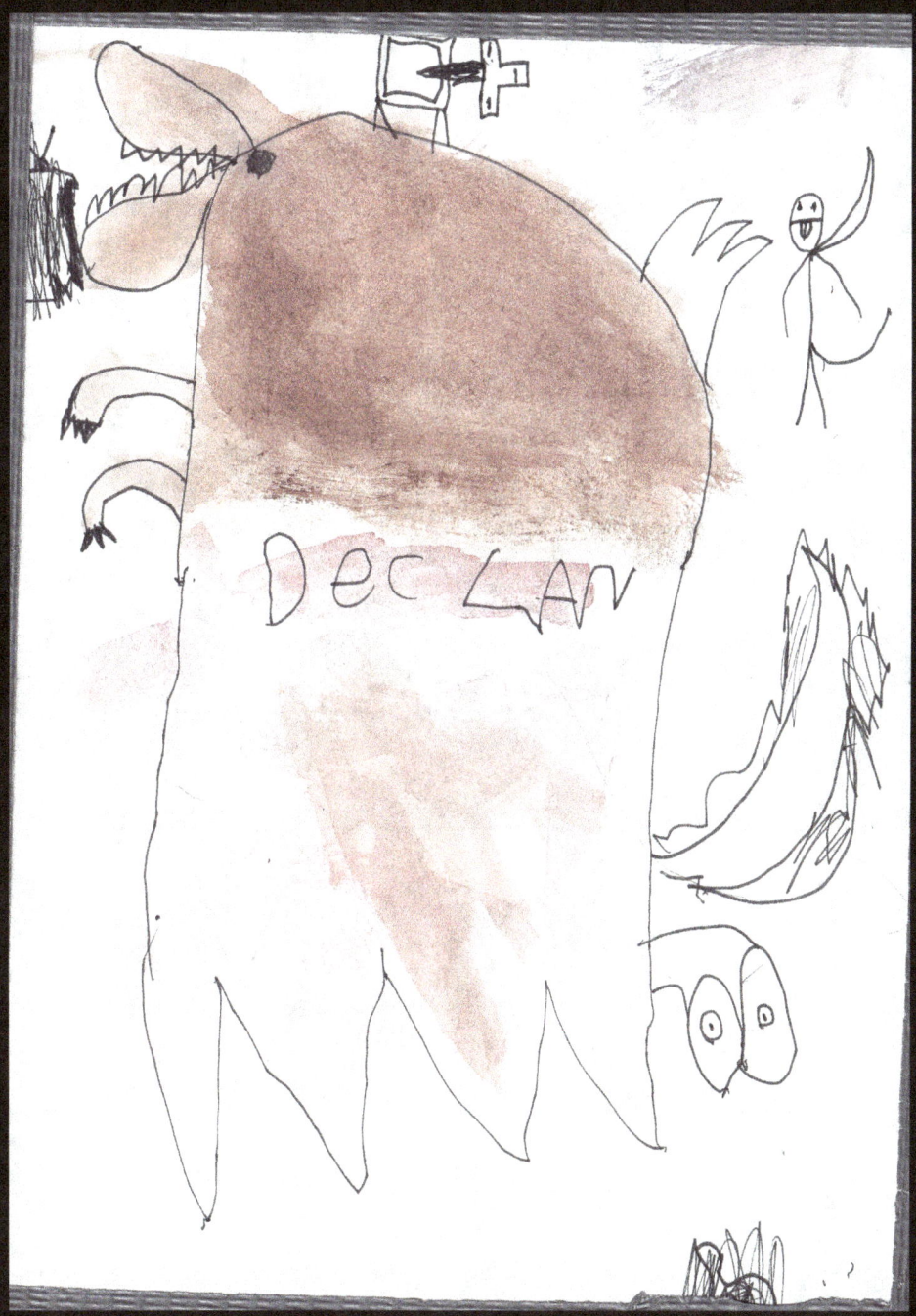

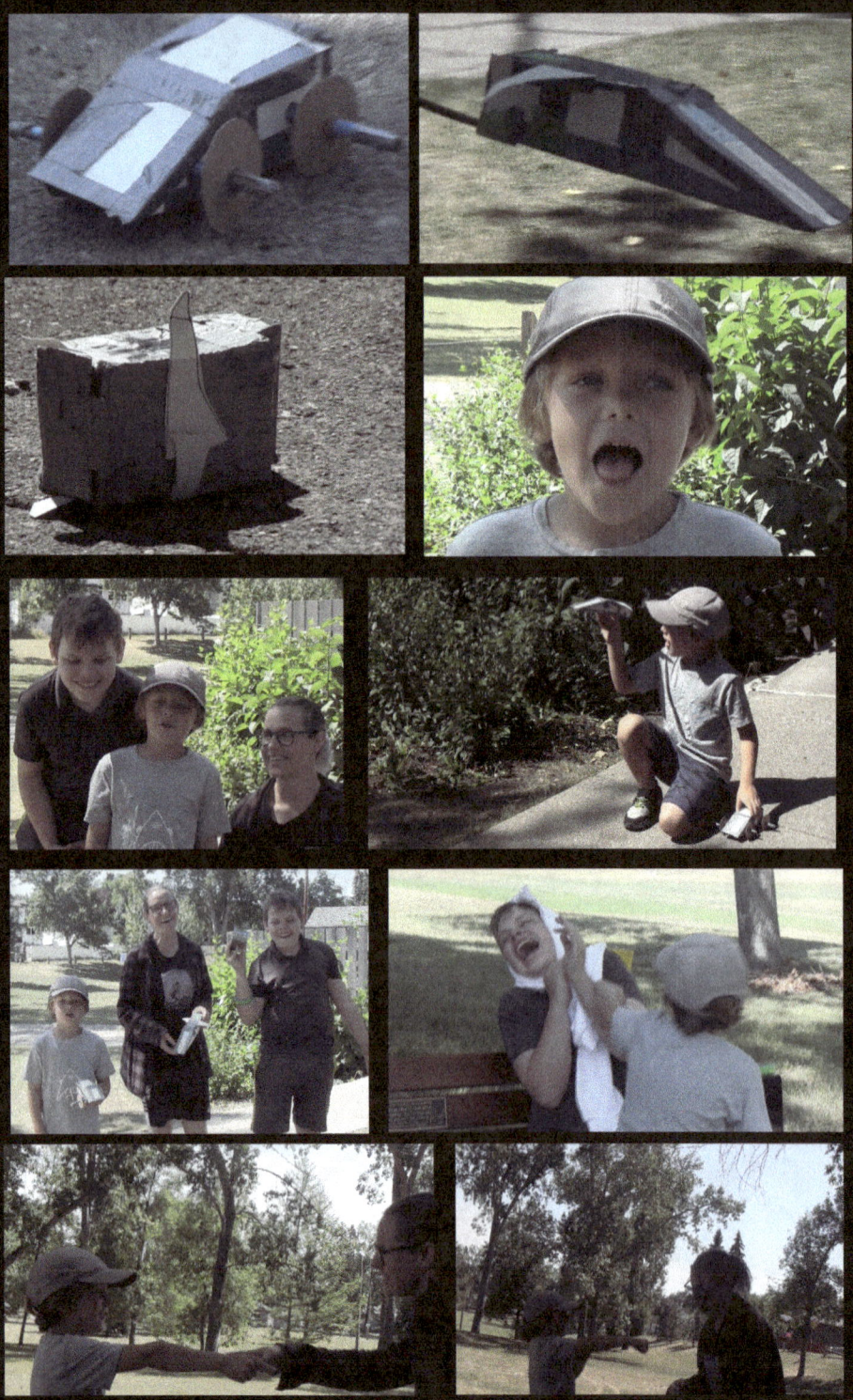

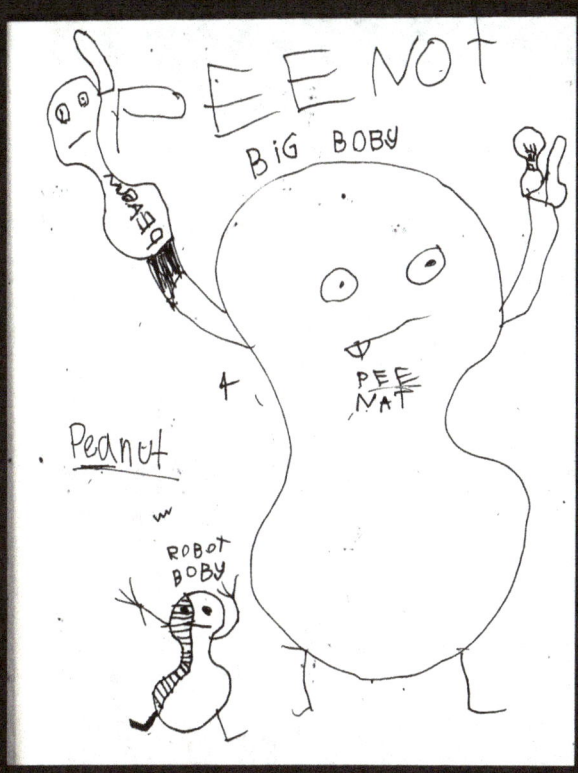
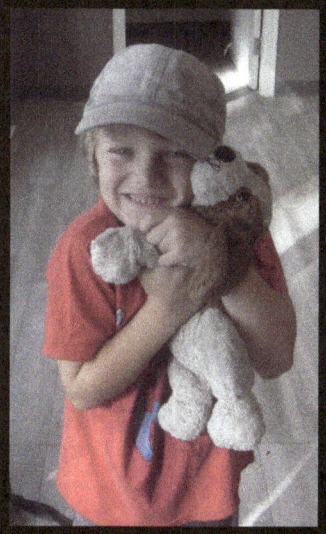
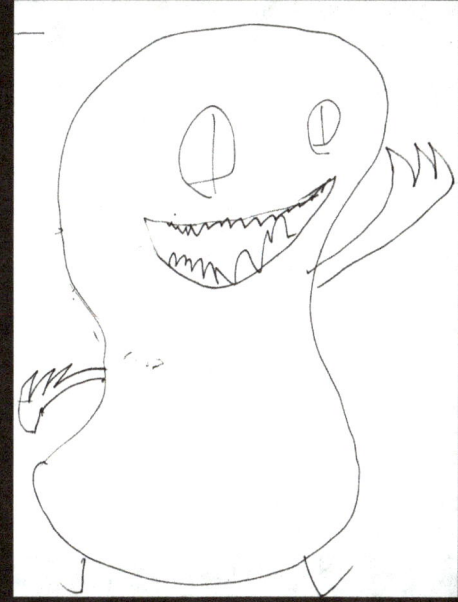
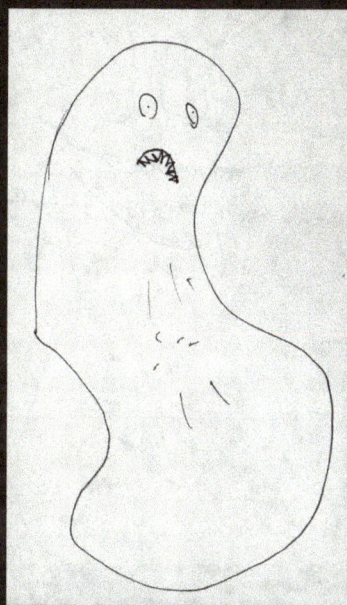

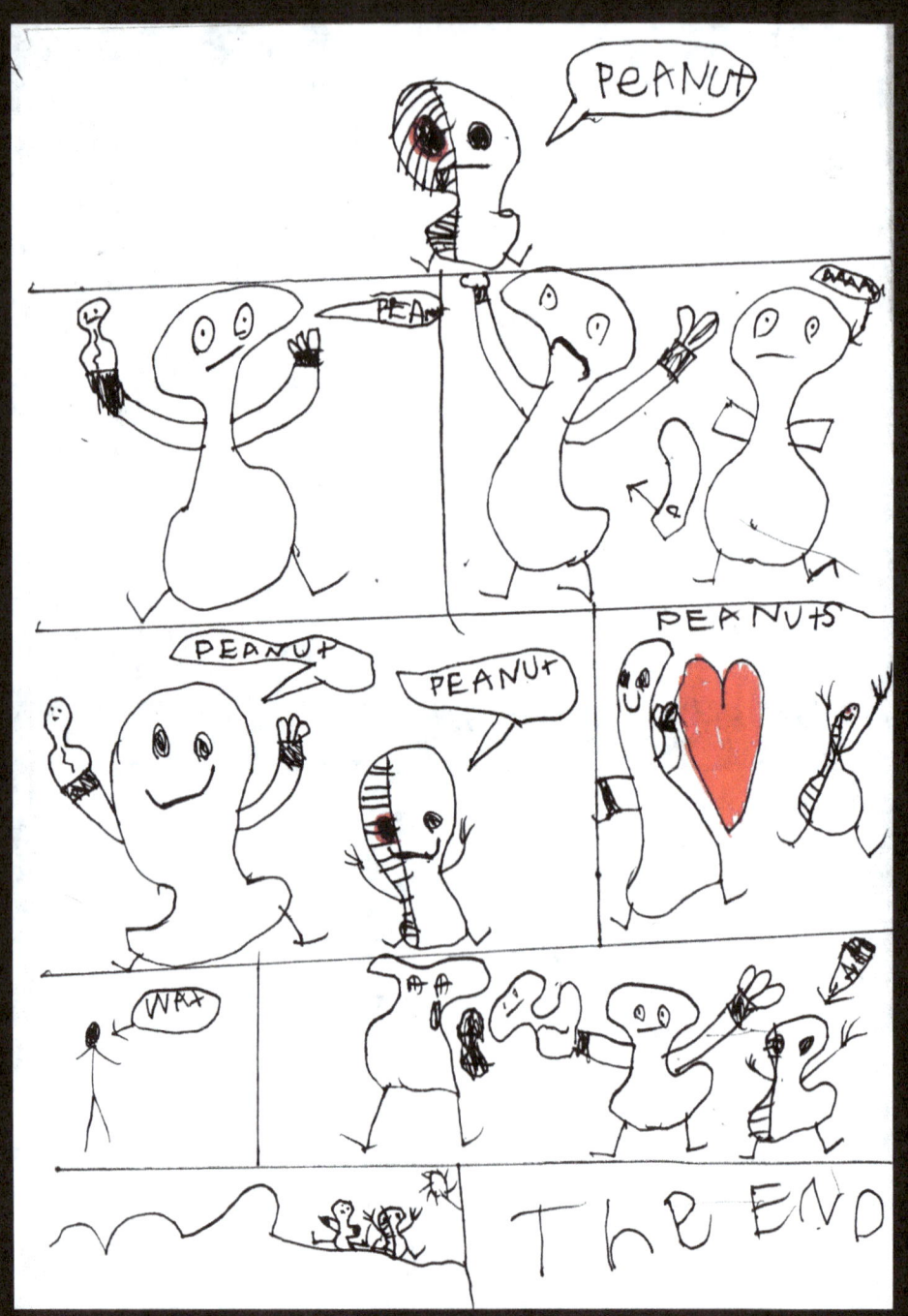

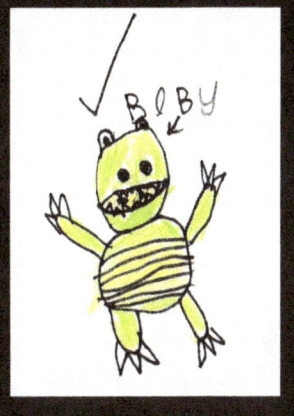
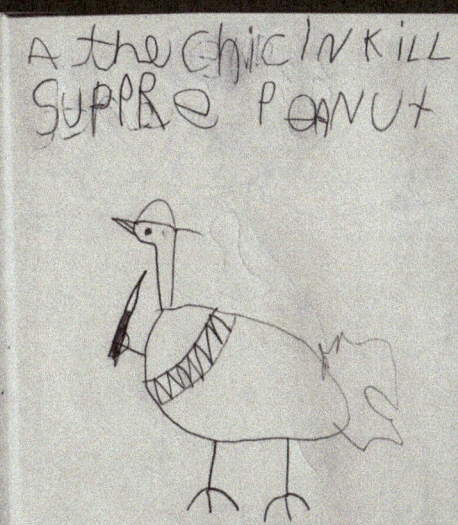
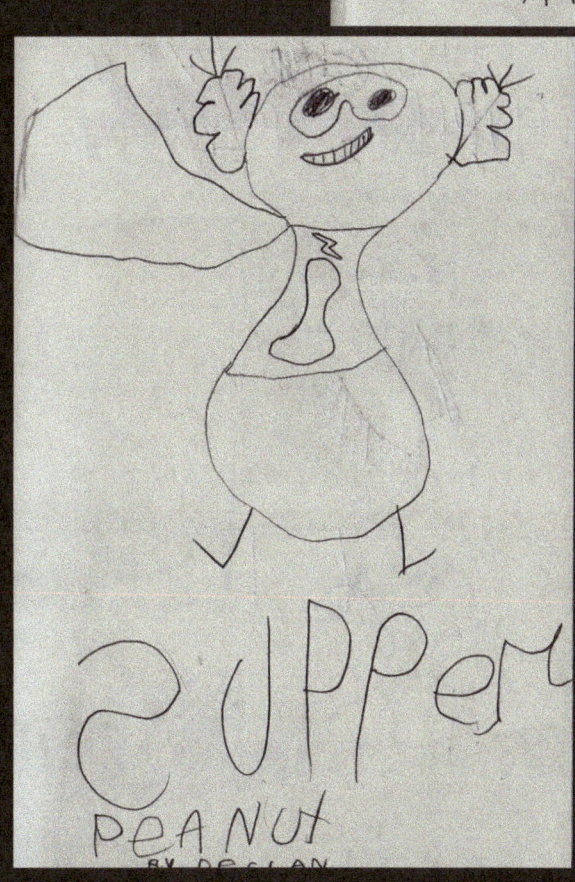

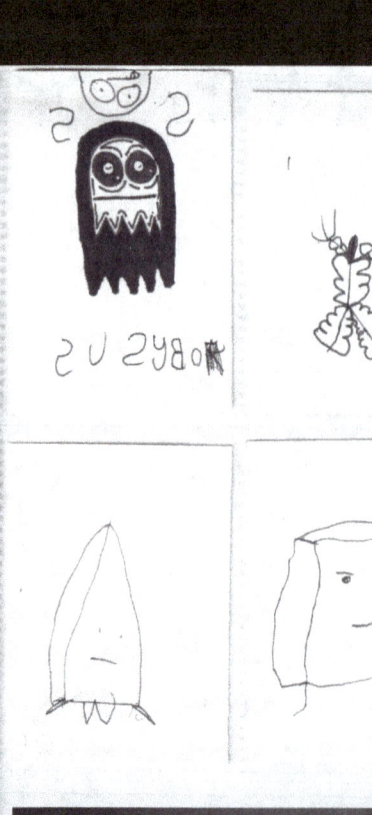
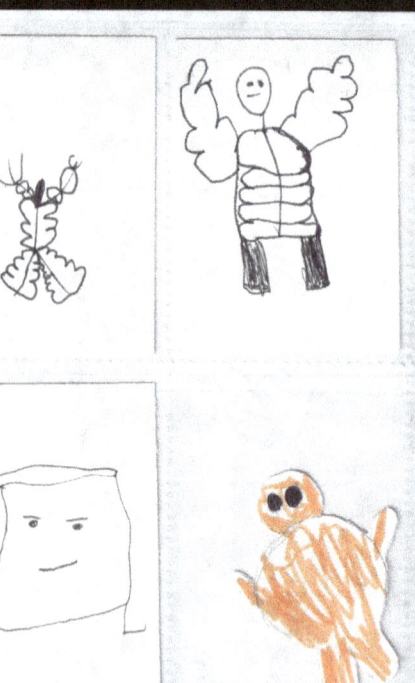
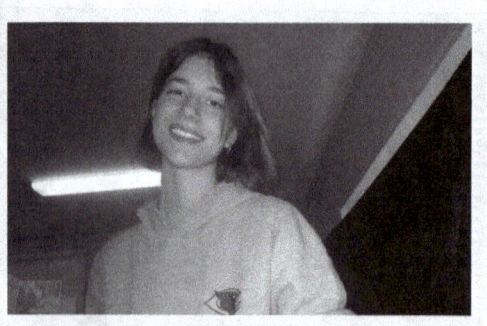
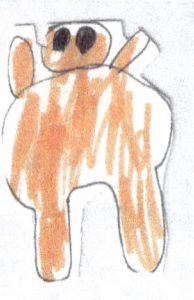
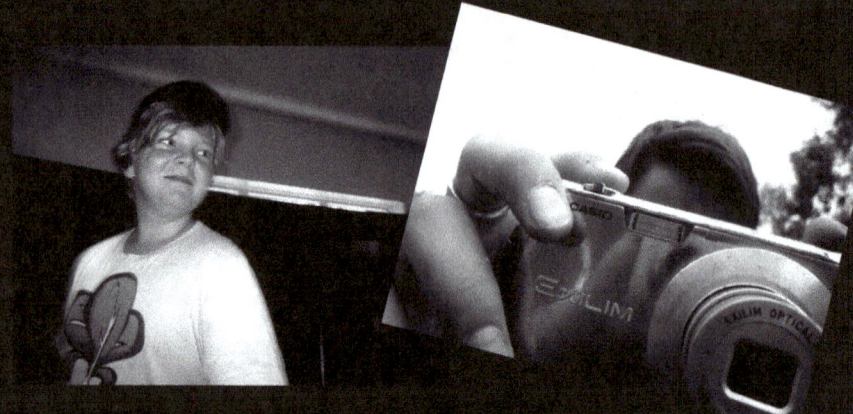

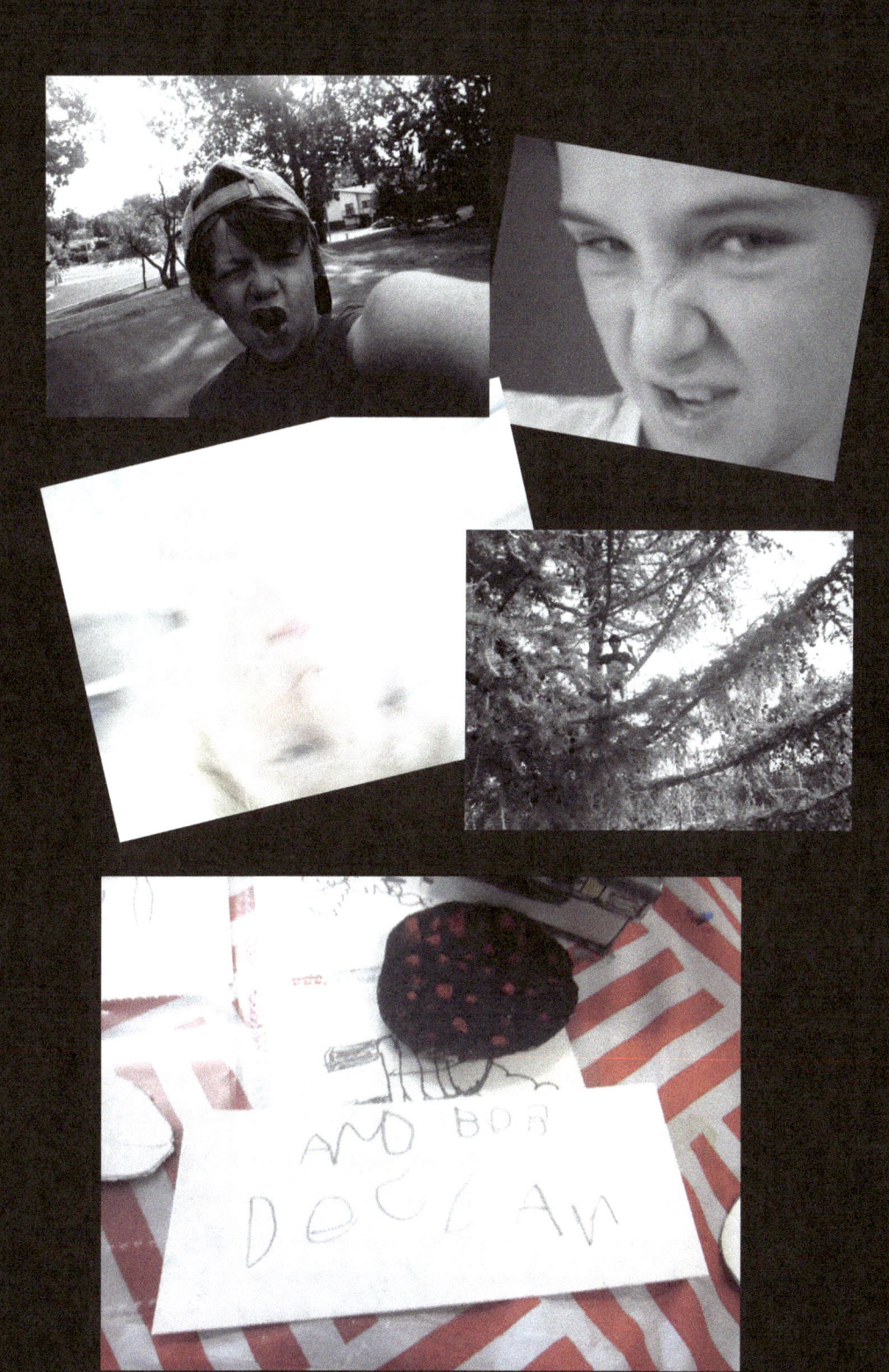

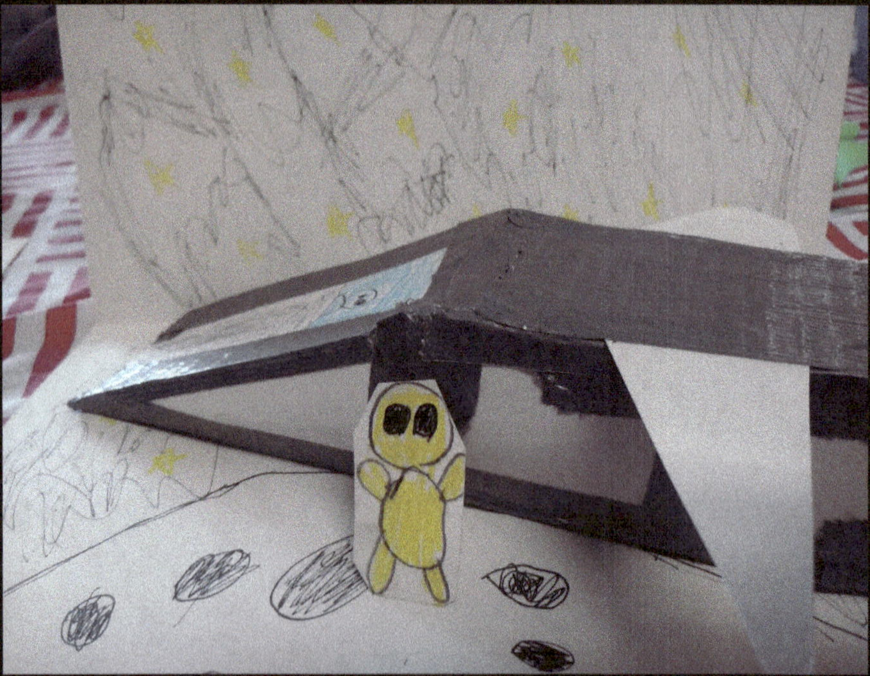

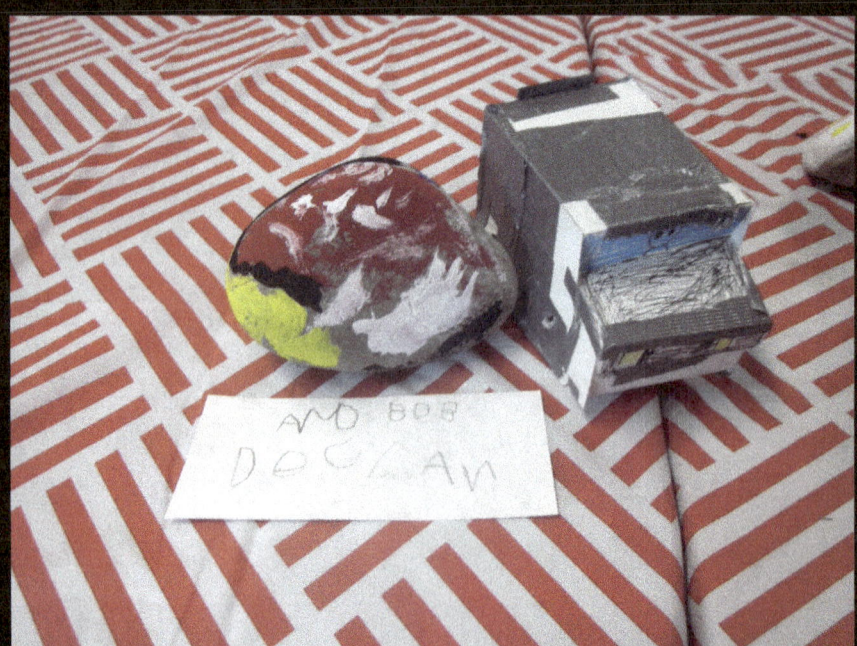

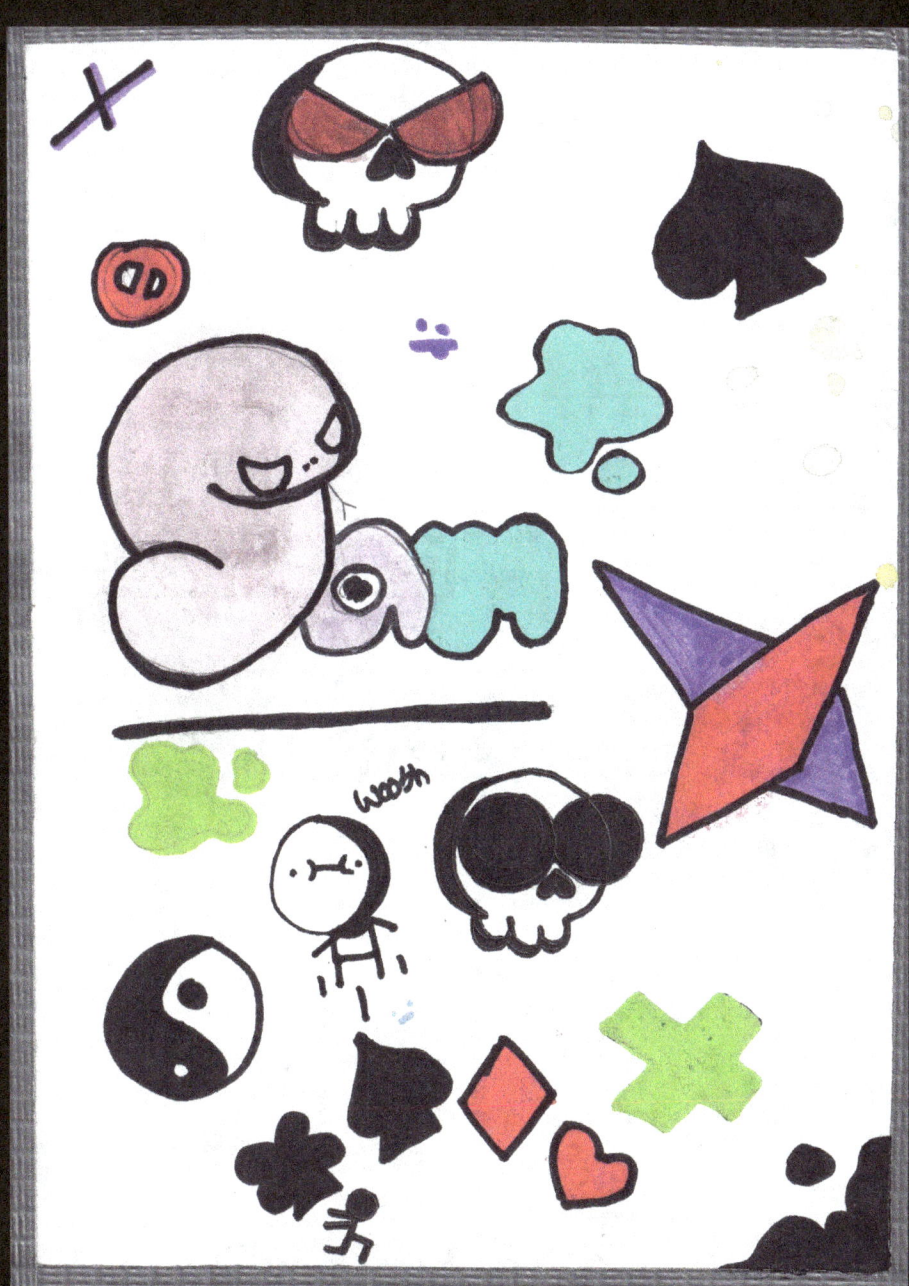

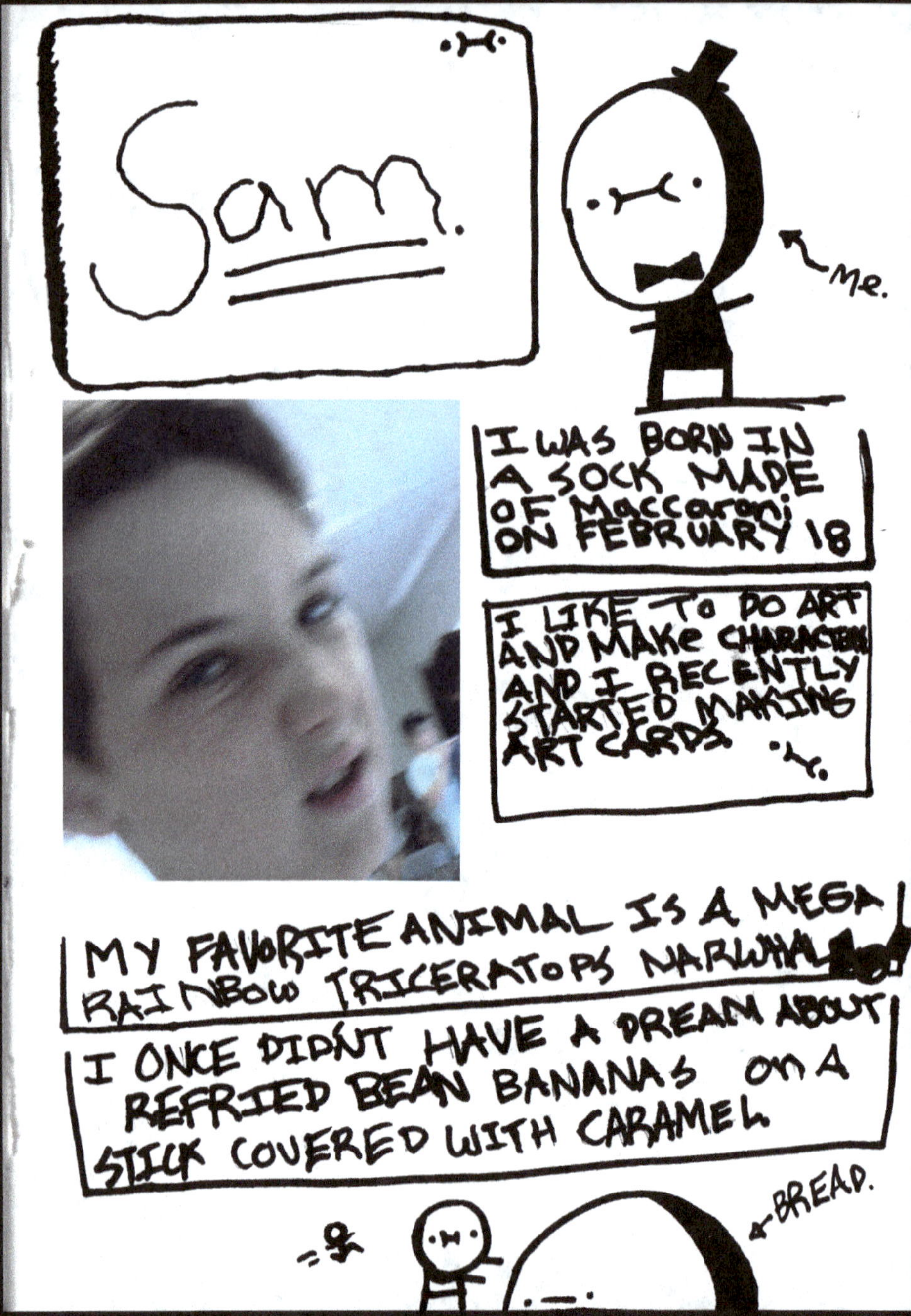

Sam.

← me.

I WAS BORN IN A SOCK MADE OF MACCARONI ON FEBRUARY 18

I LIKE TO DO ART AND MAKE CHARACTERS AND I RECENTLY STARTED MAKING ART CARDS.

MY FAVORITE ANIMAL IS A MEGA RAINBOW TRICERATOPS NARWHAL

I ONCE DIDN'T HAVE A DREAM ABOUT REFRIED BEAN BANANAS ON A STICK COVERED WITH CARAMEL

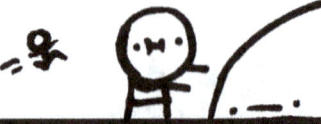

←BREAD.

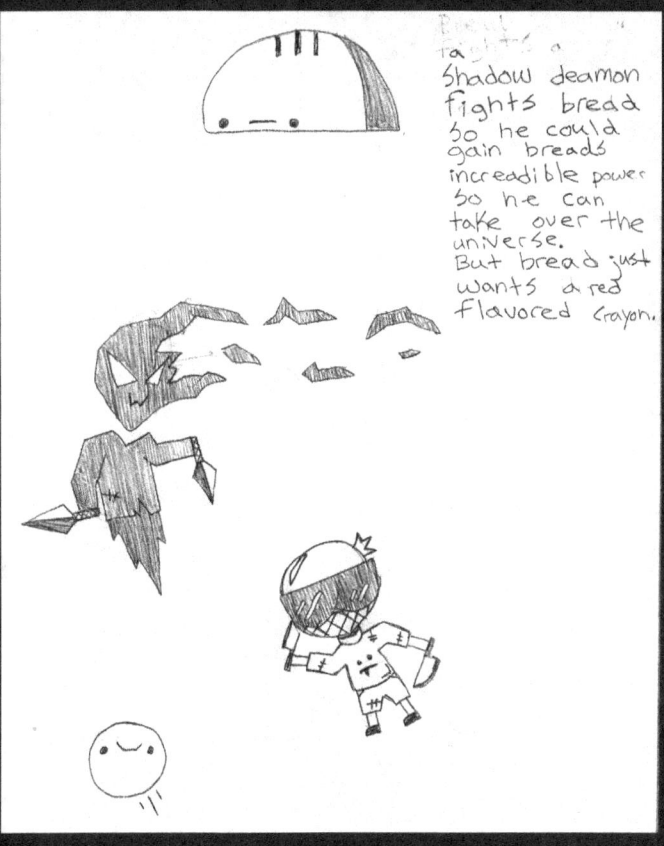
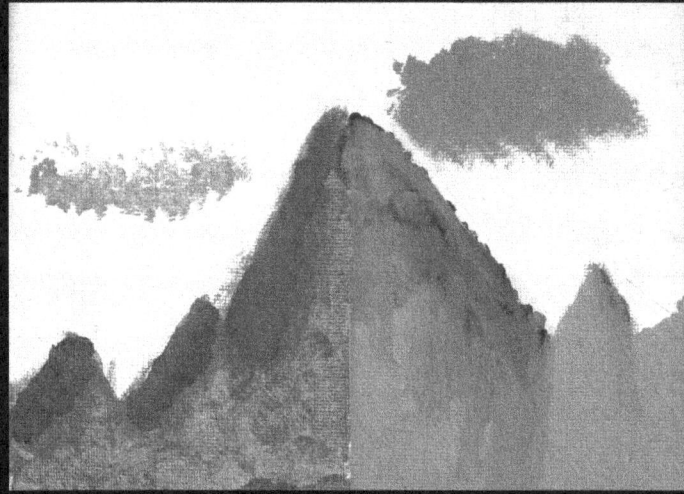

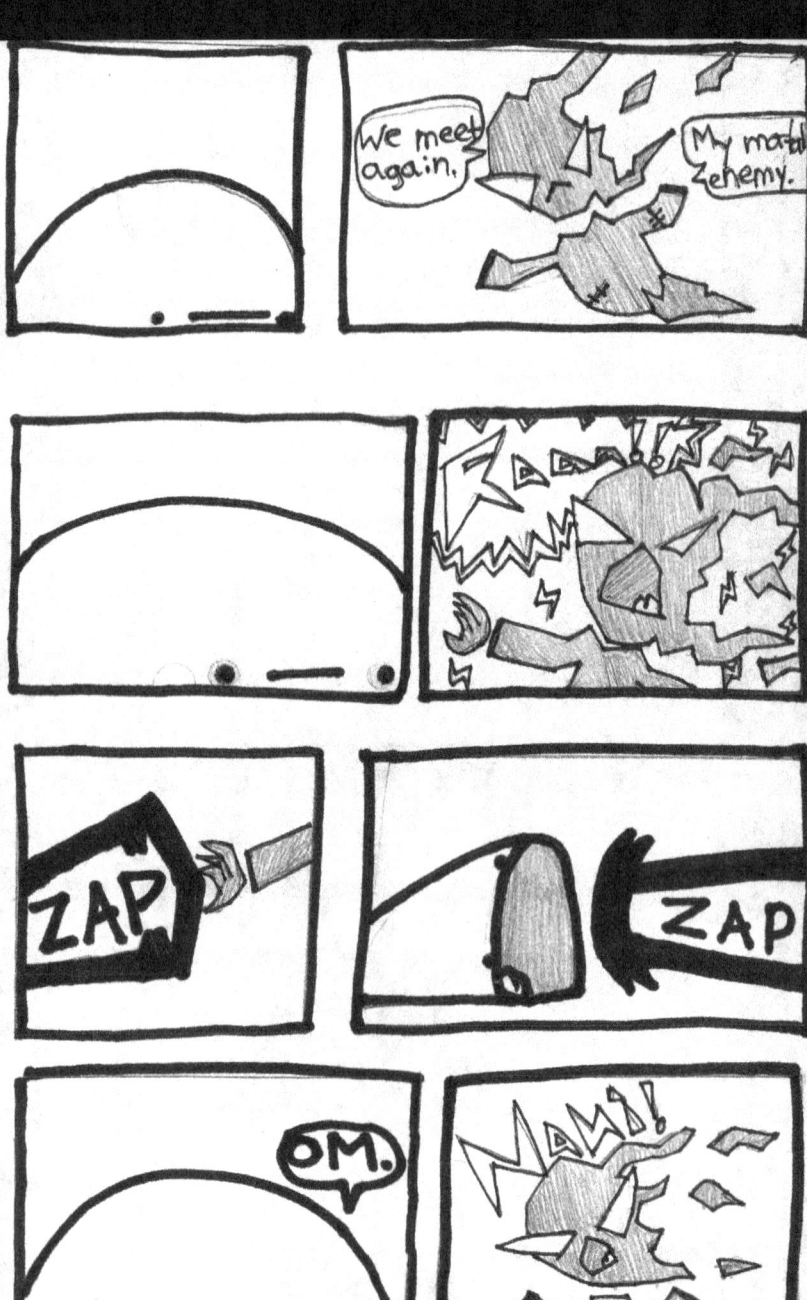

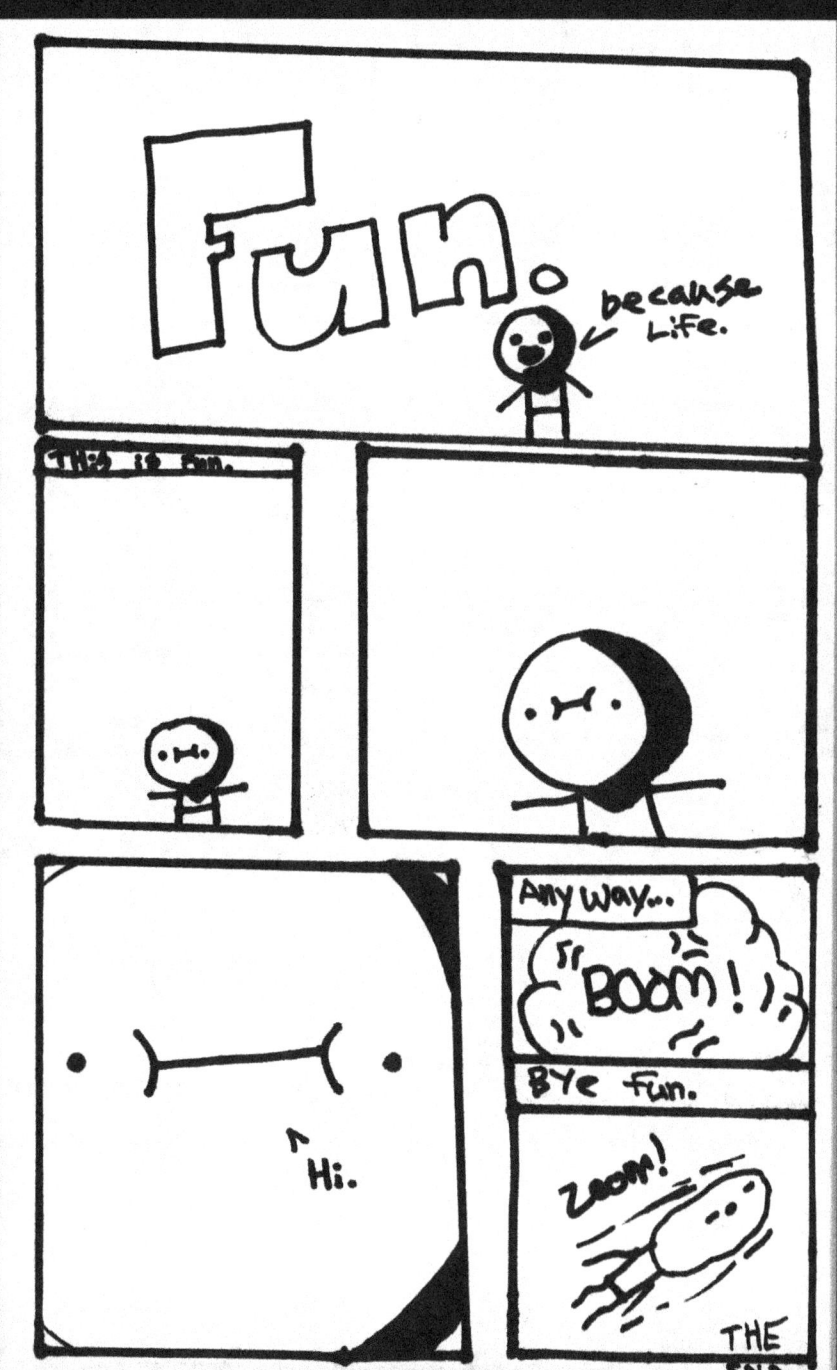

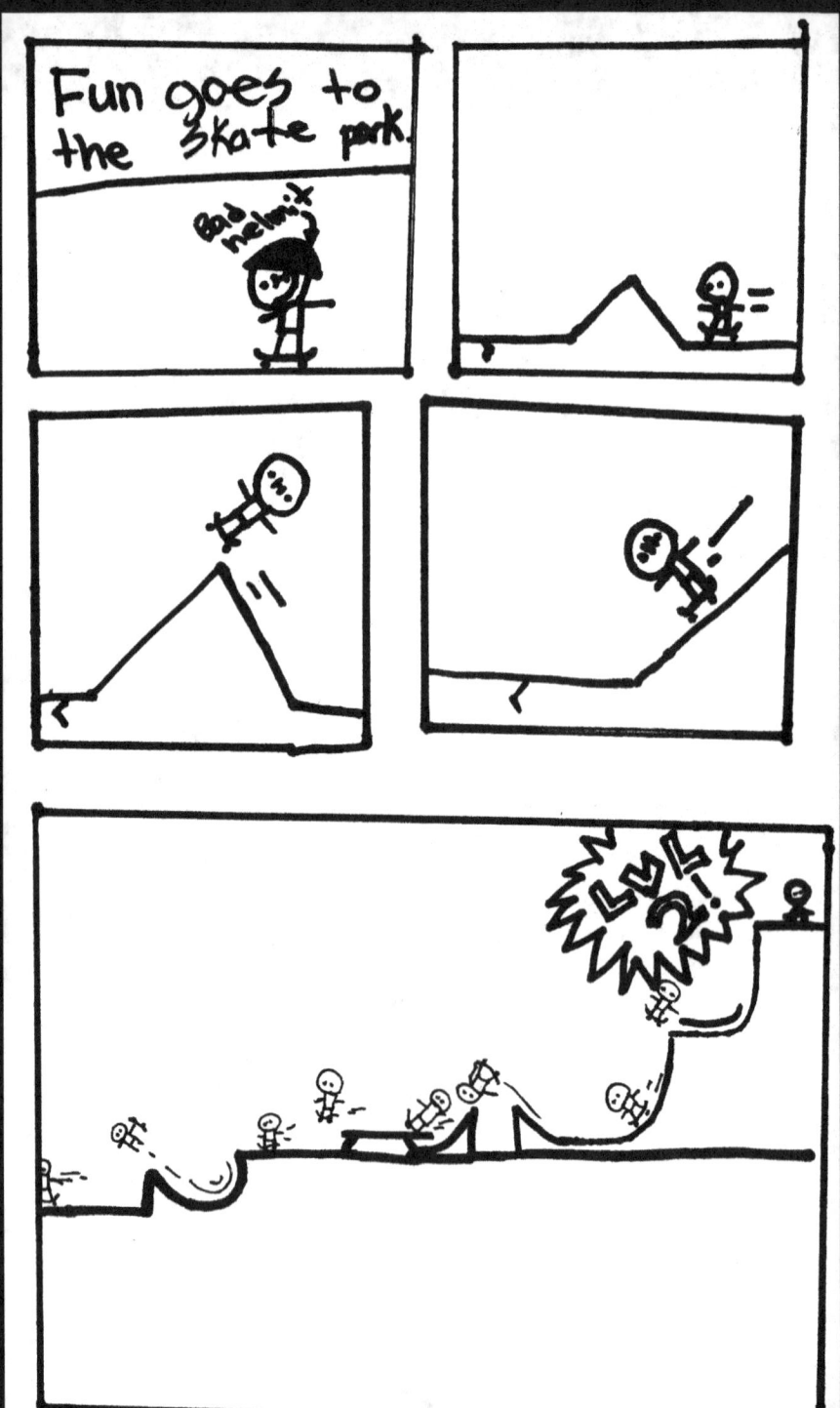

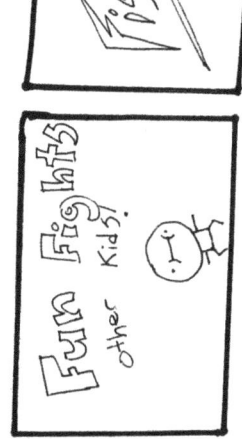
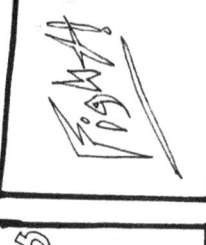
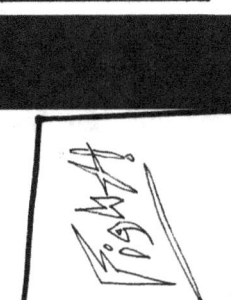
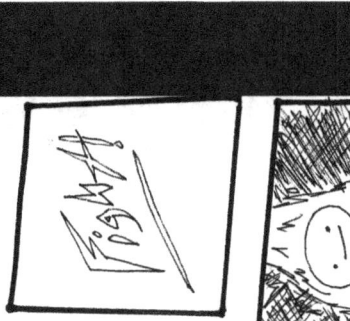
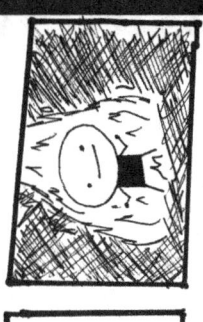
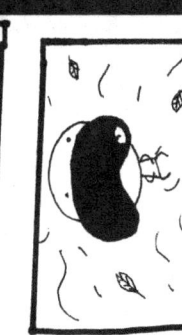
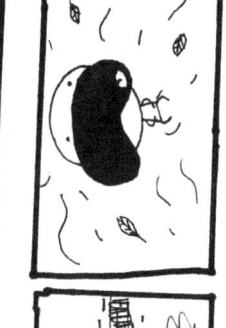

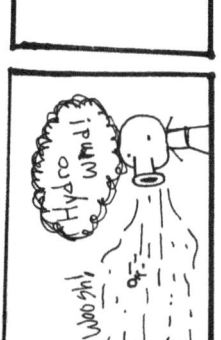
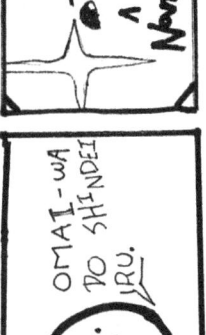
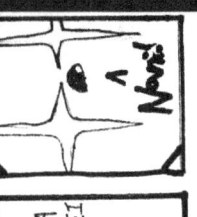
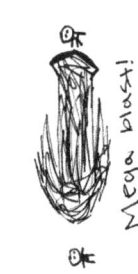
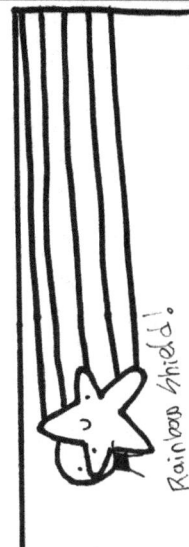

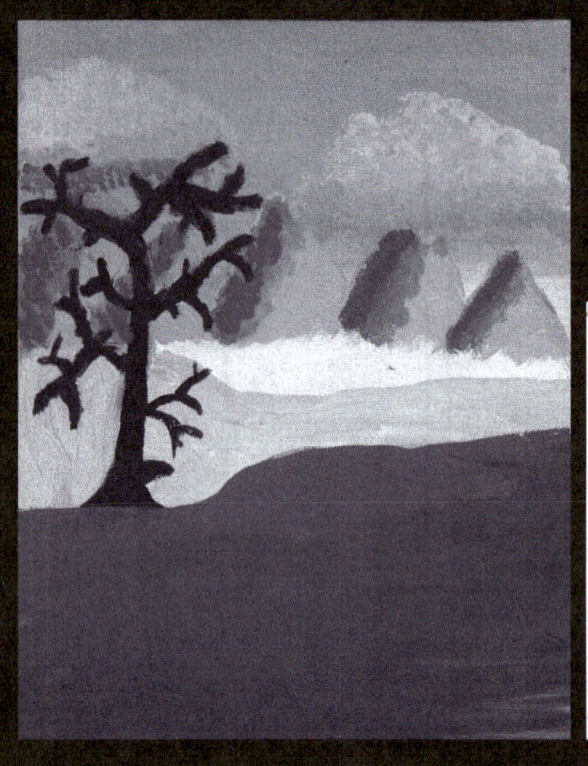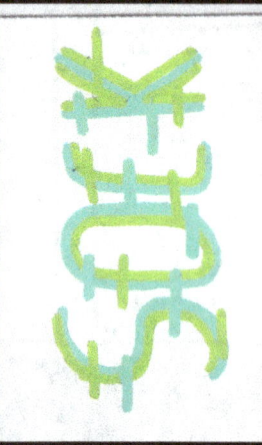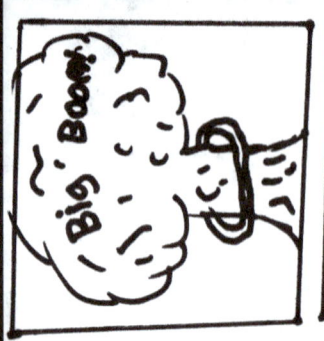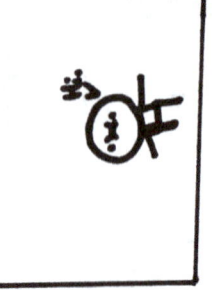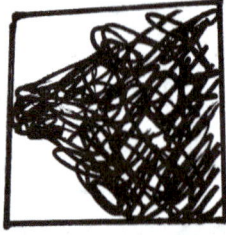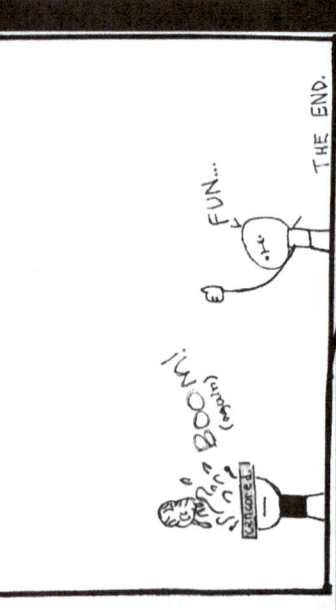

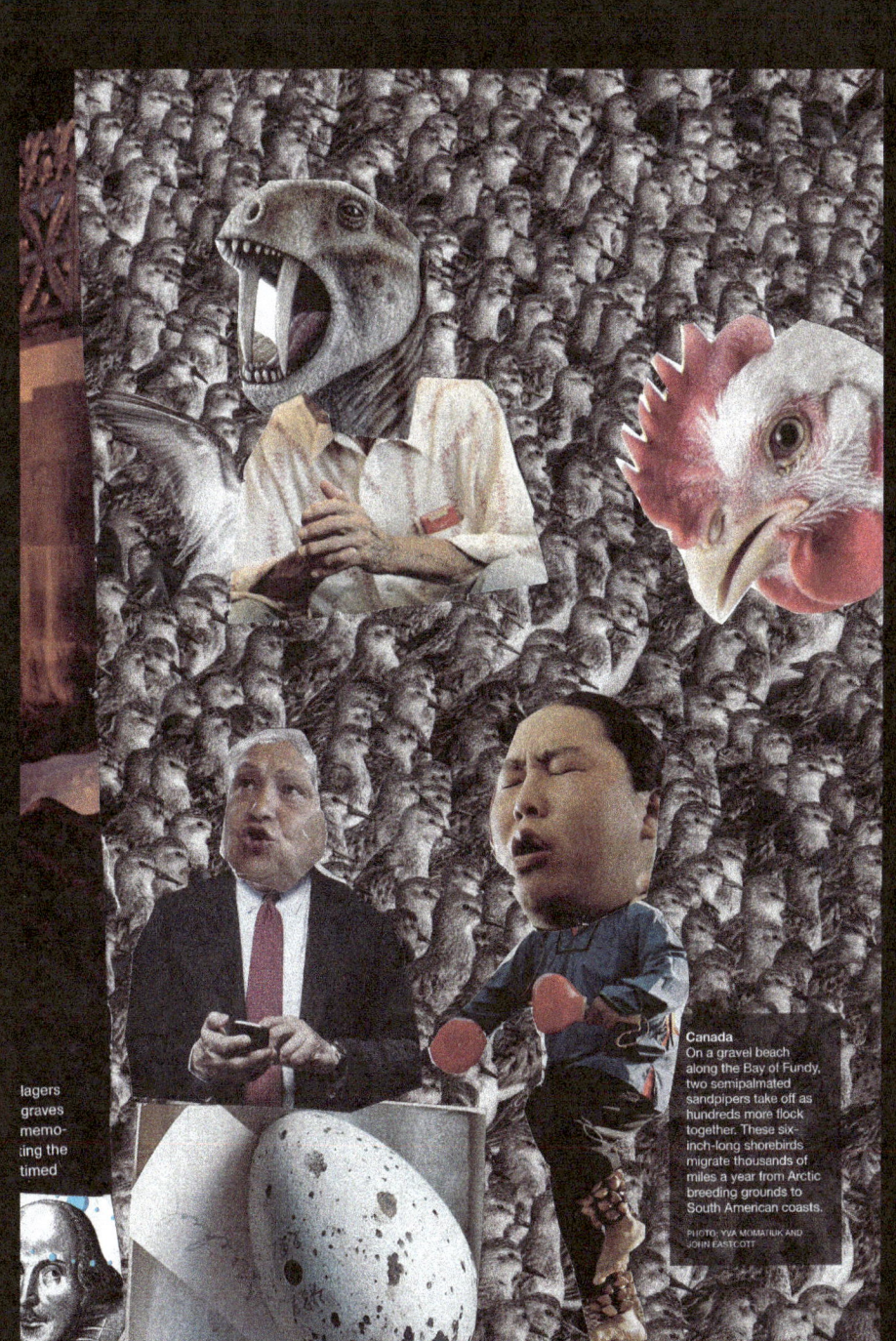

lagers
graves
memo-
ting the
timed

Canada
On a gravel beach along the Bay of Fundy, two semipalmated sandpipers take off as hundreds more flock together. These six-inch-long shorebirds migrate thousands of miles a year from Arctic breeding grounds to South American coasts.

PHOTO: YVA MOMATIUK AND JOHN EASTCOTT

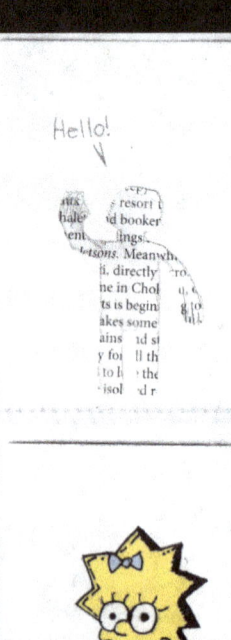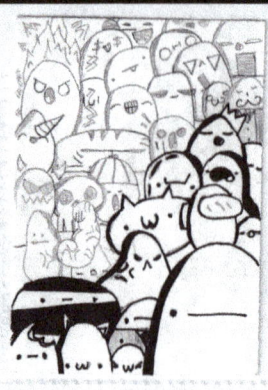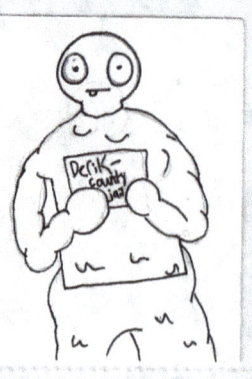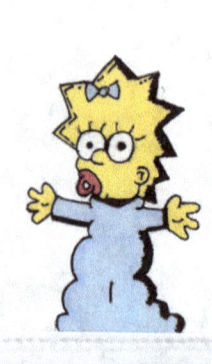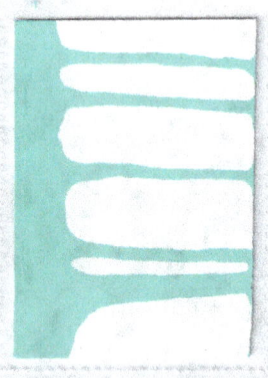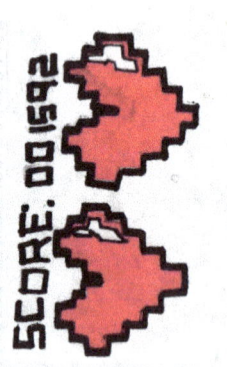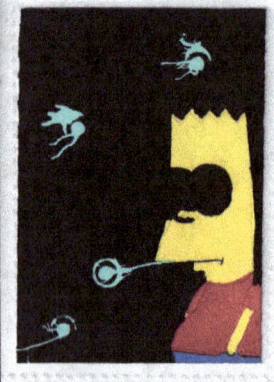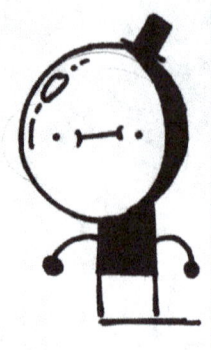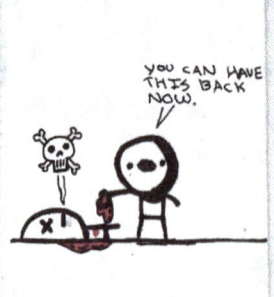

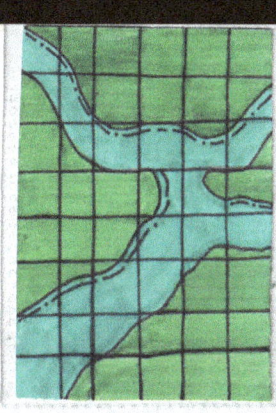
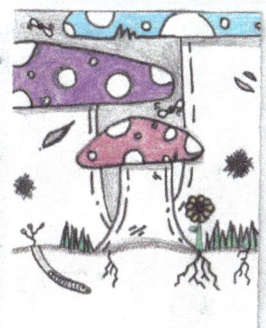
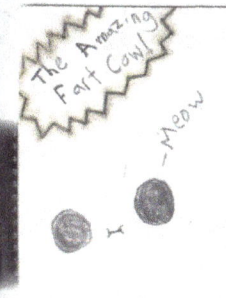
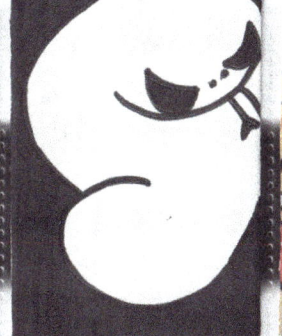
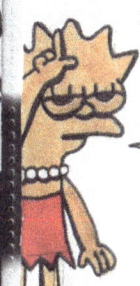

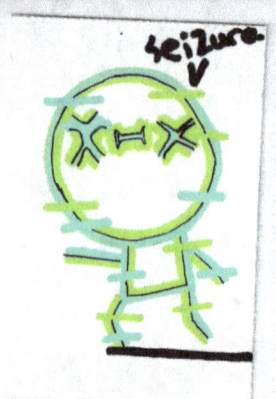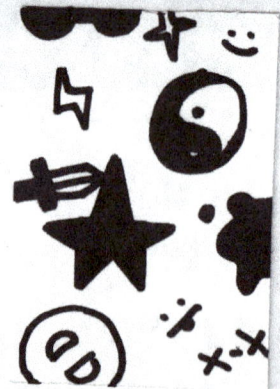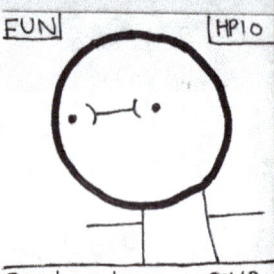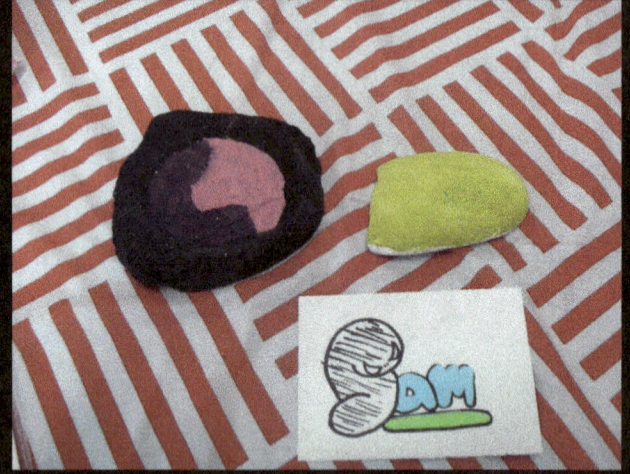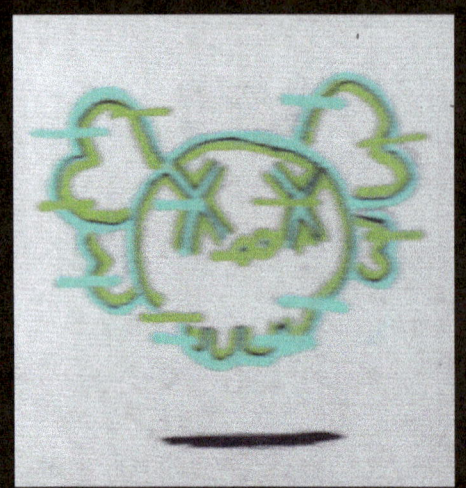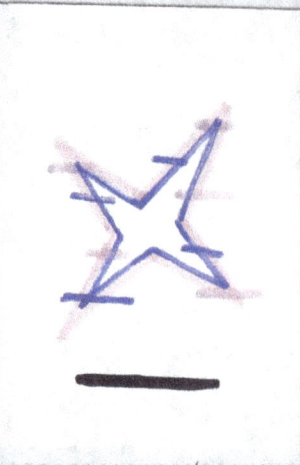

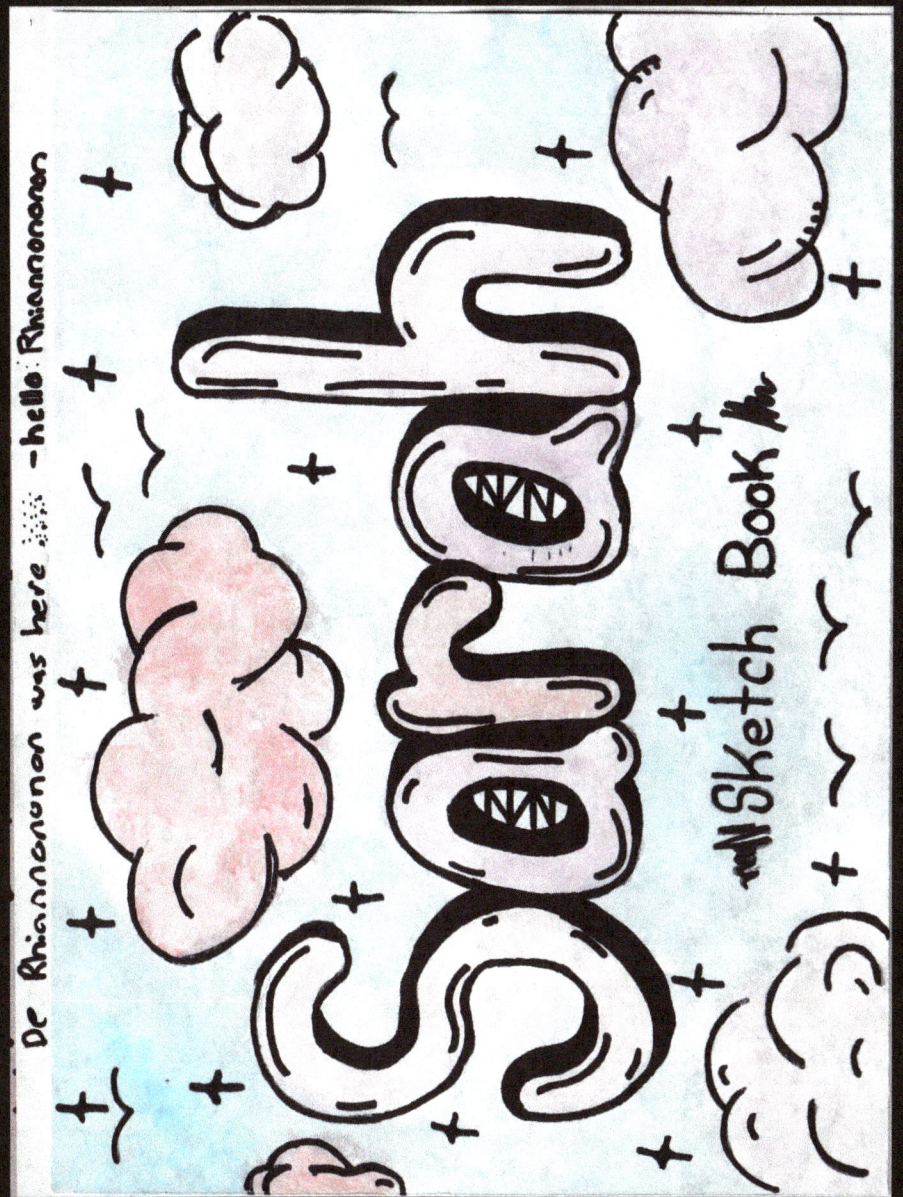

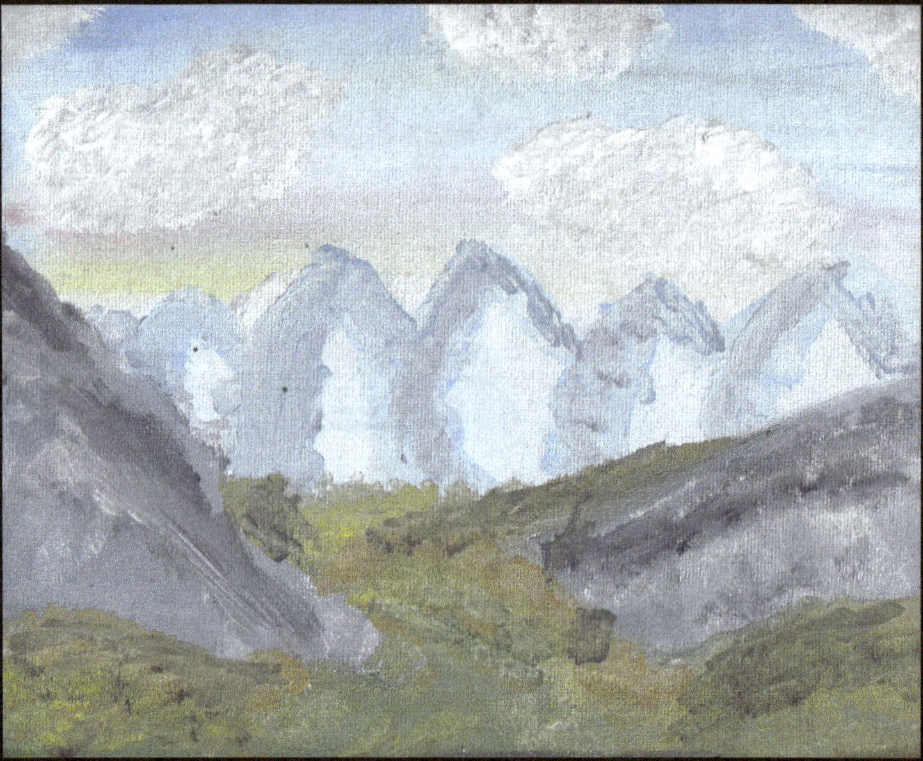

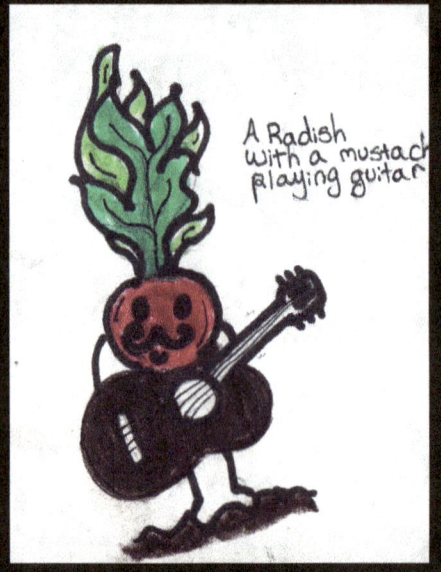

SARAH MOON

Hello! My name is Sarah Moon and I was born on January 28th, 2010. I was in Calgary Canada when I was brought into the world ☺

When I'm older I'd like to become either a nurse or teacher, as well as pursuing something musical. I'm not 100% sure yet though ☺

- I have two pets, a bird and a dog!
- Some of my favourite animals are cows ☺
- I love music AKA playing guitar and singing.

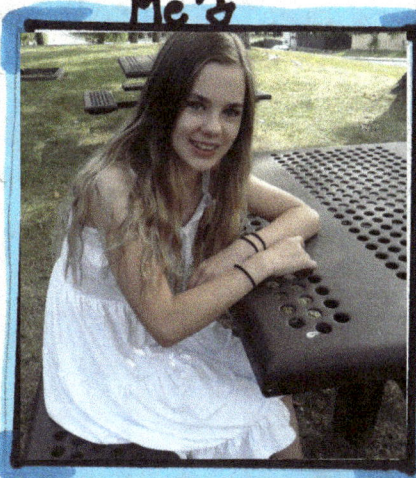
Me ?

Some answered questions

Favourite animal(s): Cows, Birds, Dogs.

Strange Dream: I had a dream where there was a competition to make your toothbrush bristles the straightest, needless to say it was very weird ☺

Another dream I had took place in a gymnastics center with my friends. We walked around, it transformed to Christmas, and we all had kids.

Some cool things about me!! ☺

- My favourite colors are Blue, green, purple, and red.
- I have done over 5 styles of dance.
- All my friends call me "Sawaha"
- I like cooking and baking!
- People say I have nice writing ☺

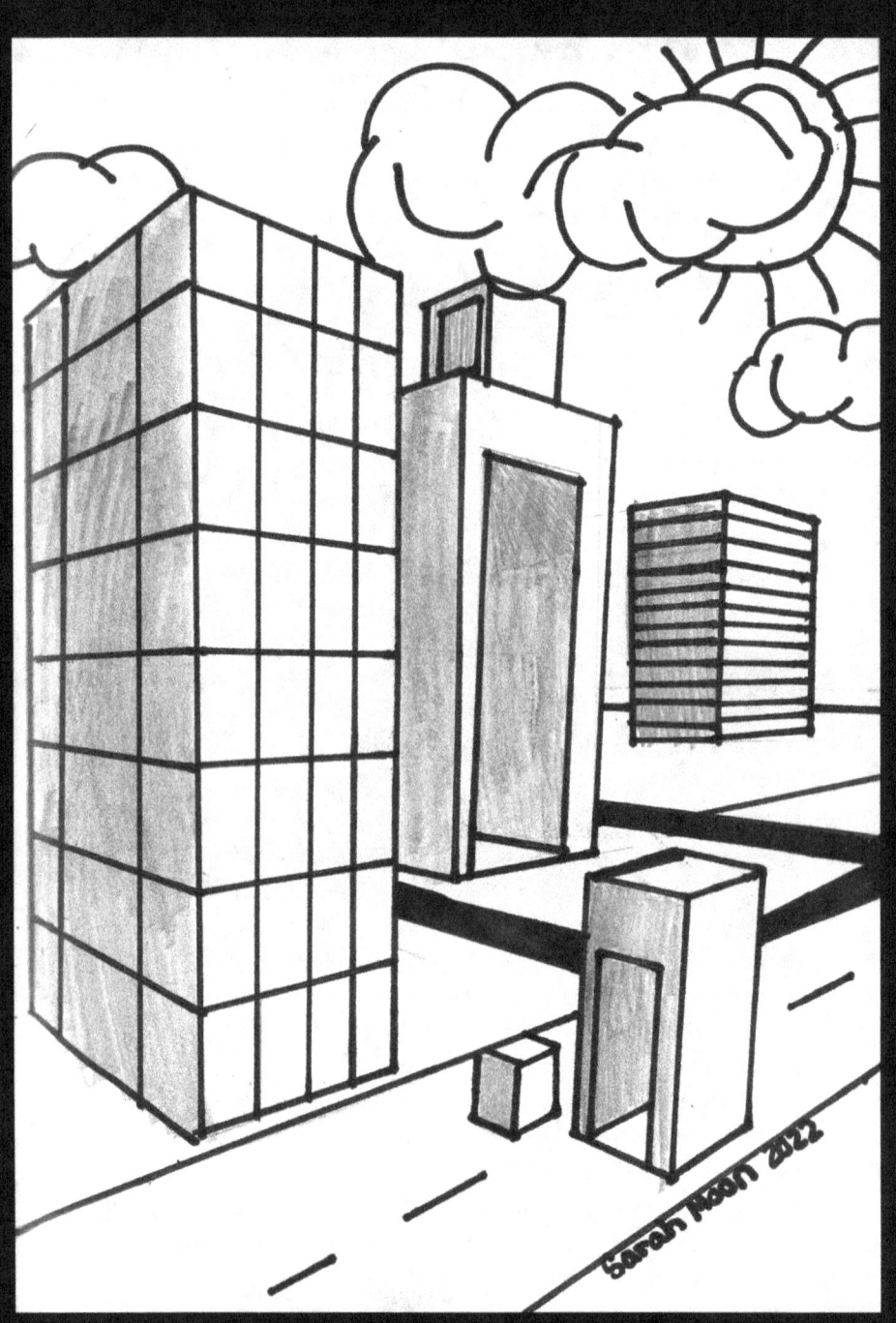

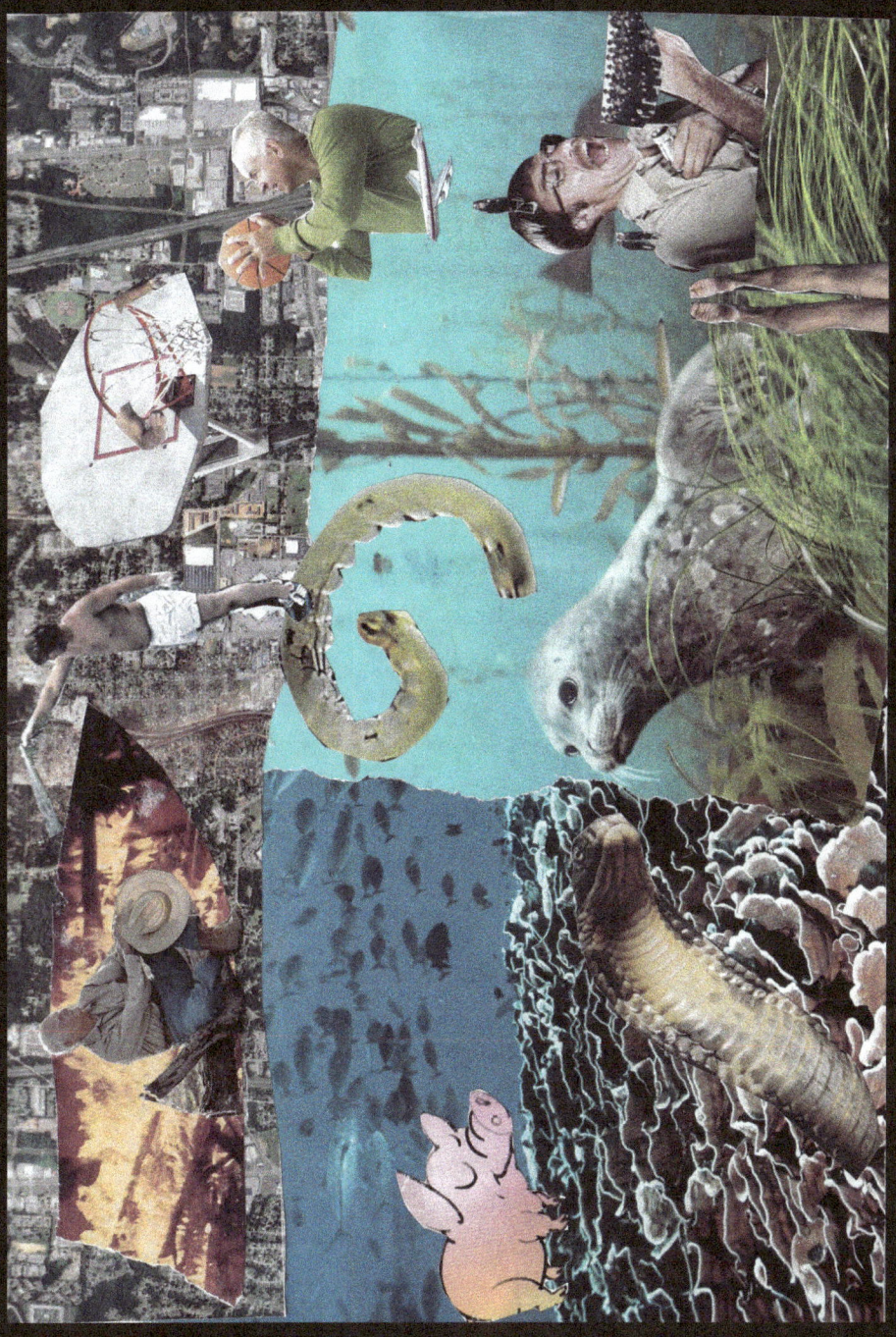

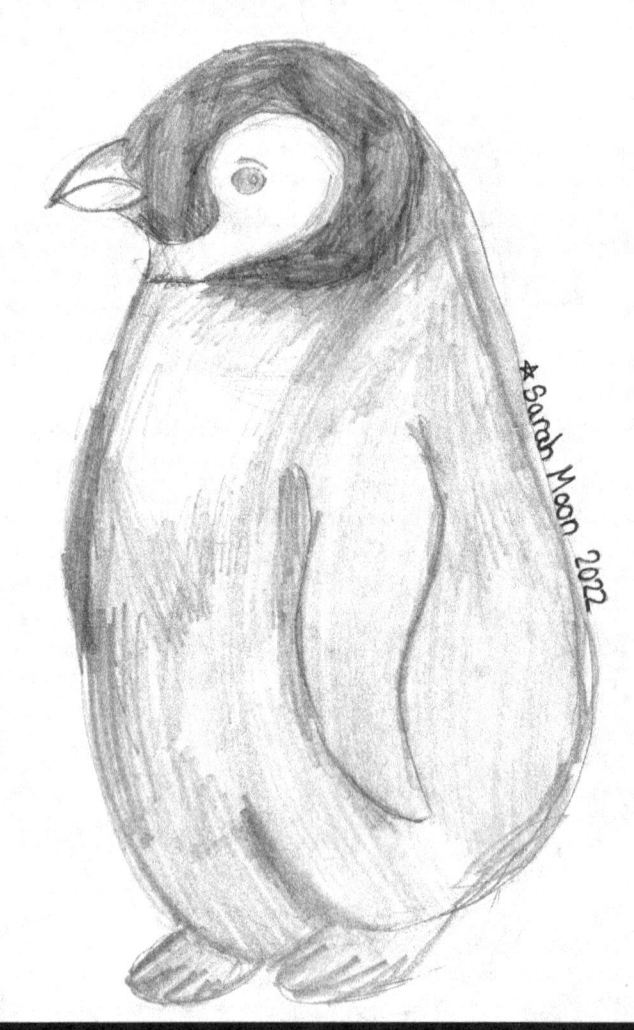

There was once a dog on new york's eve taking on the world. Take thes monkeys he said, twisting a tortice who was making a meso on saturn.

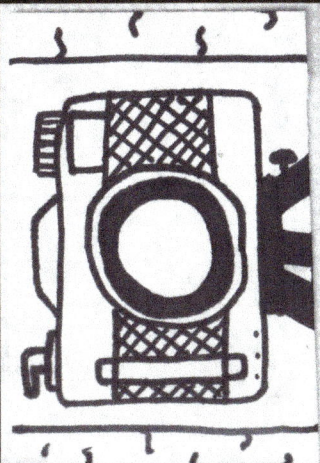

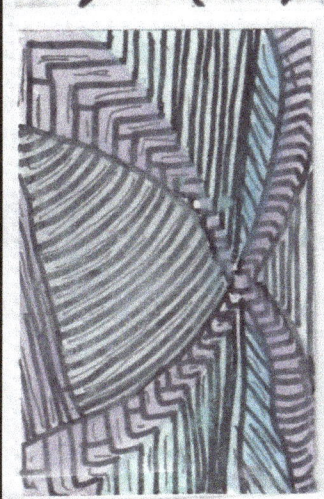

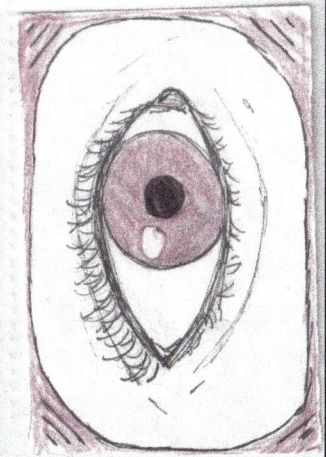

There was a shiny turtle making cookies as he was dancing to disco music. They wanted to arrest a dog he made to be dead. Lovely knife he said. The porcupine laughed Numer a was making papertowel as paper came into the car. "Normal weather" he said, while crushing a bag of onions. To be alive makes you cucumber, Lots of furnaces die these days. You must tell the bride about nature and how it is a devil. Hording telephones make for good decision in later life. Designer thumb nails are in your future. Let them be a dog. Telepathic furnature makes me think you love you. When are you going home he said, monsters coming out of the depth. Terrifying stories of a lamp, curling her hair while making majic. They lived to be content.

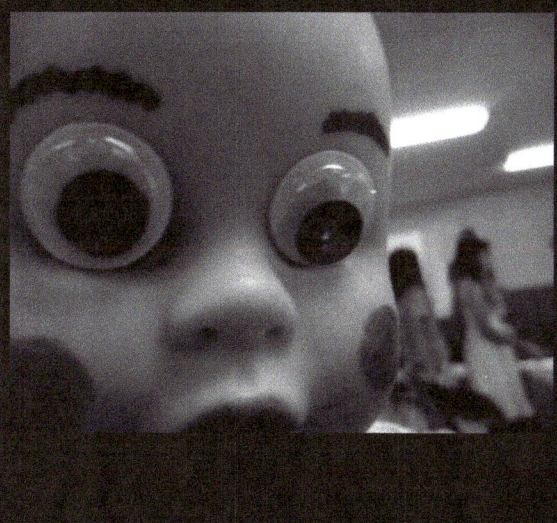

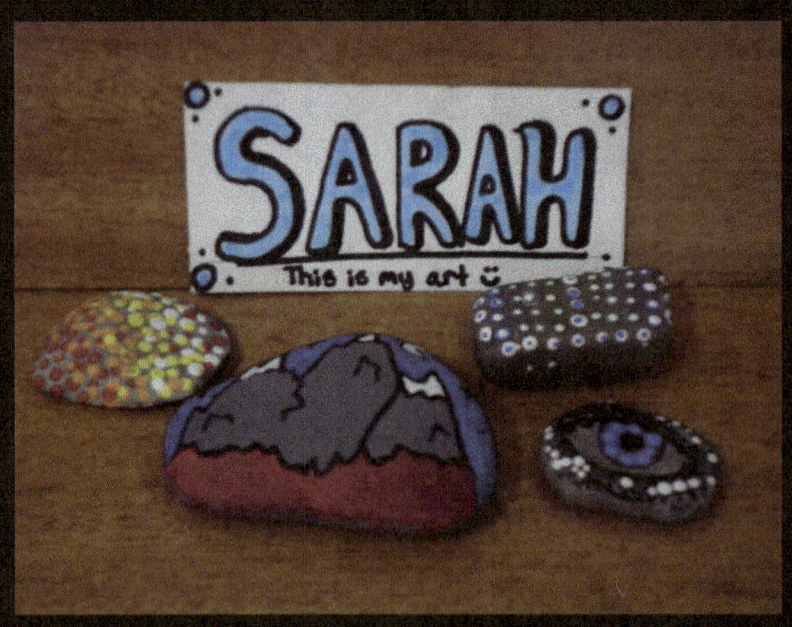
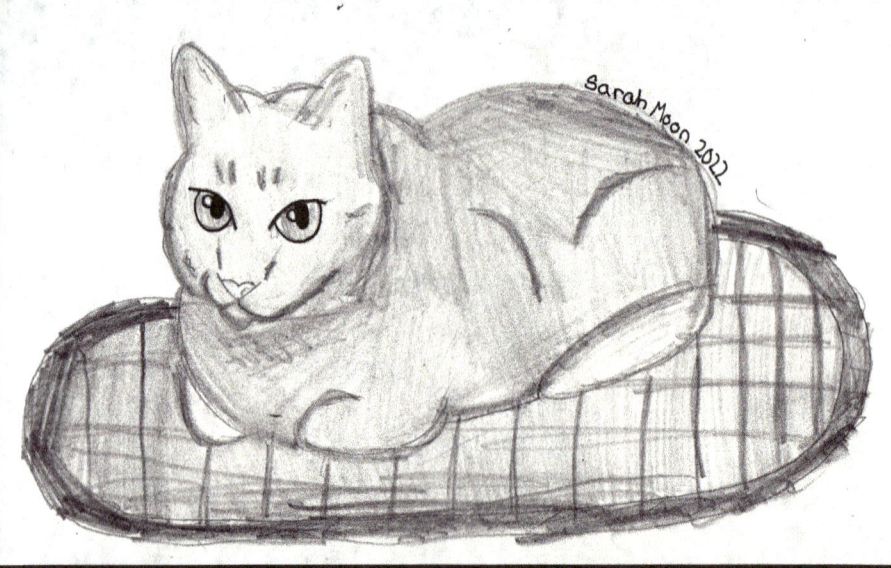

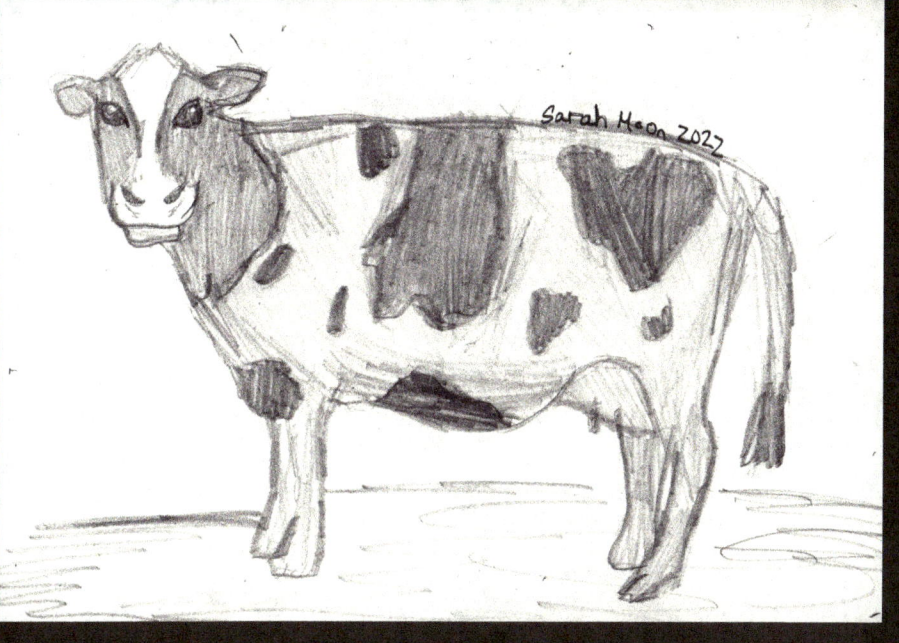

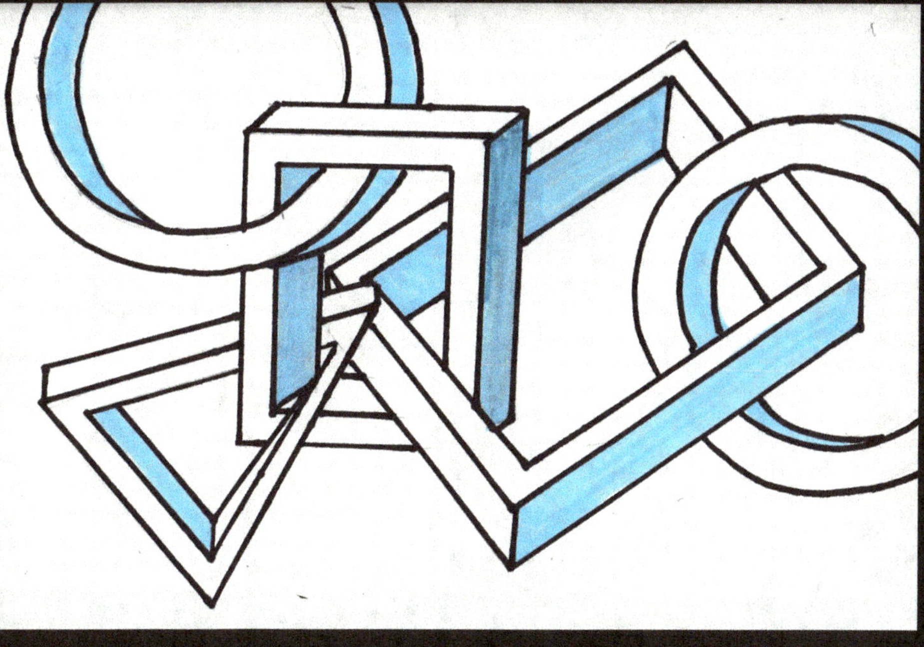

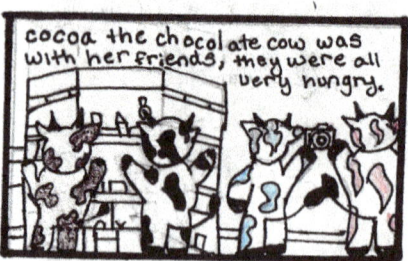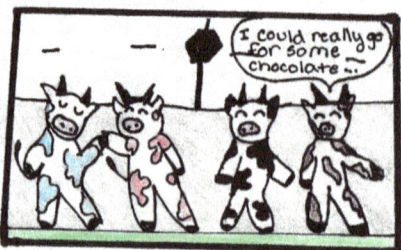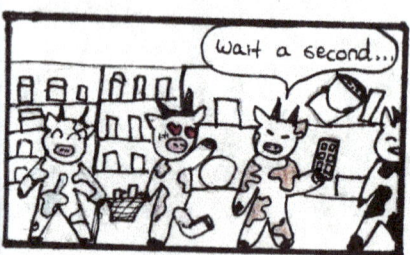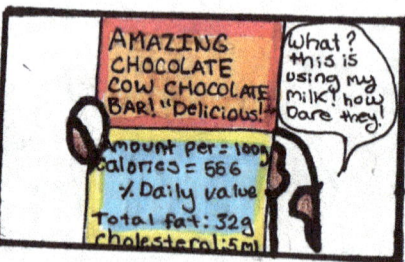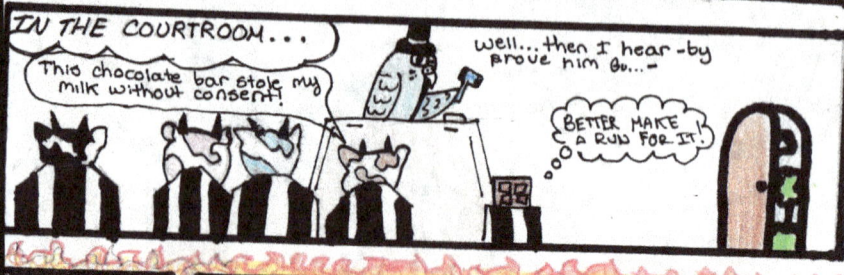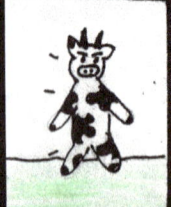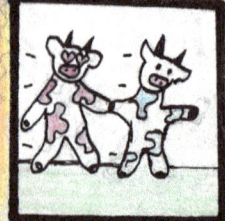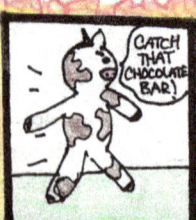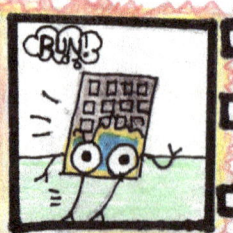

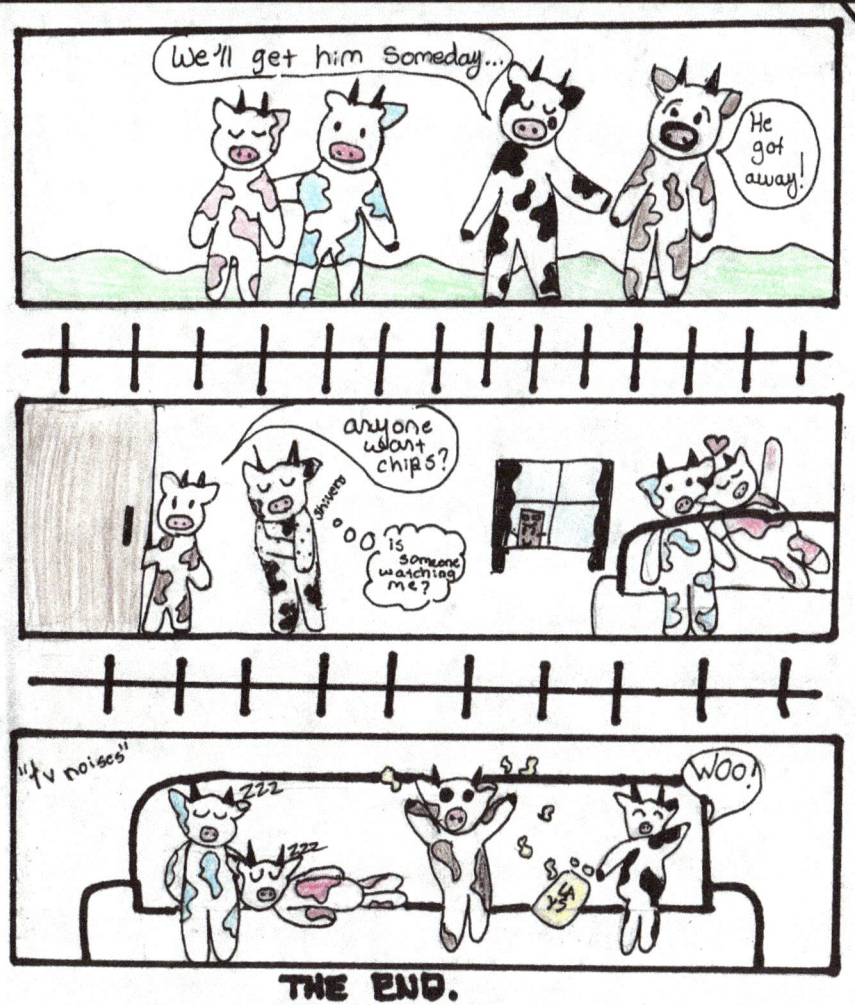

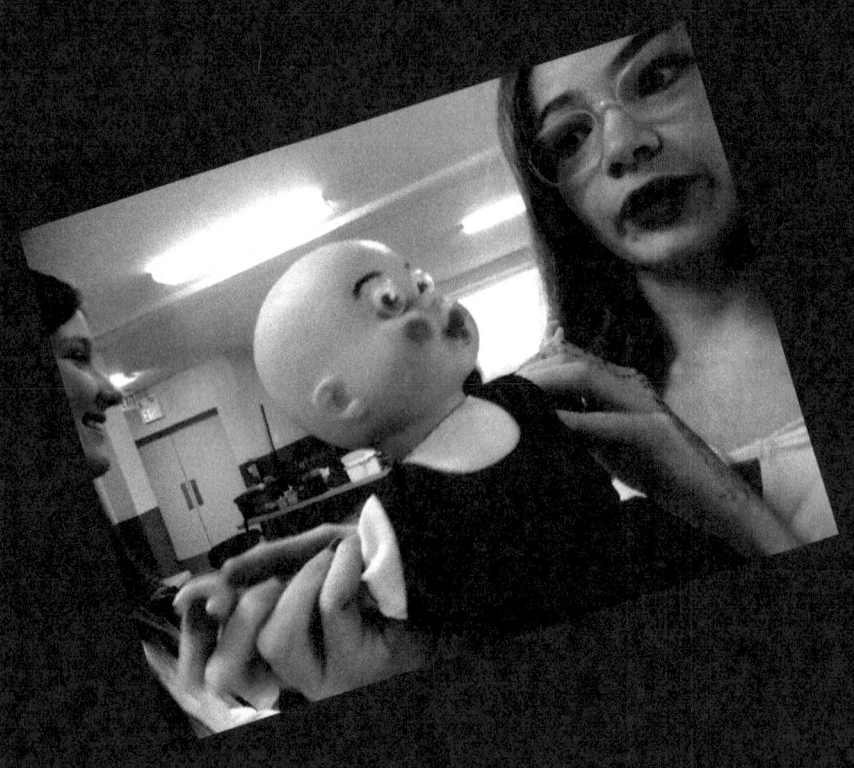

Sophie

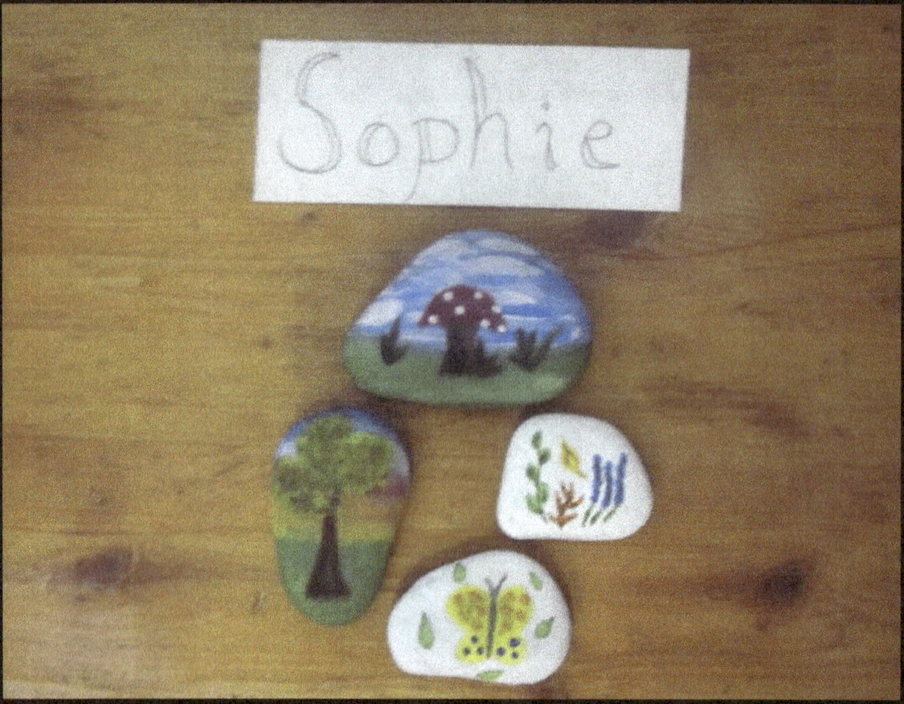

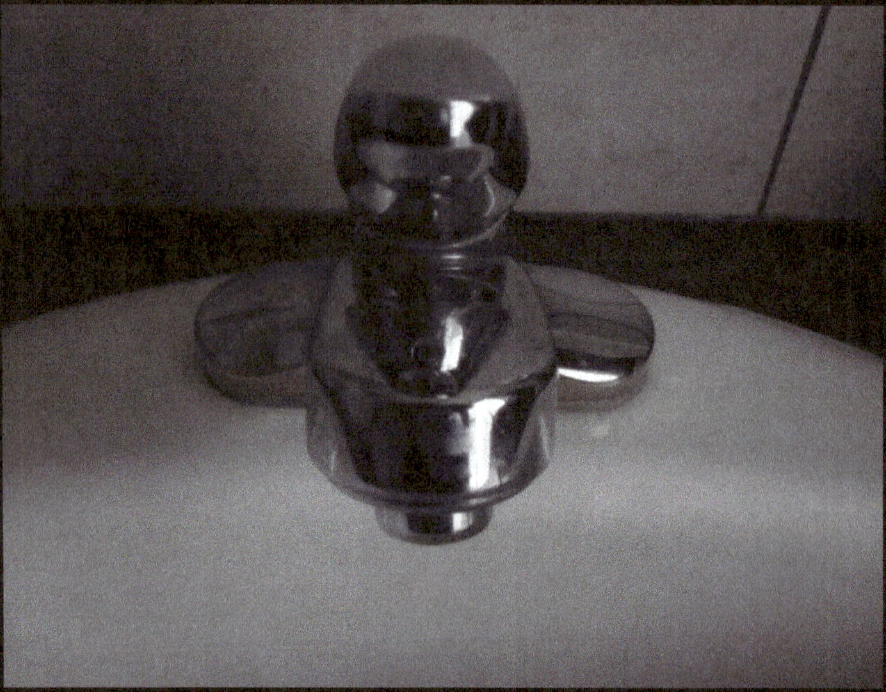

Sophie.

I love to spend time in nature and the mountains.

My favorite instrument to play is the ukulele.

I love the colors blue, turquoise and purple.

My favorite animal is an owl.

I have many pet fish.

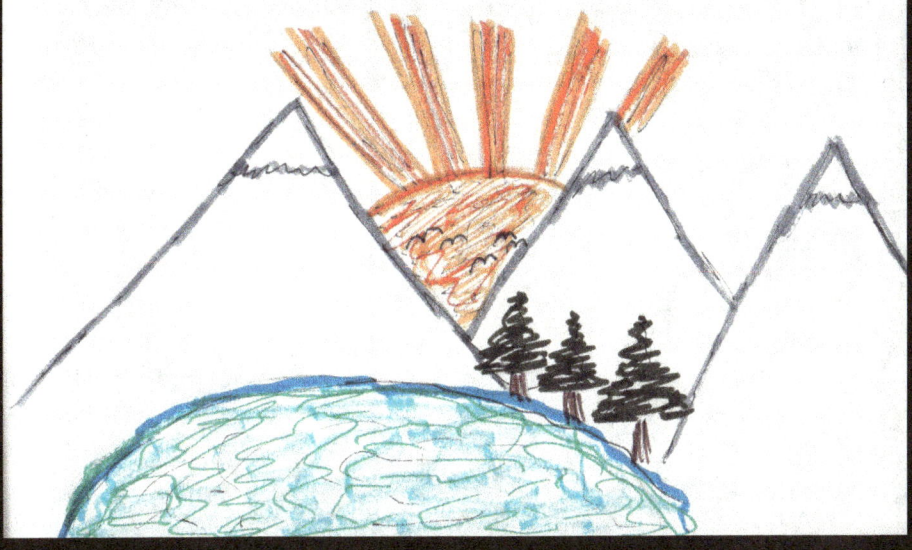

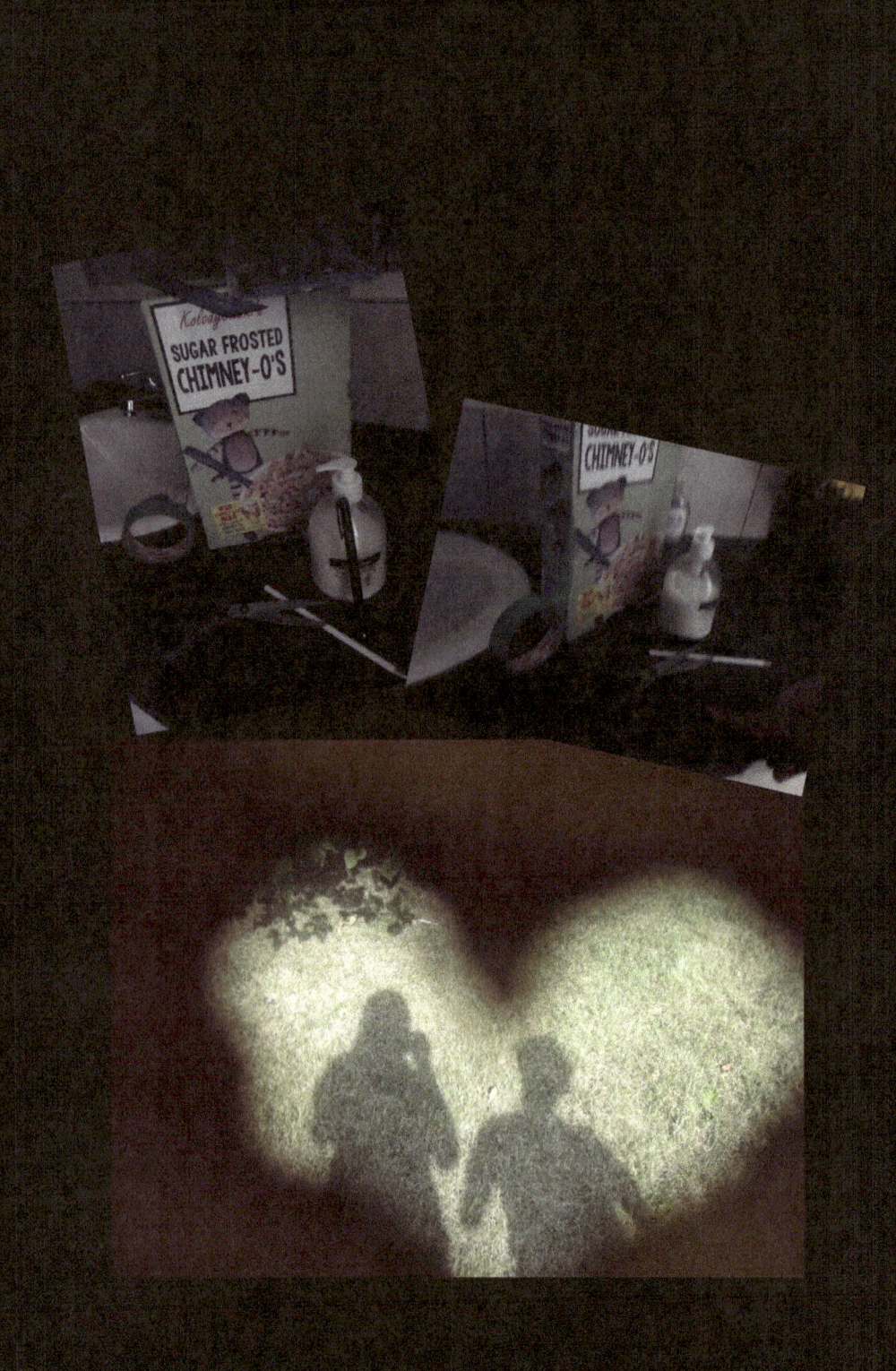

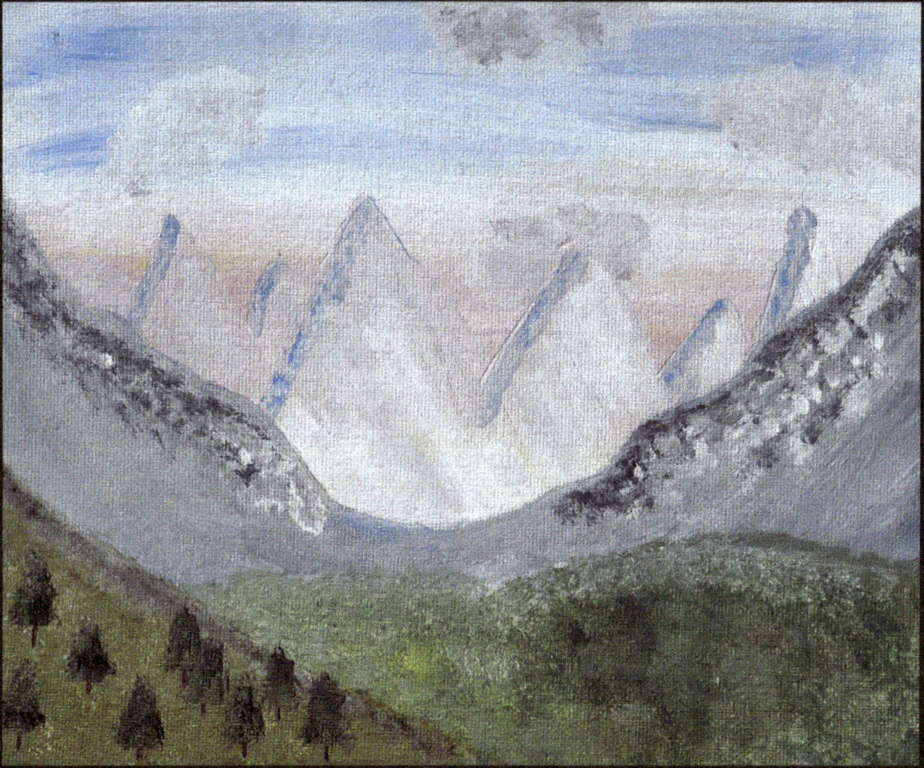

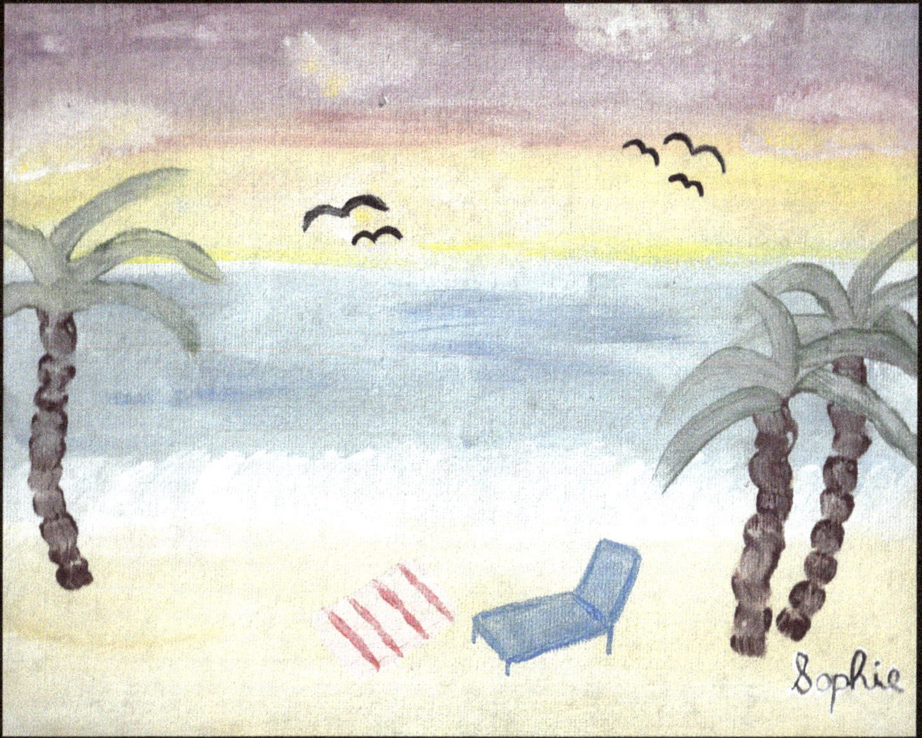

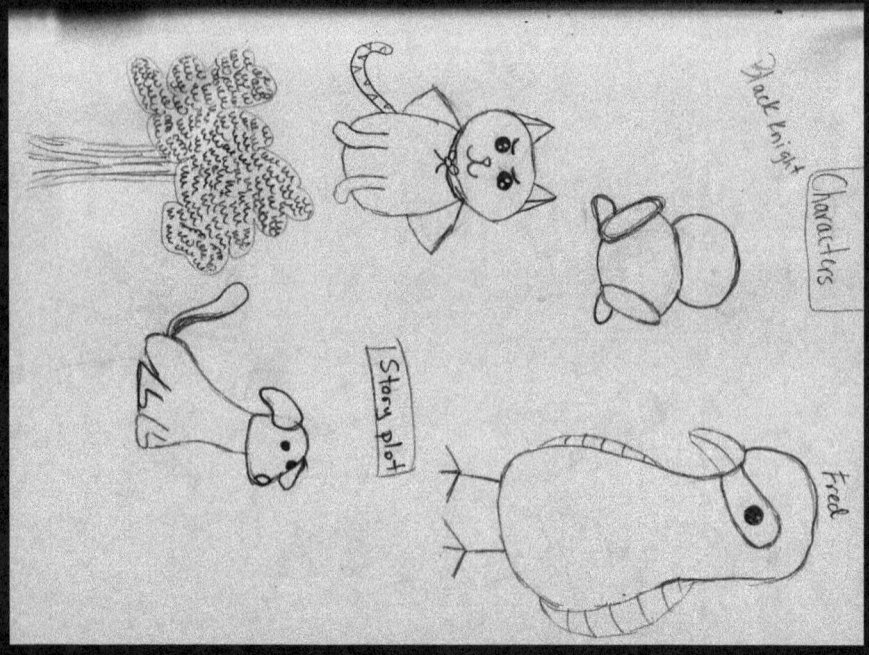

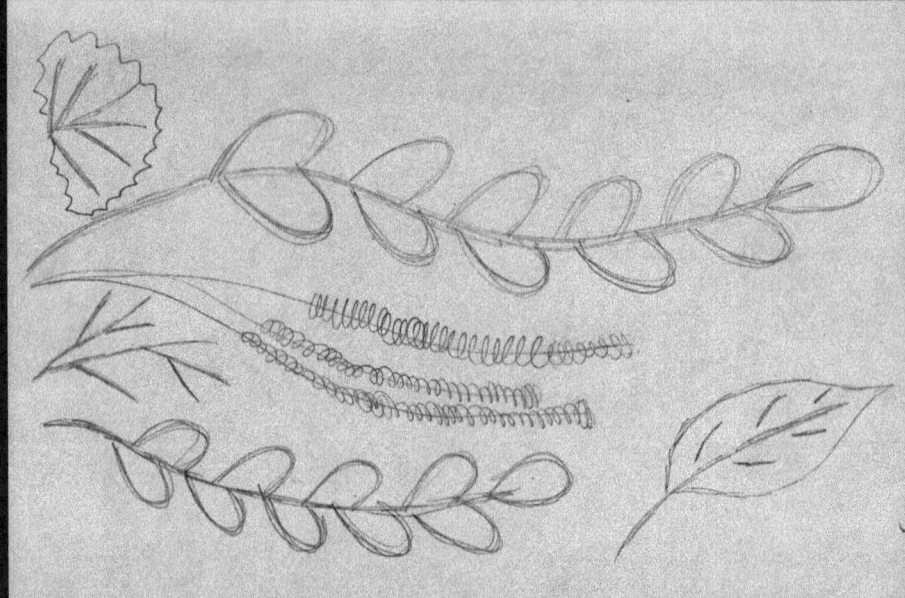

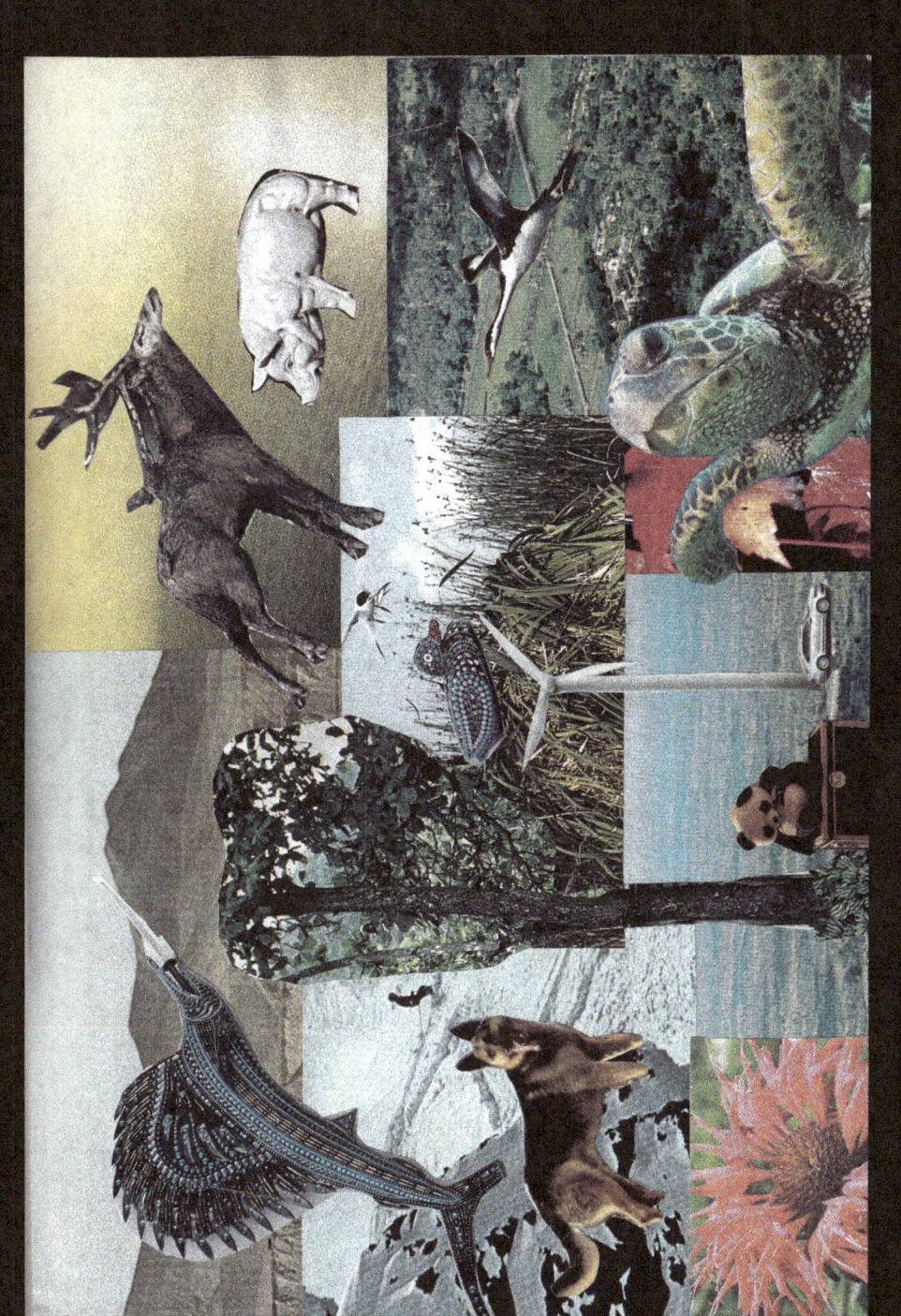

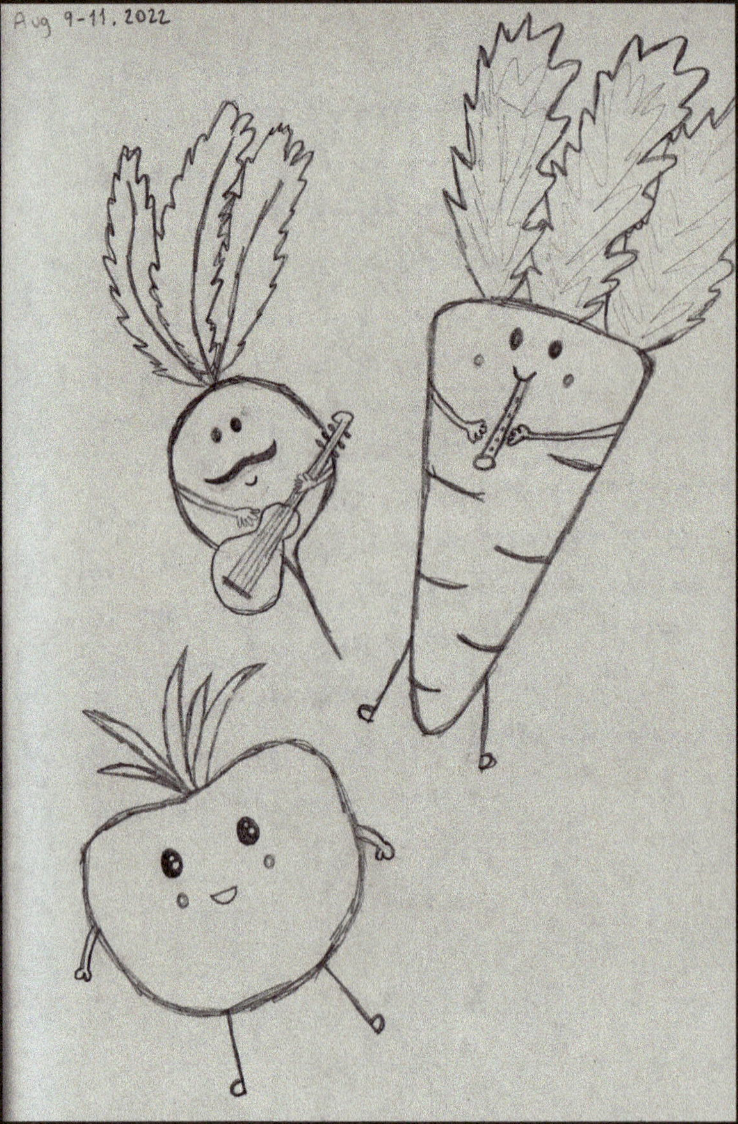

Aug 9-11, 2022

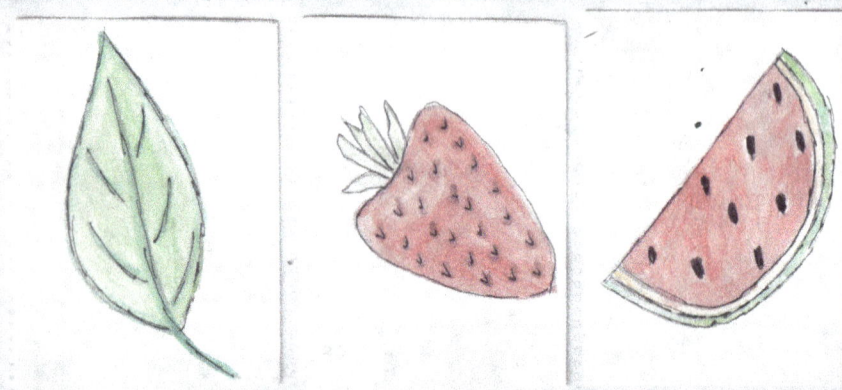

There was a swimming pool and in that pool there was a dog. There also was a cat by the dog, and the dog said "how'd you do, I'm Rex!" The cat looked so confused at what the dog said, so the cat left the pool and went outside by the tree where there was a railroad track. The cat heard the train sound the horn and got so scared of a sudden when the cat jumped up and purred. The cat was so calm that he then realized there was no train horn sounded or no train even coming. The next day the cat met a man named Fred and followed him everywhere he went, to the store, and then Fred walked into the swimming pool building and the cat purred and walked away purring.

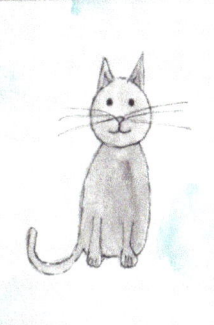
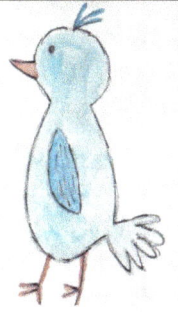
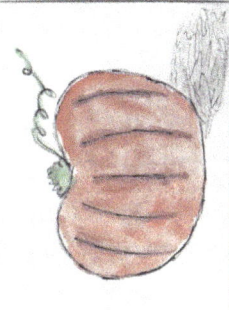
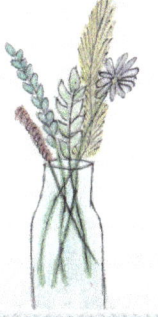
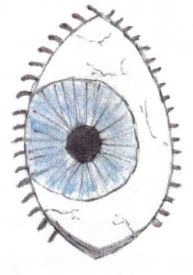
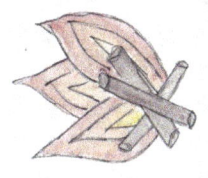

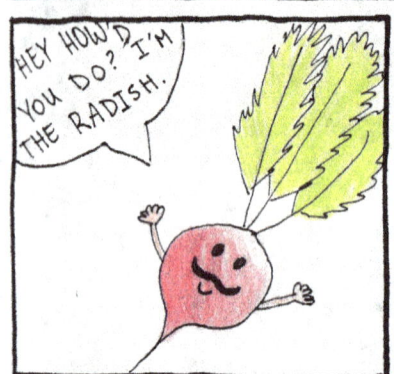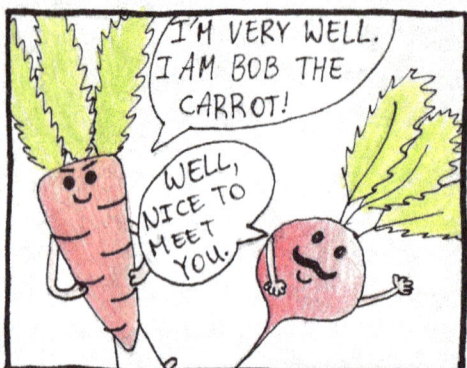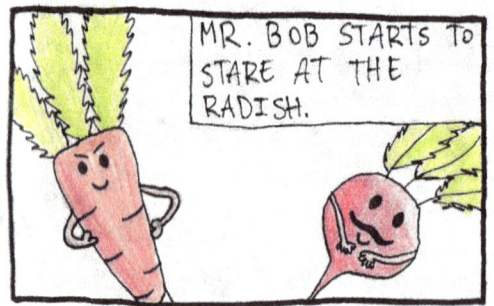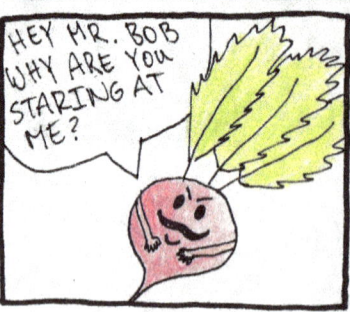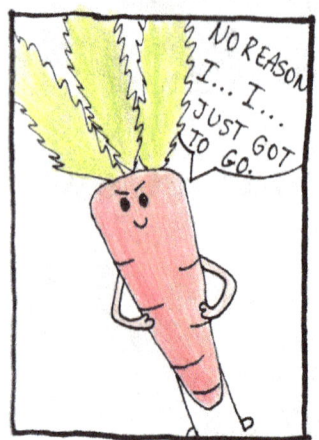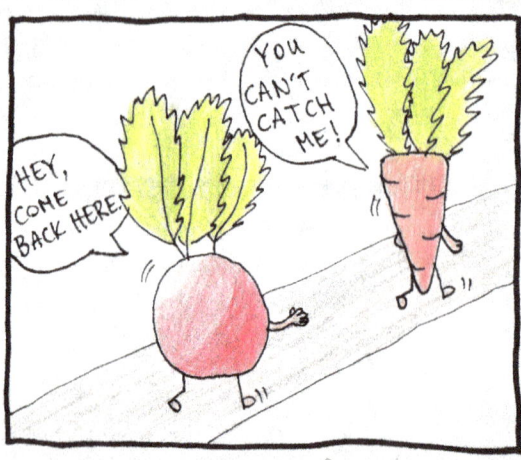

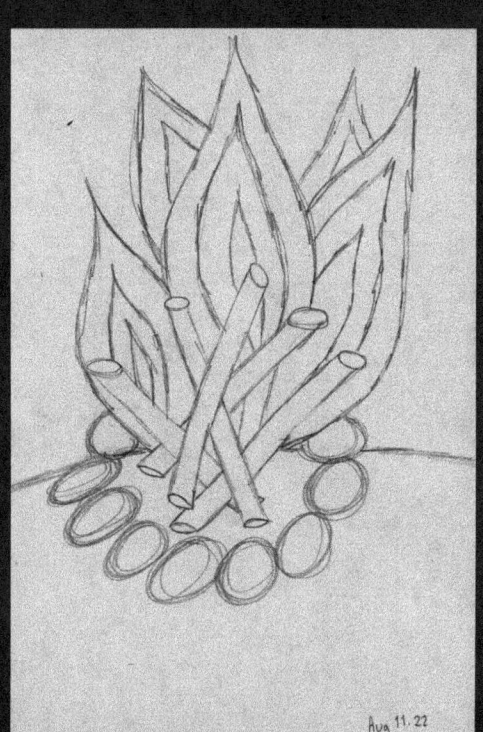
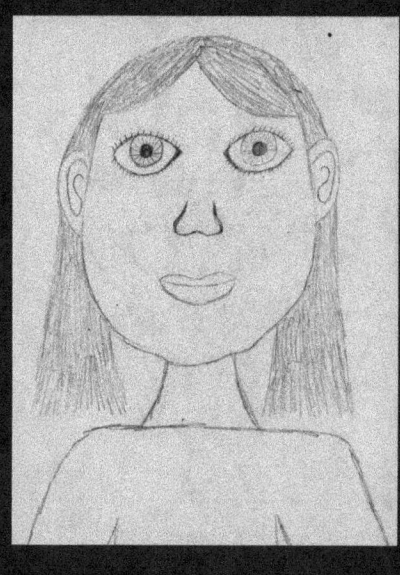
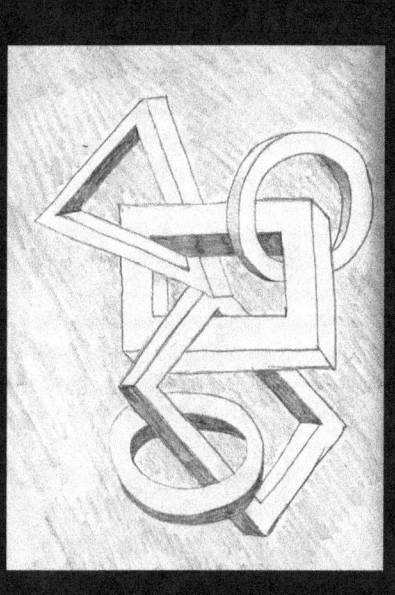
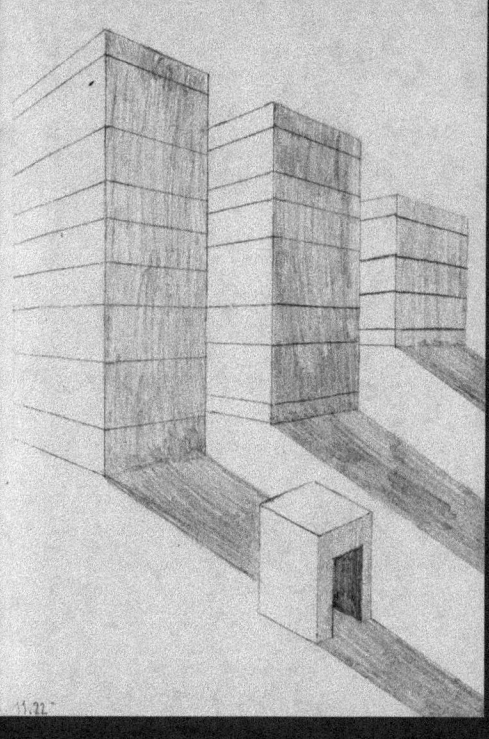

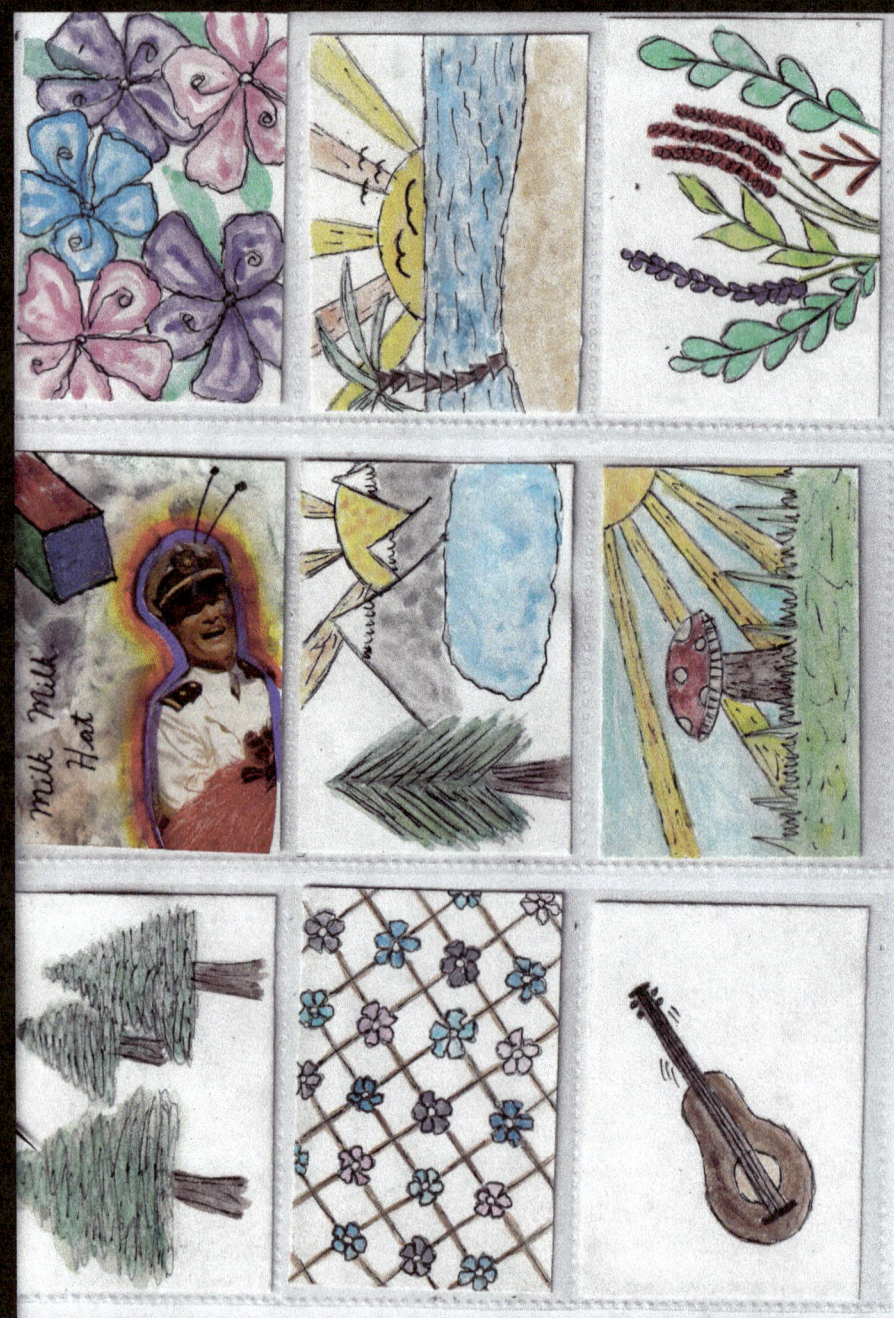

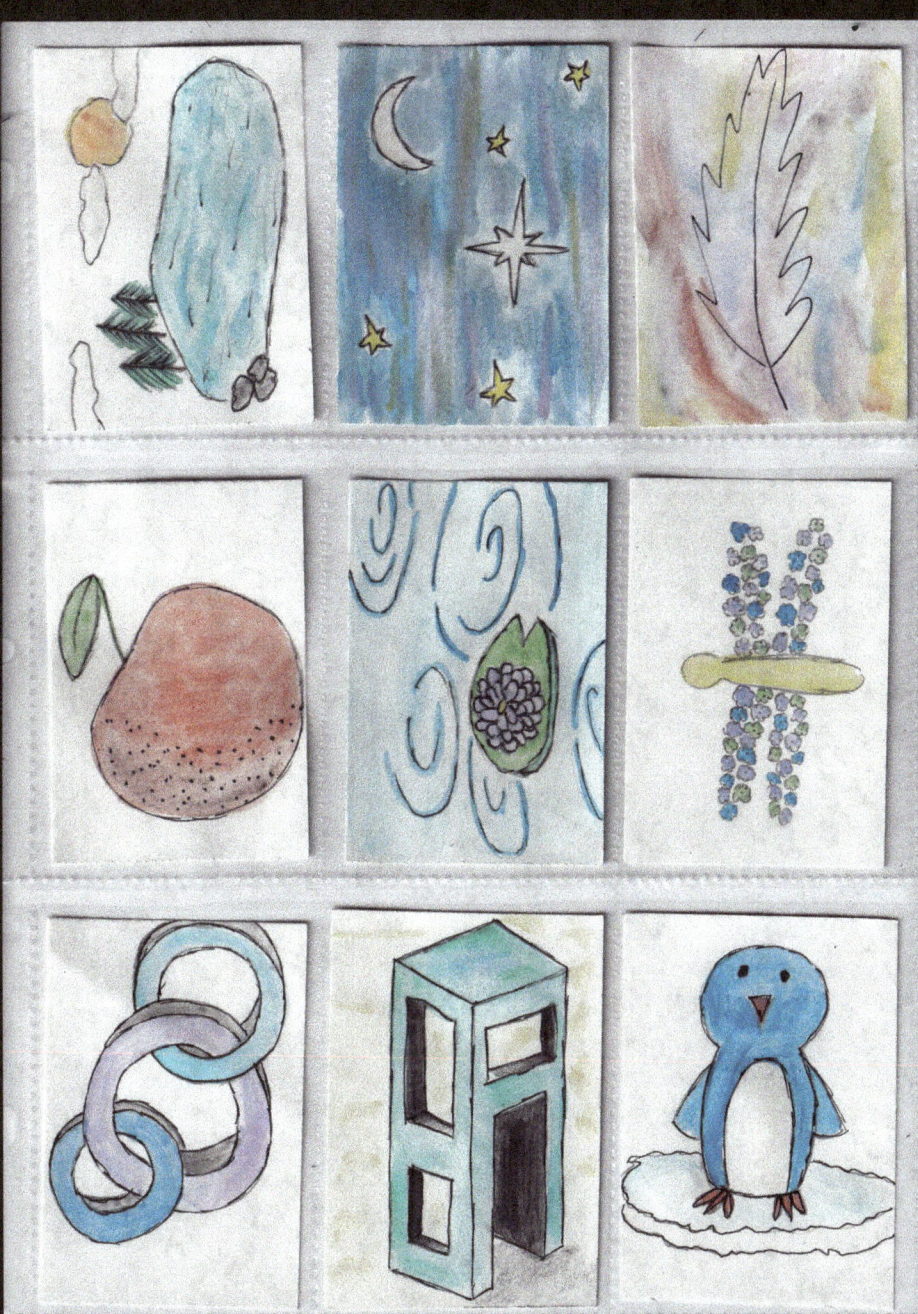

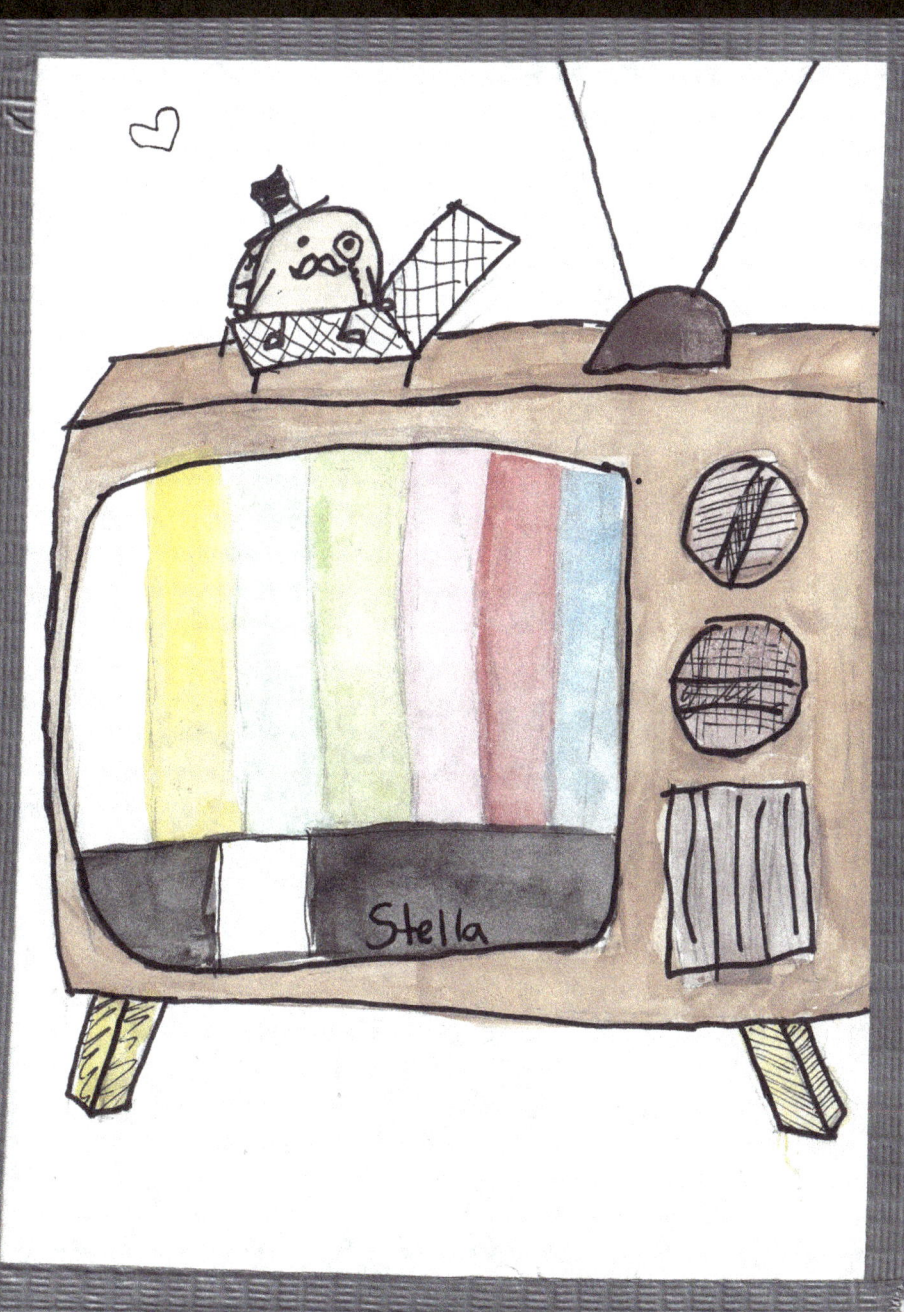

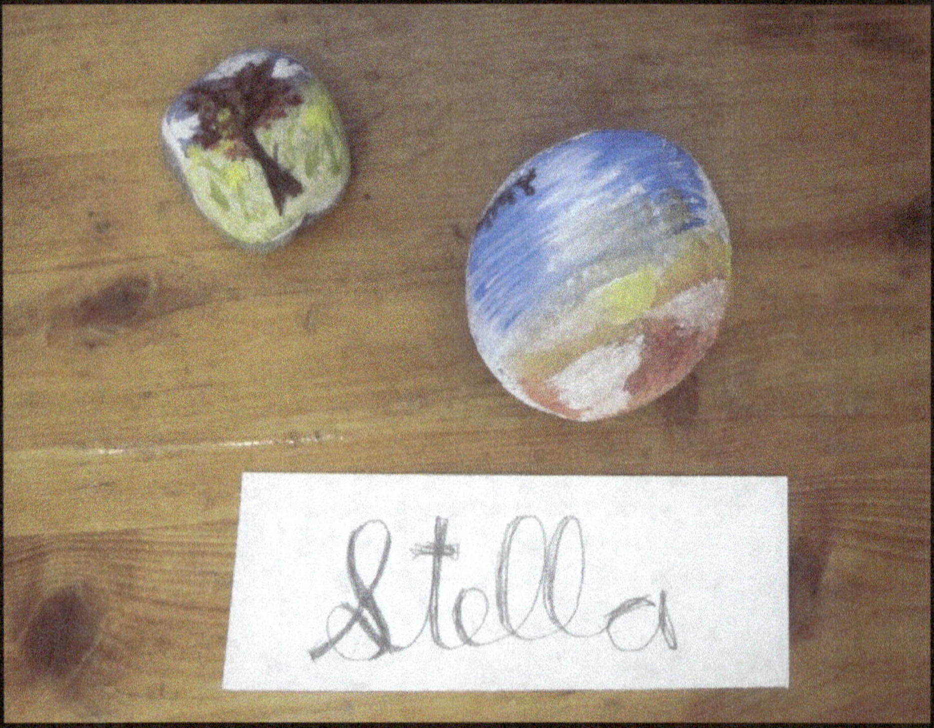

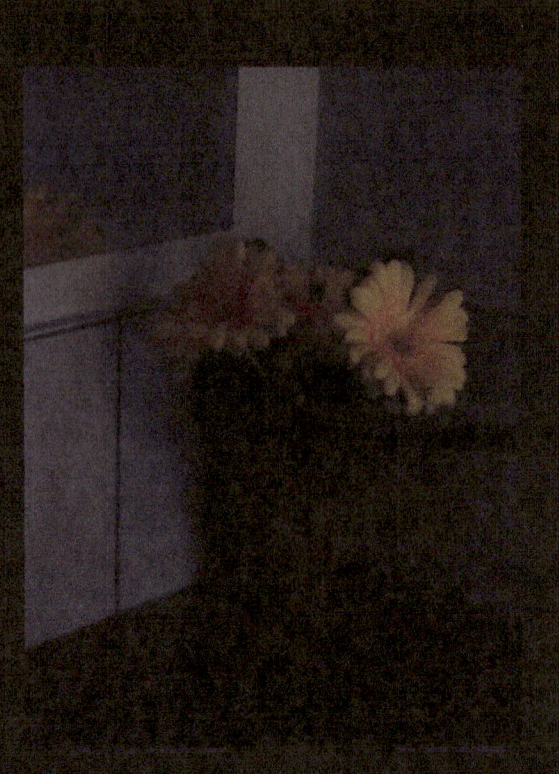

STELLA

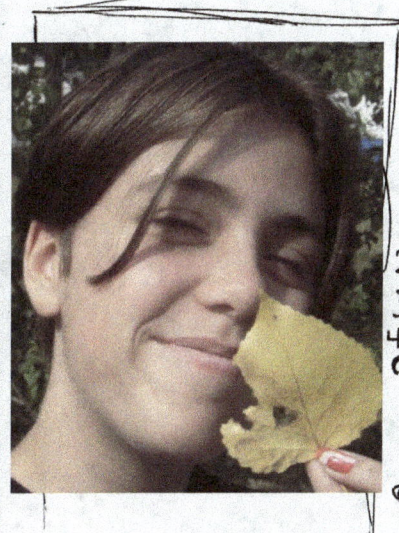

Hello! My name is Stella. I am 14 years old. My birthday is May 29th. My Top three favorite songs are
1. Prom dress by Mxmtoon
2. We fell in love in october by girl in red
3. This Side of paradise by coyote theory
4. Care by Midwxst (thanksgus) (because i want to)

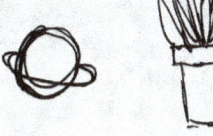

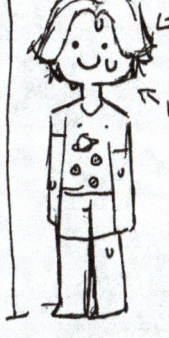

↑ I love bracelets

5'0 ft tall

← Not very accurate
← me

Ⓛ

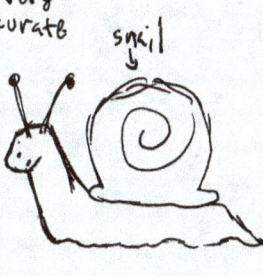

snail ↓

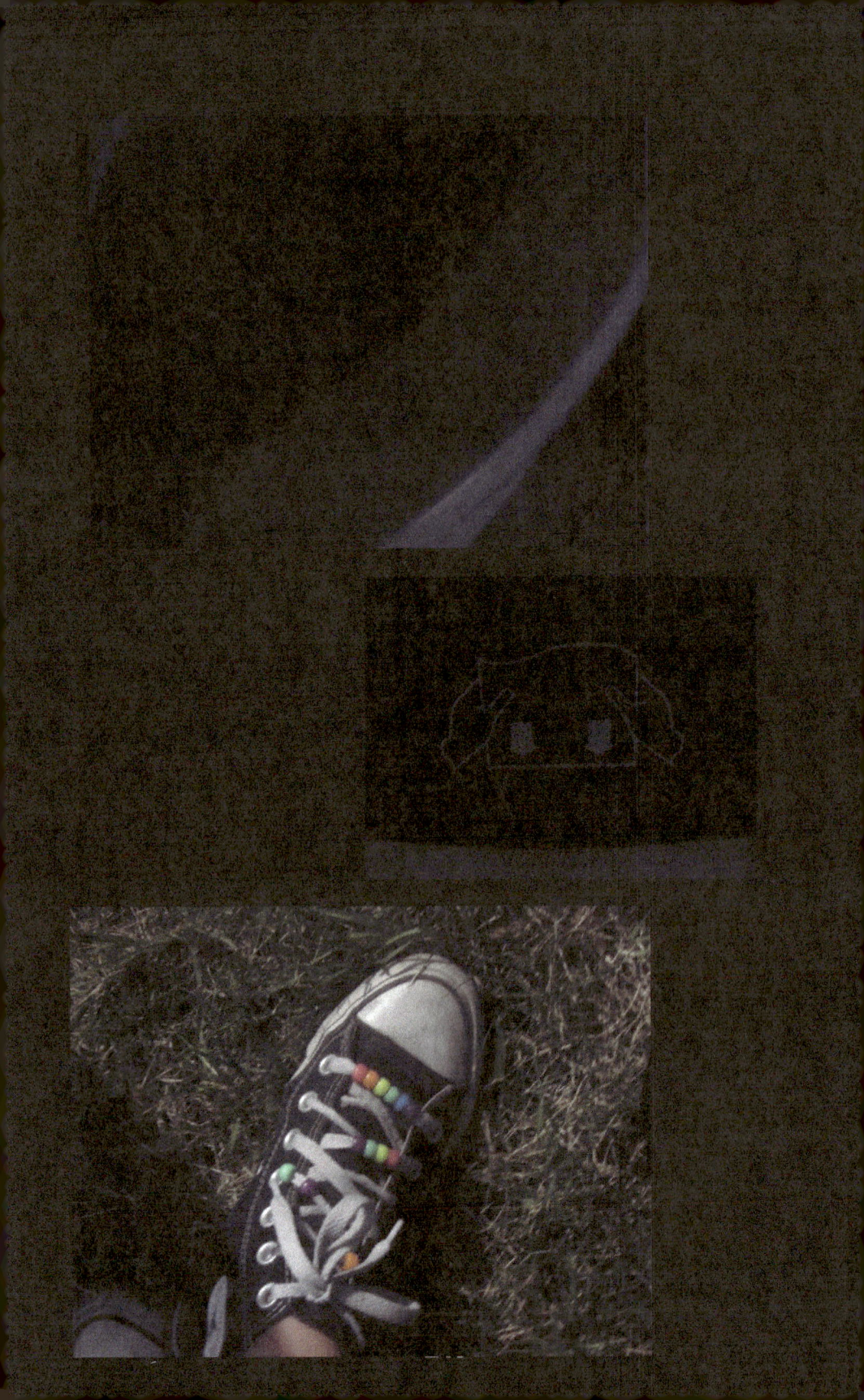

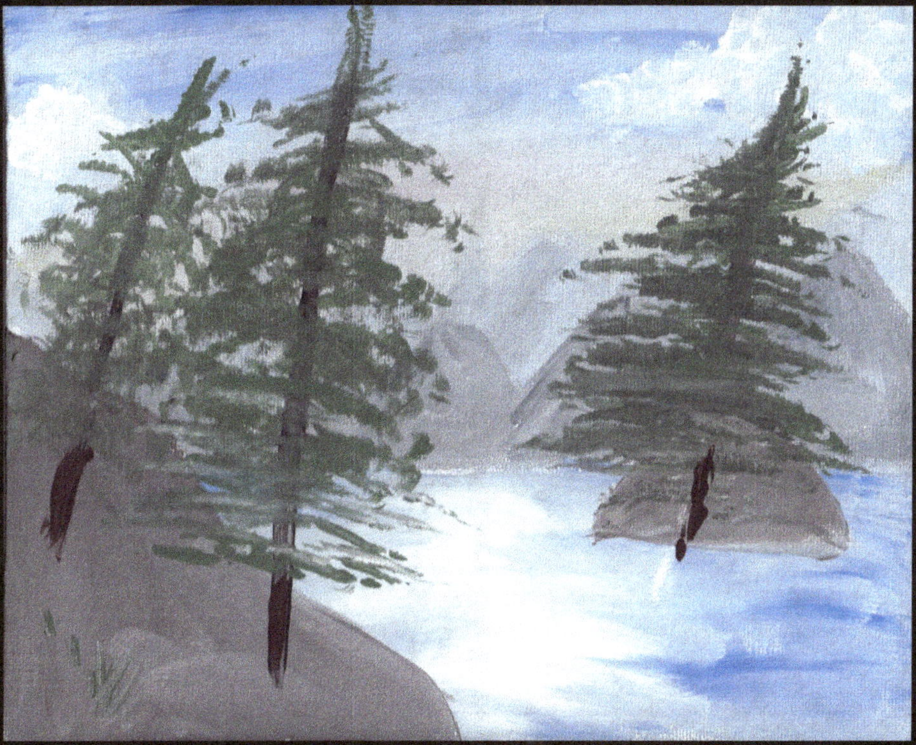

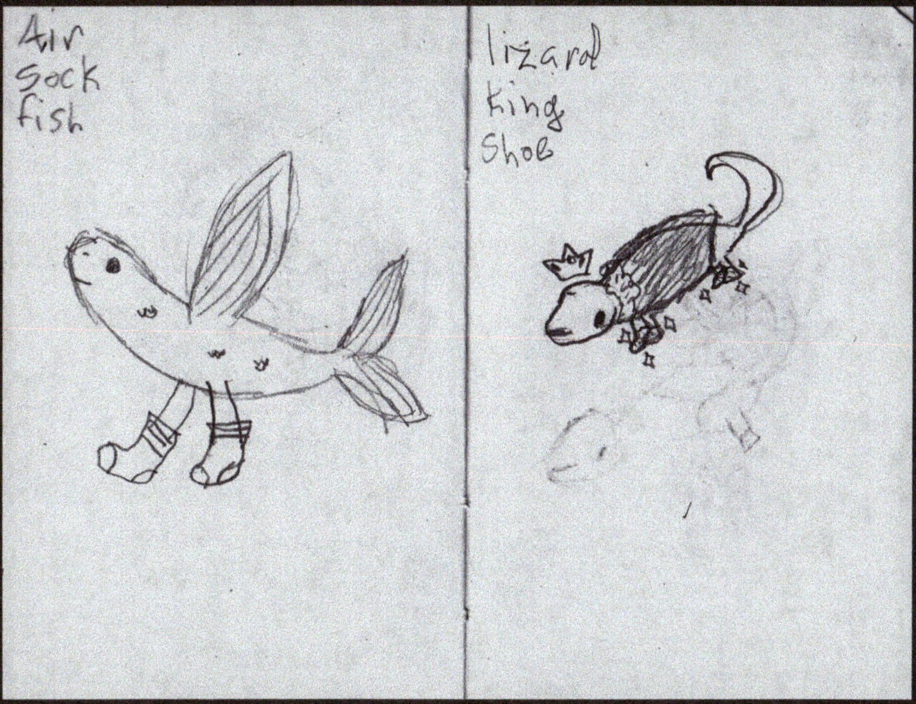

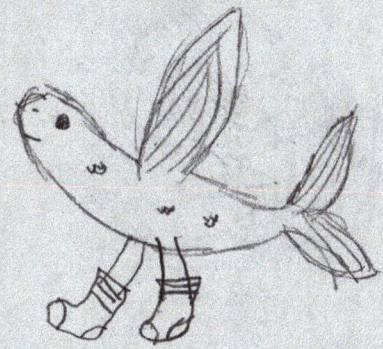

Air
sock
fish

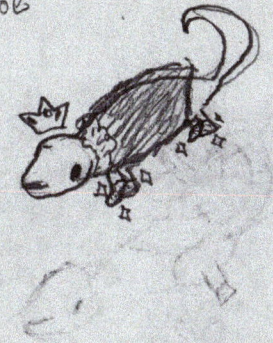

lizard
king
shoe

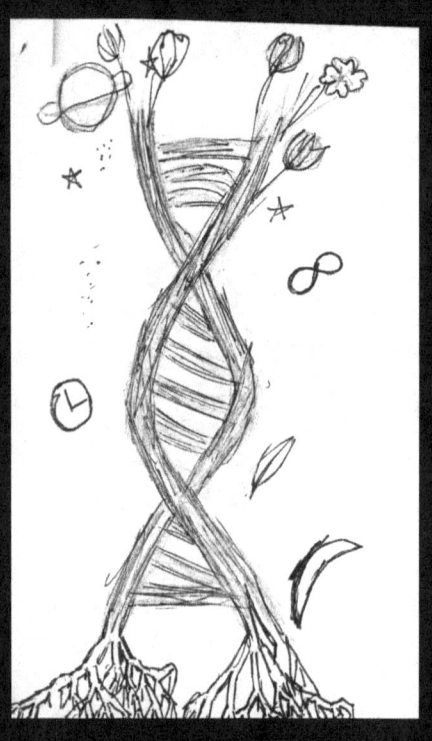

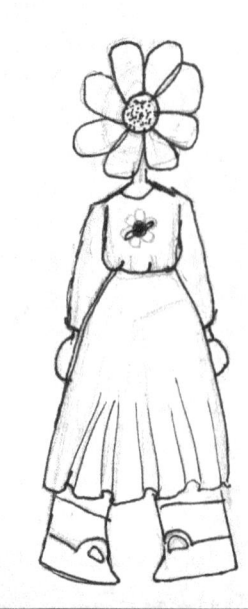

'Pancake
bird
Octapus

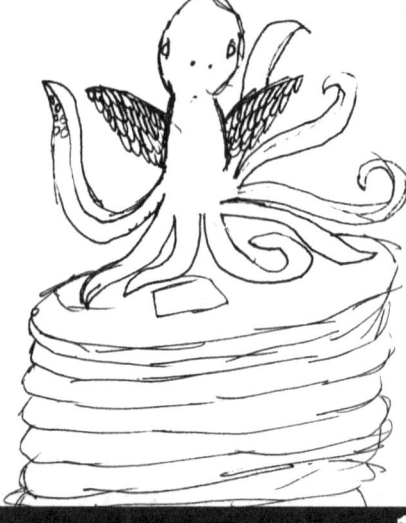

Charecters

Name: panda

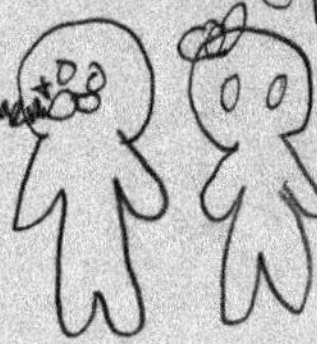

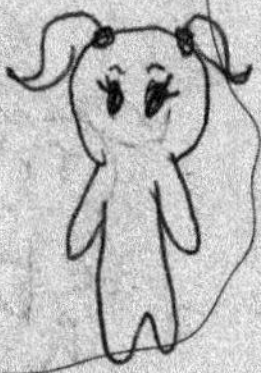

Name: little girl
age: 9

Main

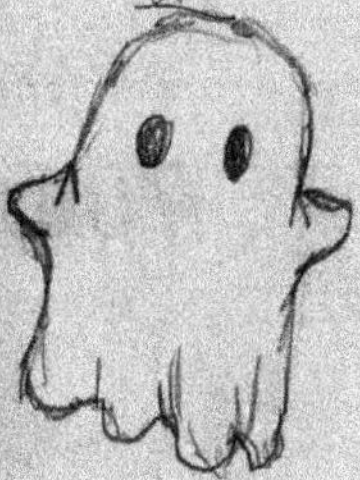

Name: billy/marcus/debbie
age: 5

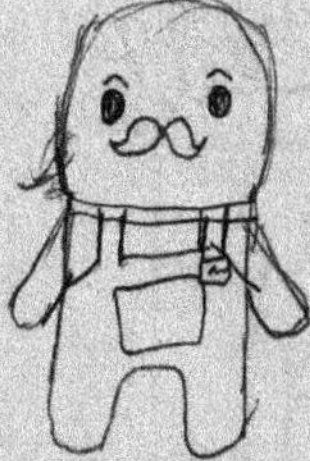

Name: store clerk/
warehouse worker/

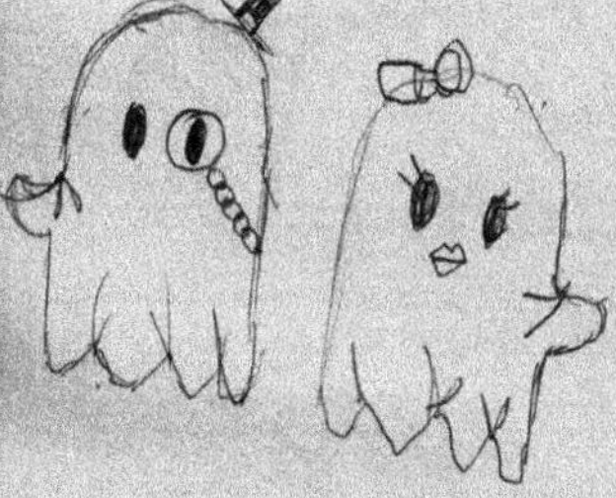

Names: Dead parents
Age: 48, 56

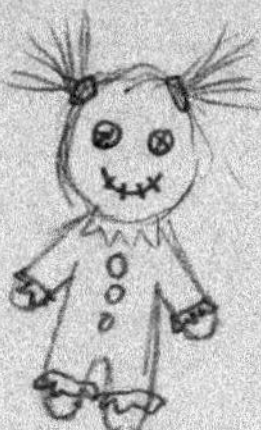

Story

a ghost is trying to find a doll from the house she and her parants deid in by murder but the house was alredy sold to a differant family. So she has to go find the doll so she gos to the store but they dont have it so she go to the warehous and steals the doll

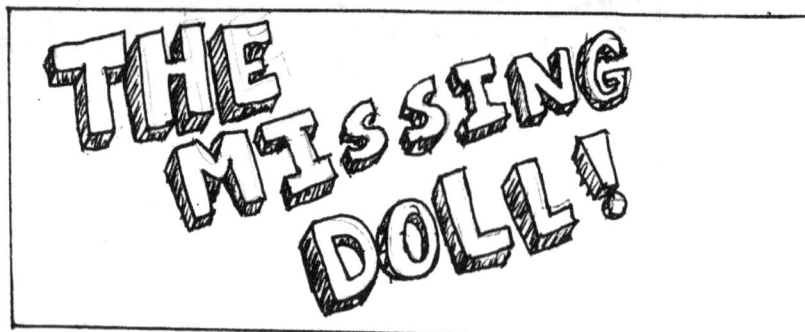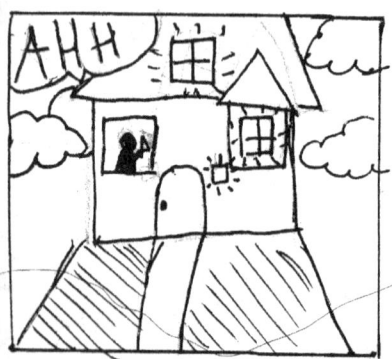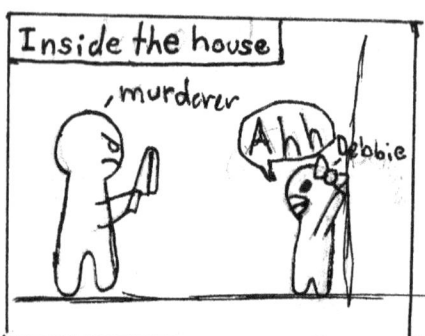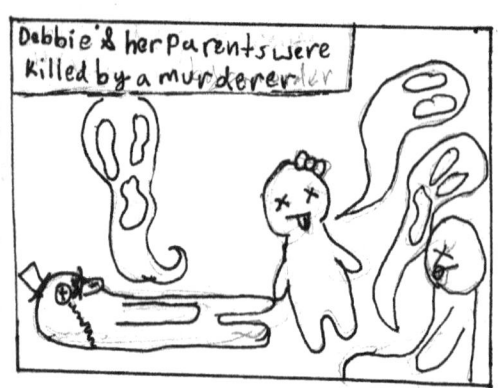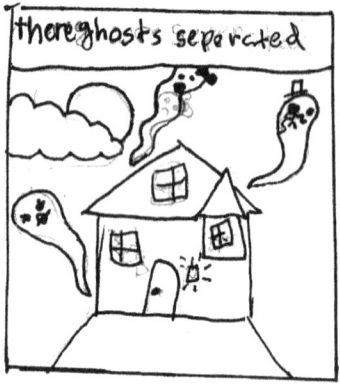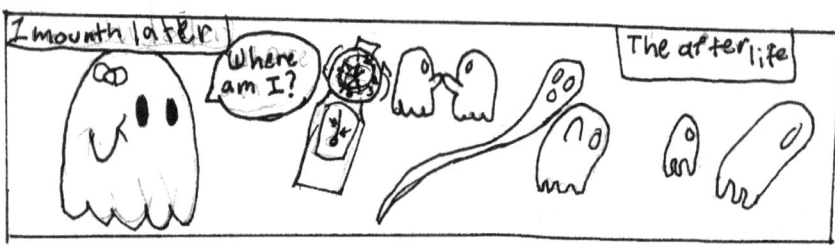

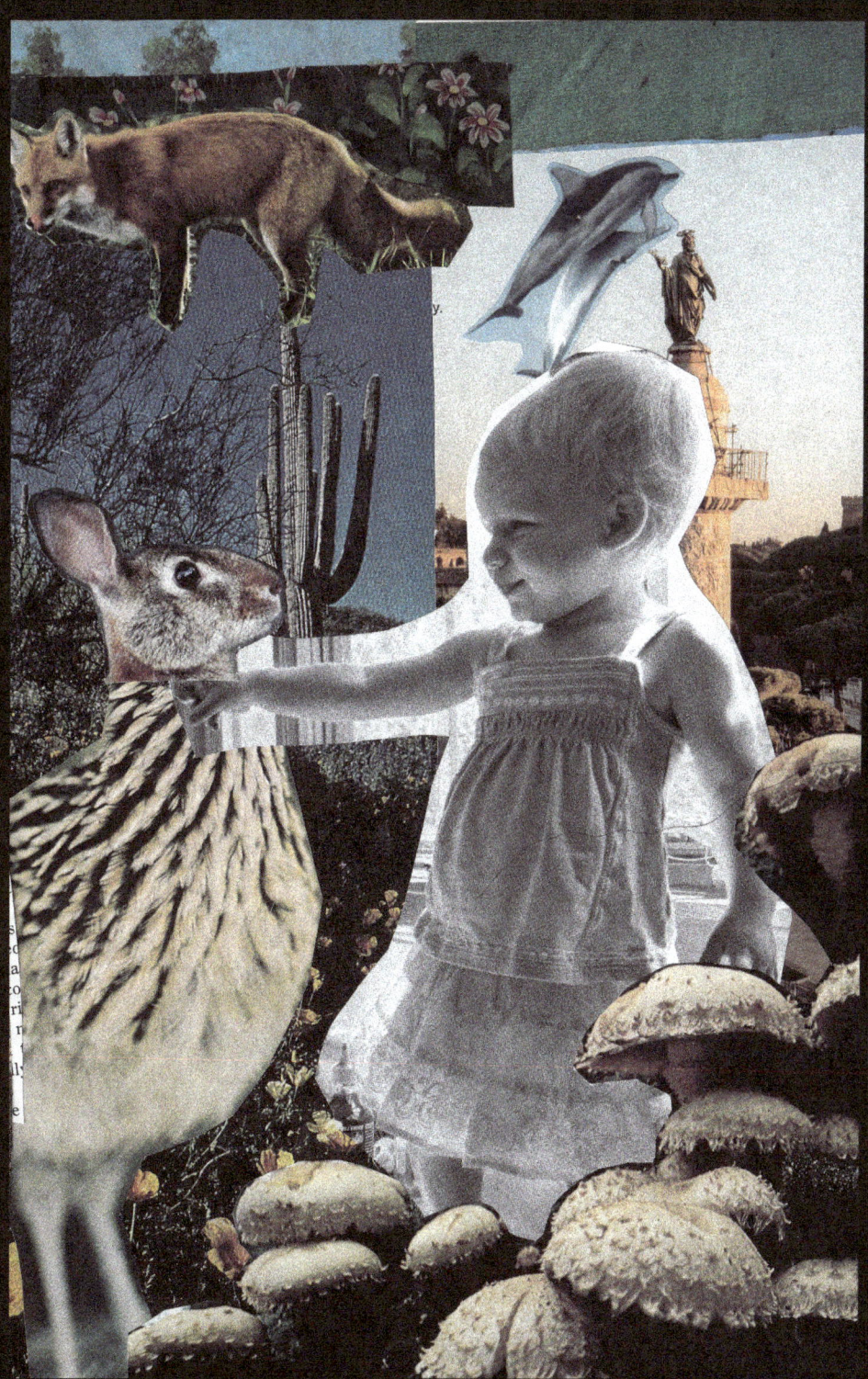

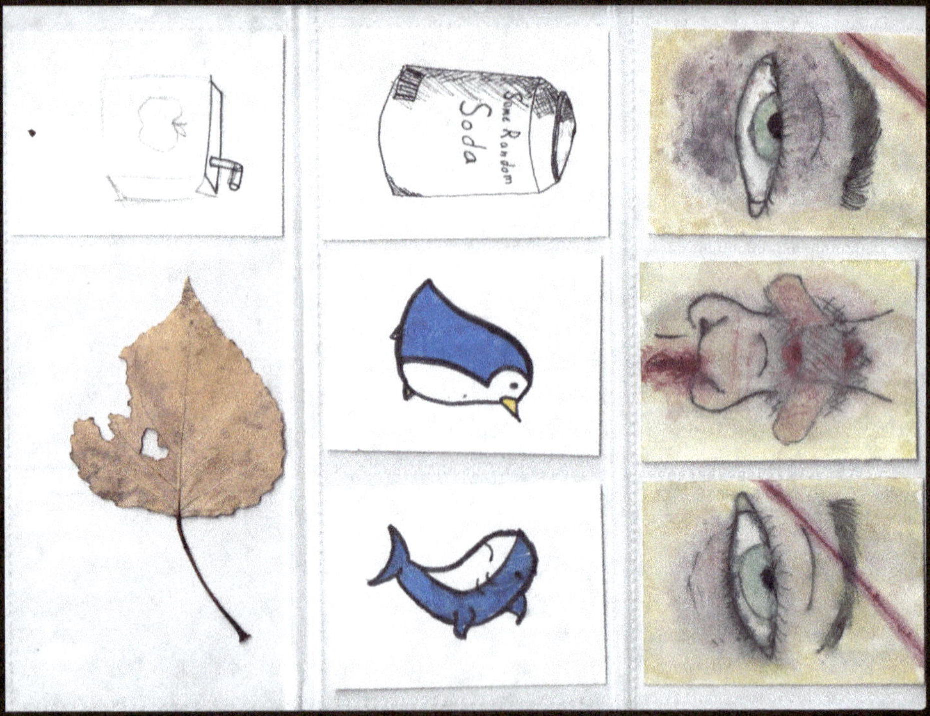

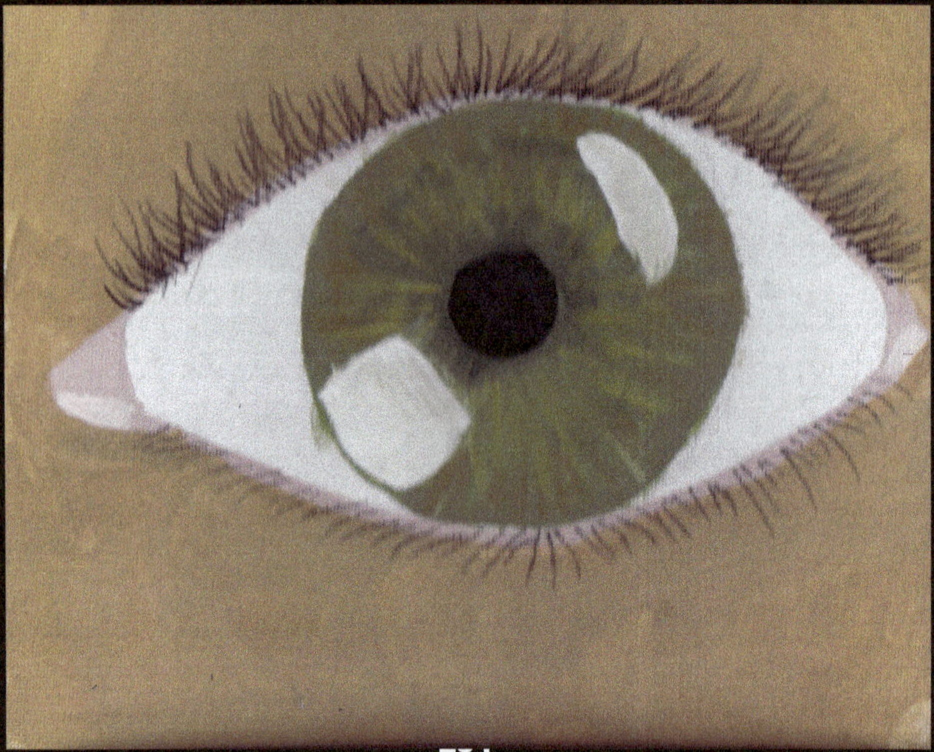

TOMATO PIE

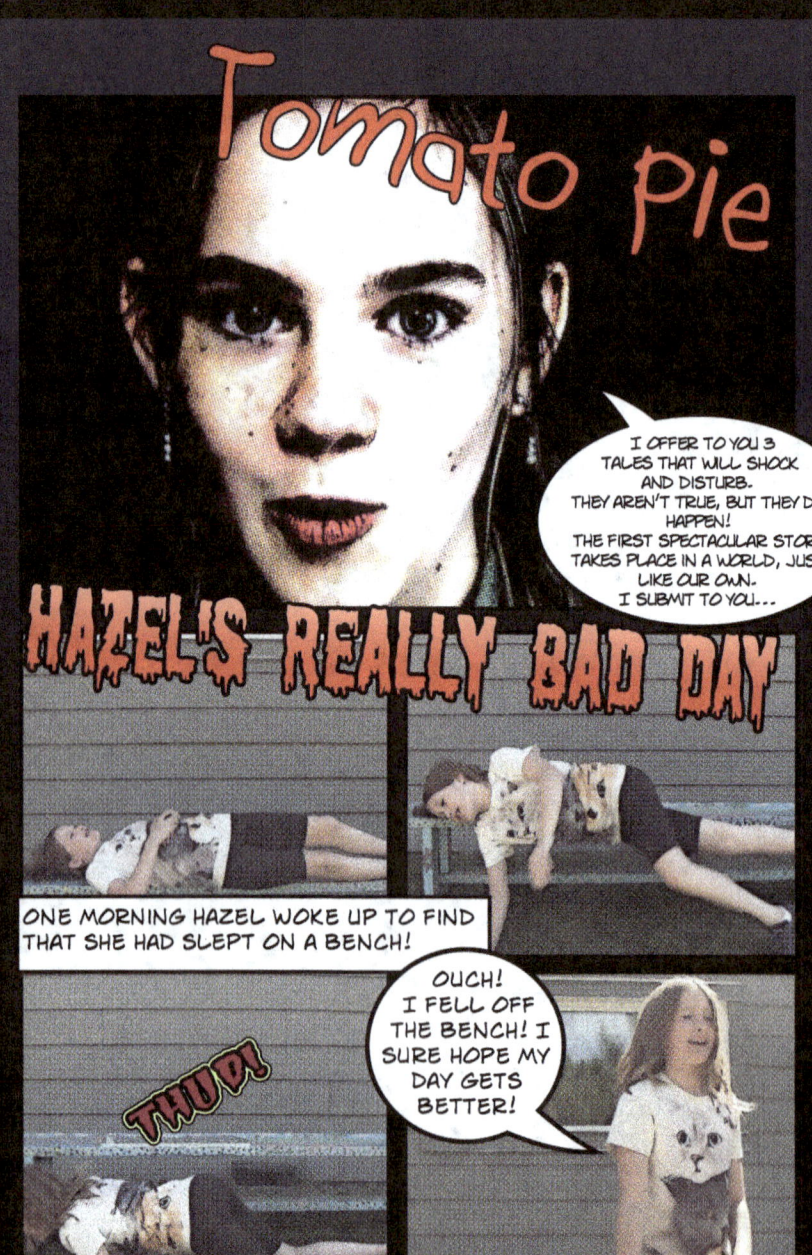

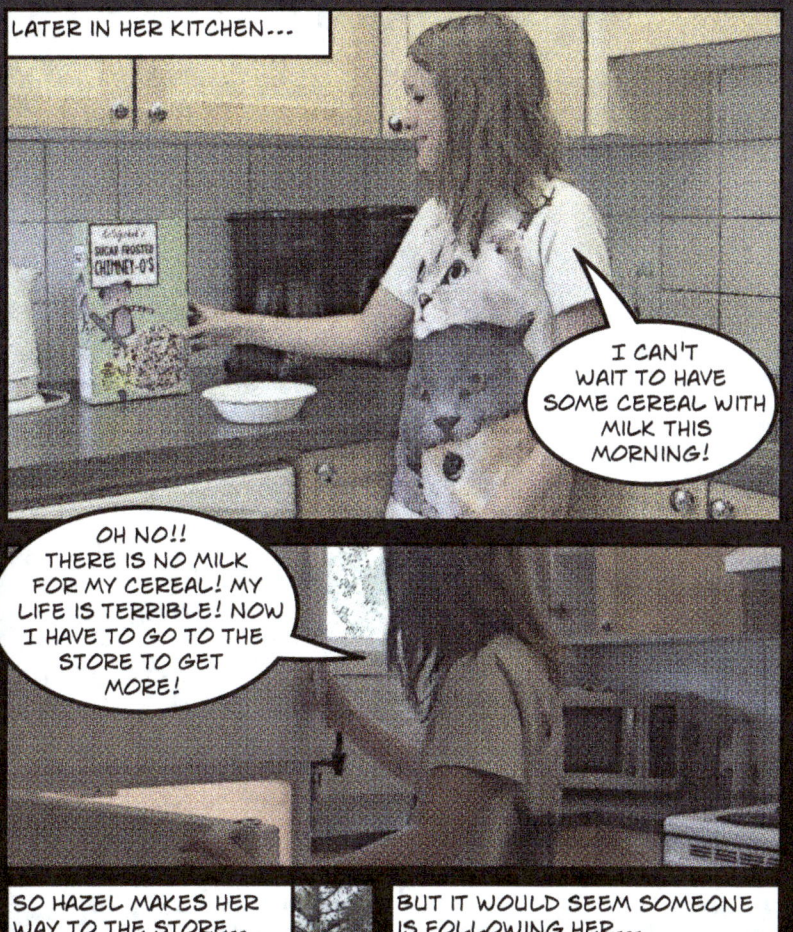

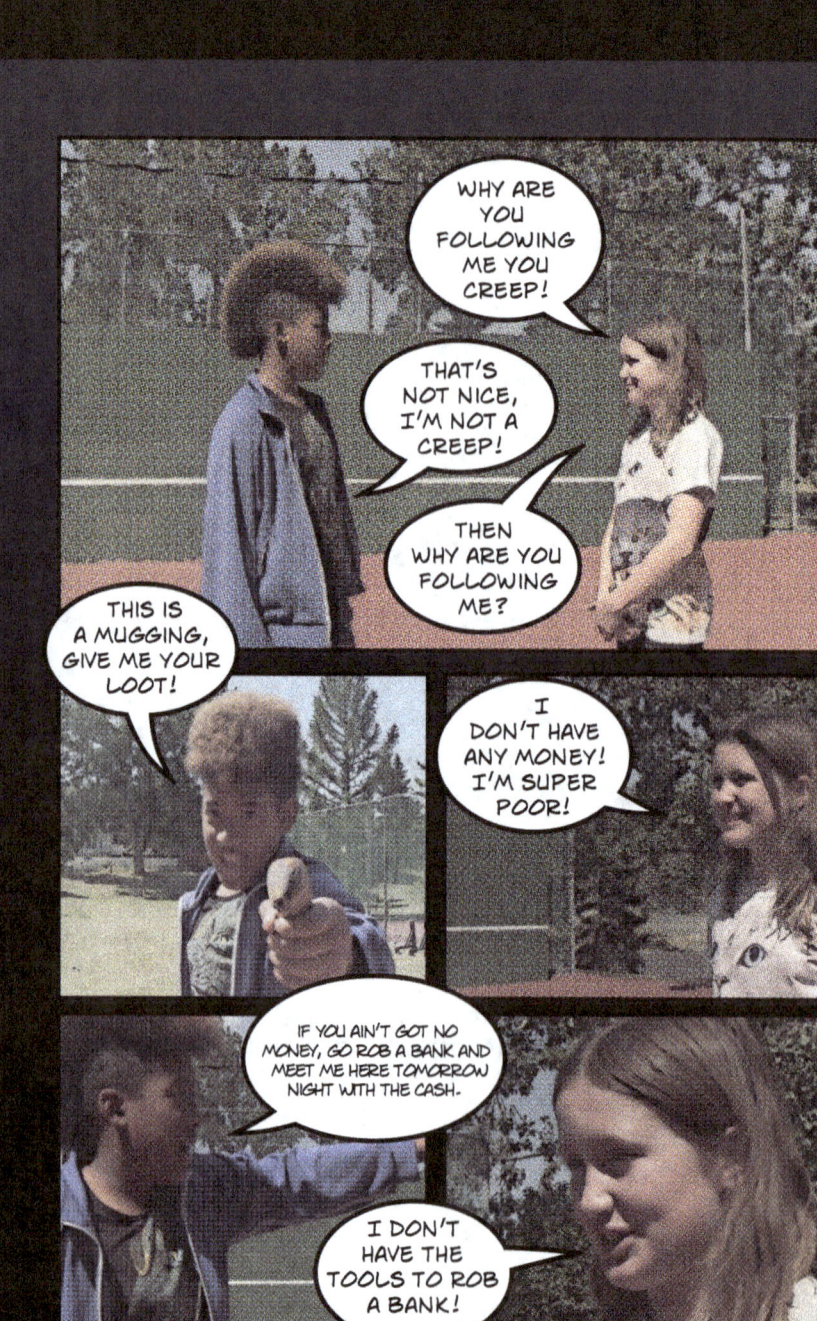

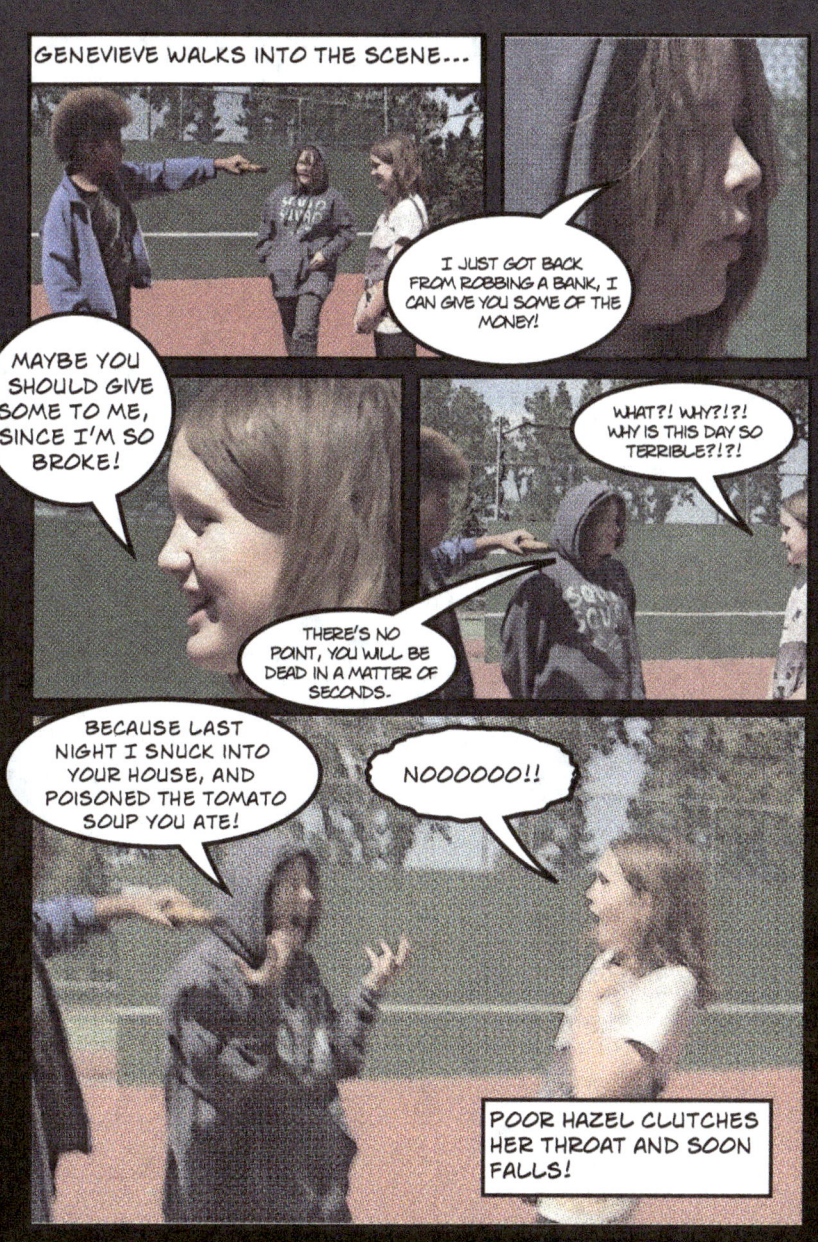

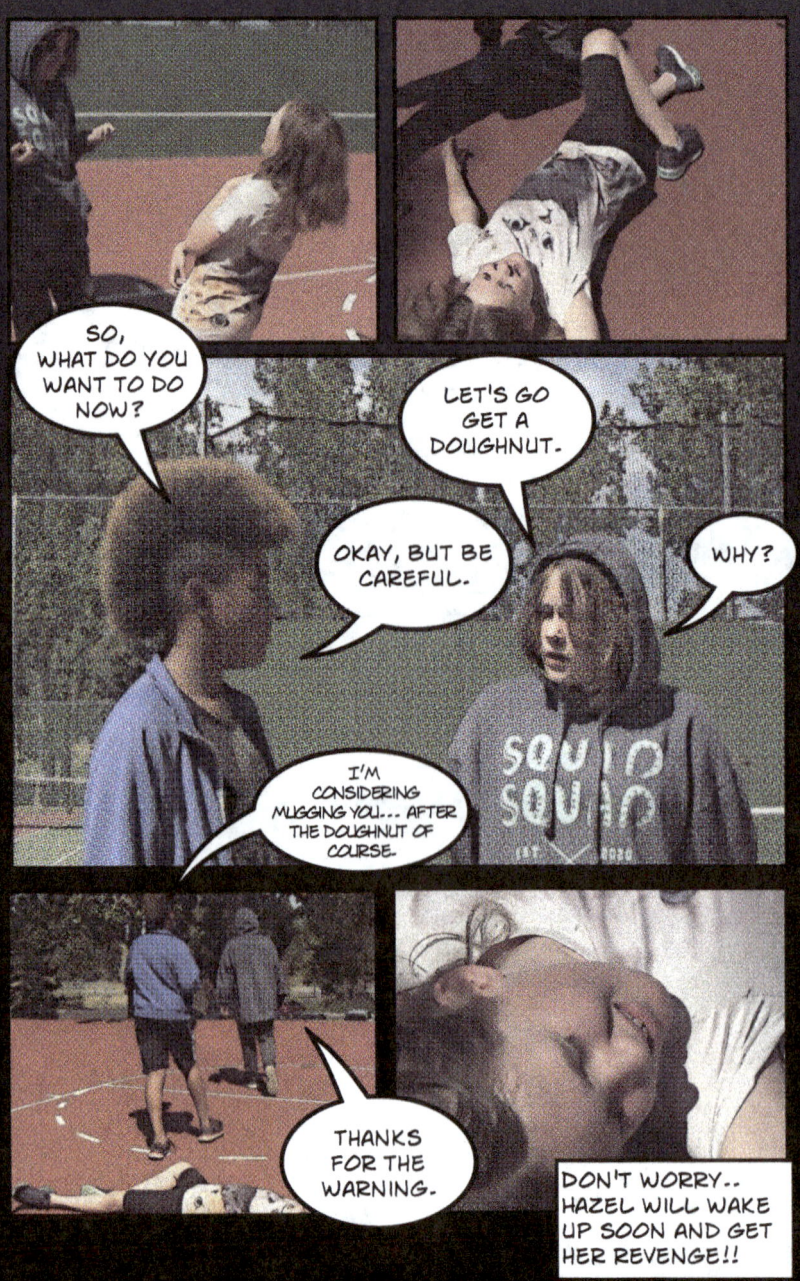

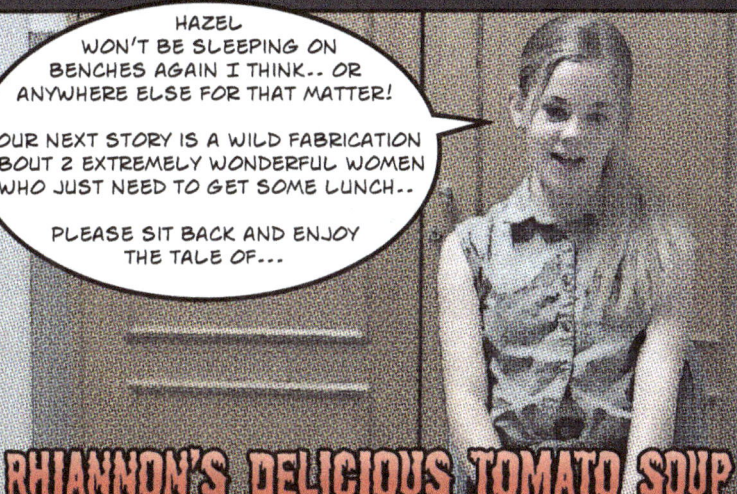

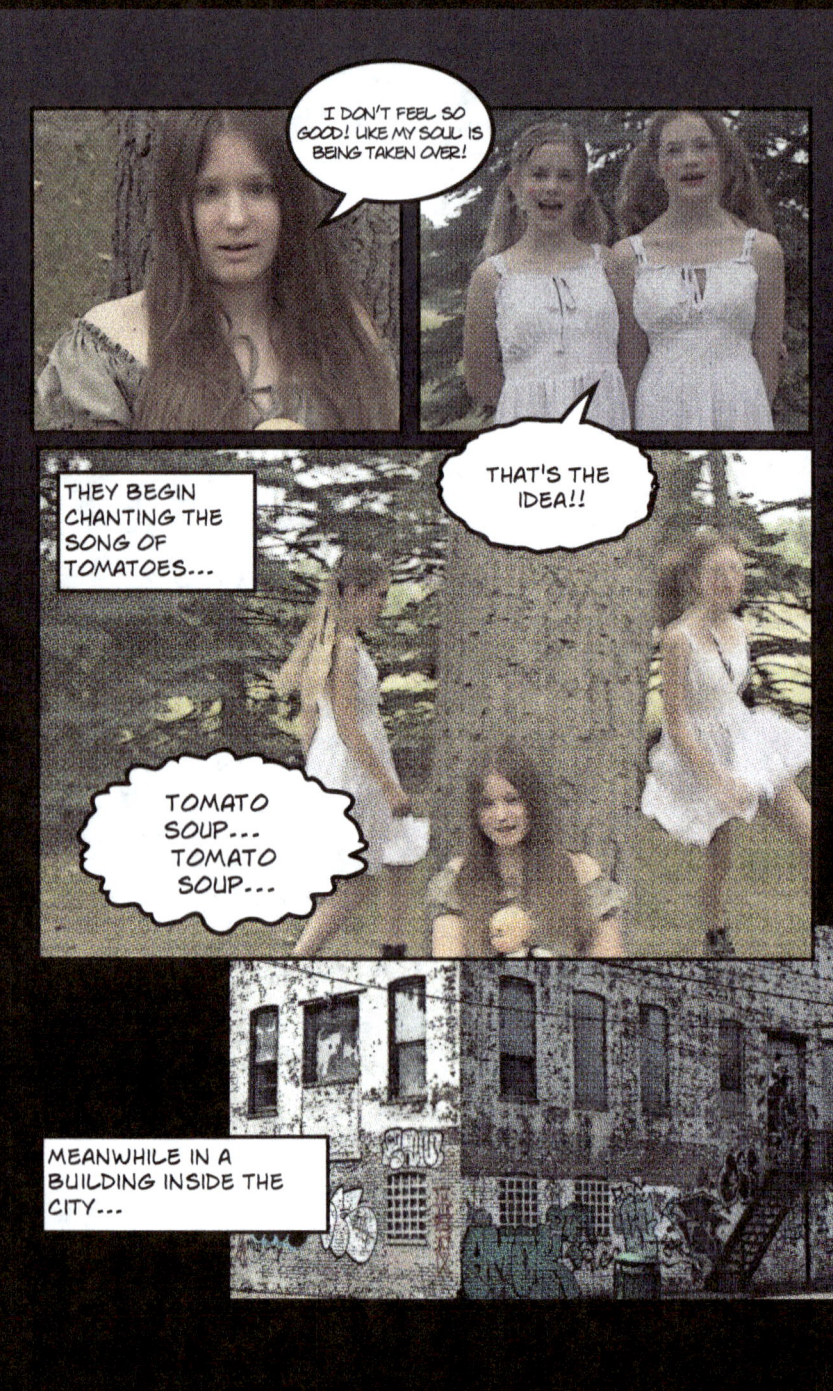

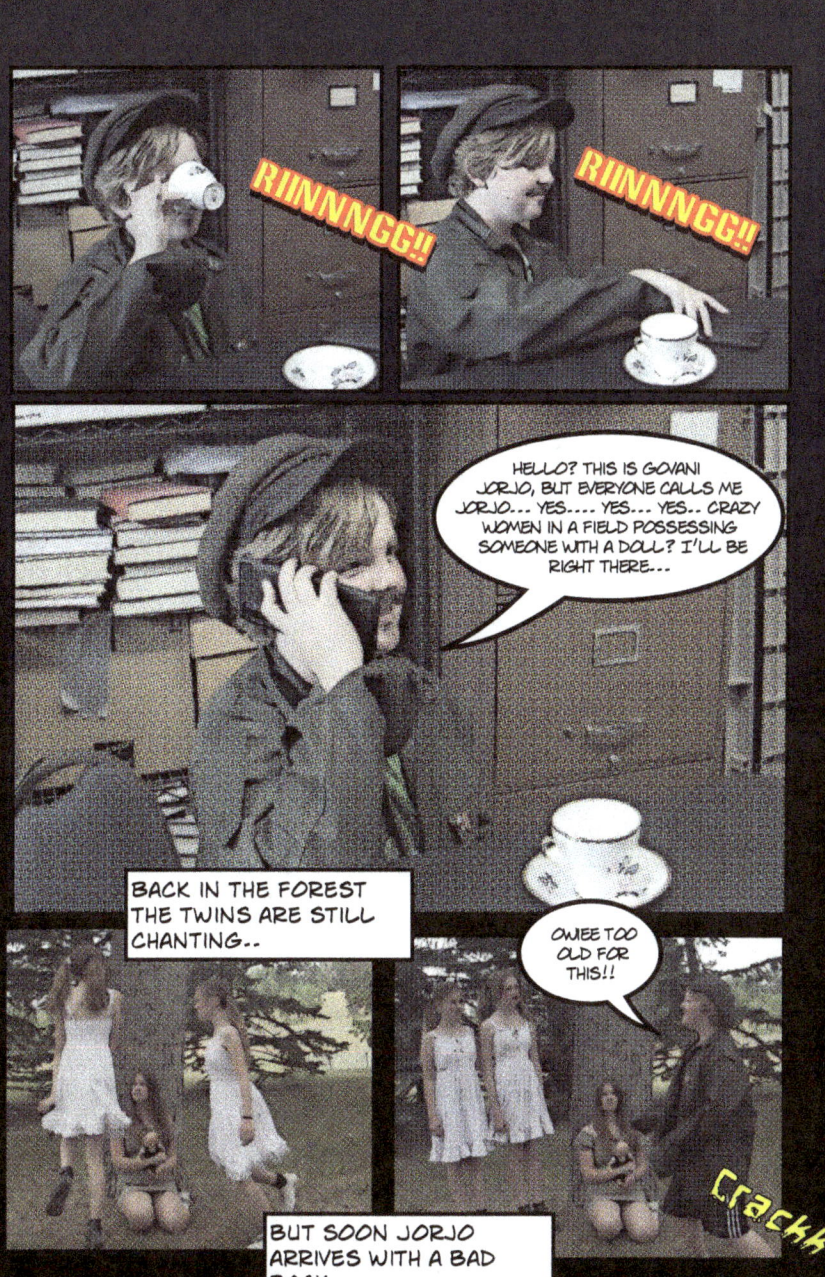

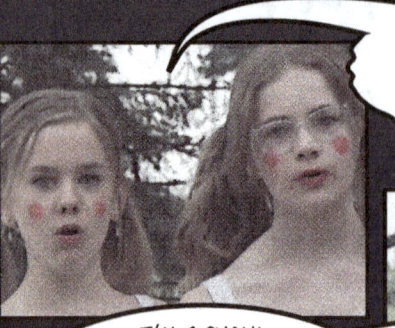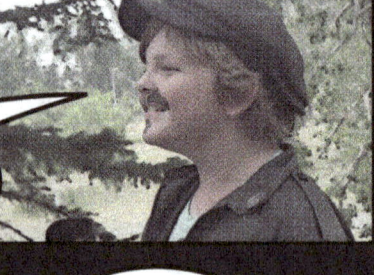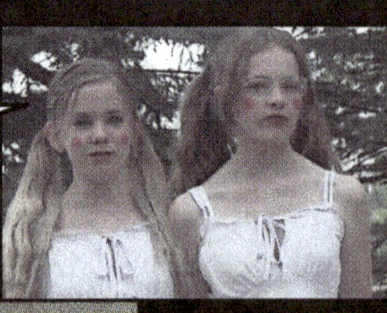

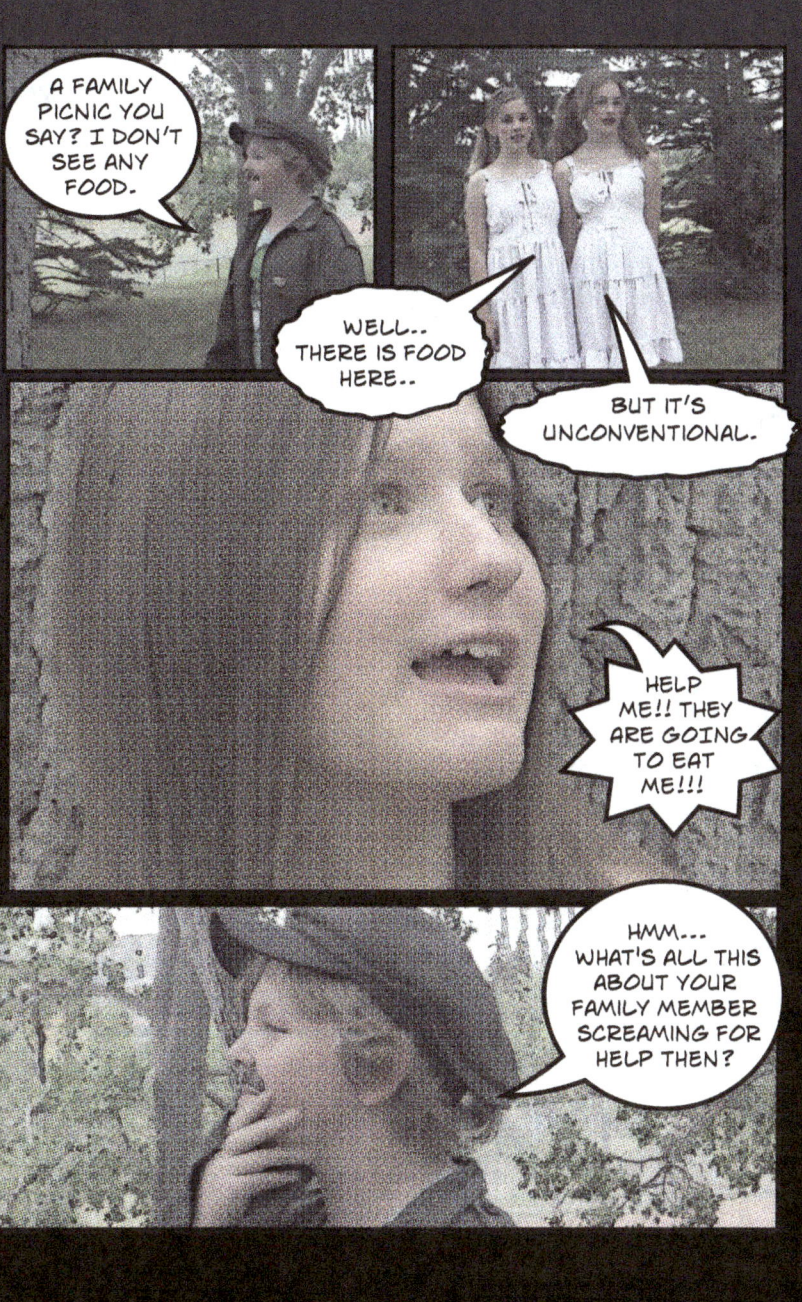

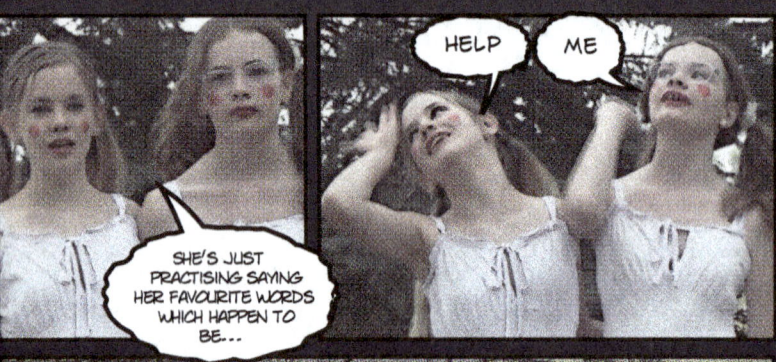

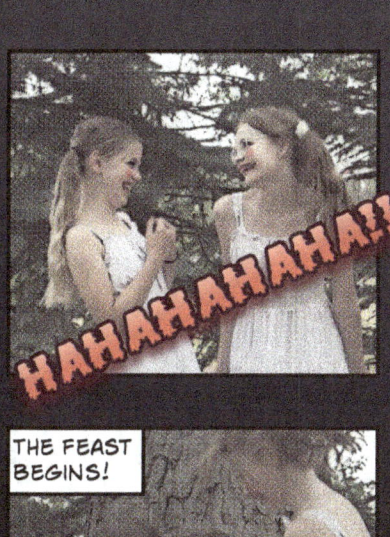

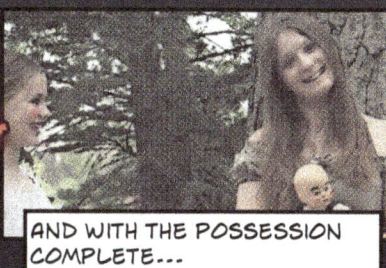

AND WITH THE POSSESSION COMPLETE...

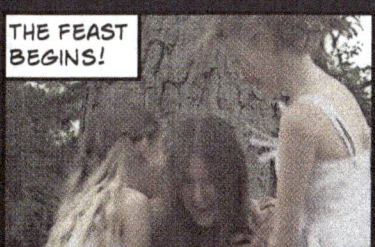

THE FEAST BEGINS!

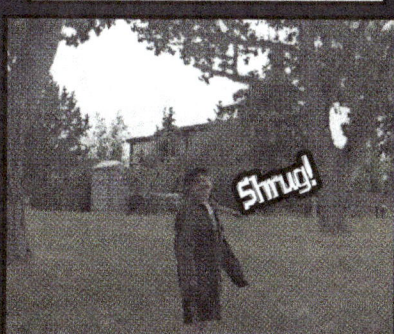

I'M SURE GLAD THAT TURNED OUT THE WAY IT DID. YOU WOULDN'T WANT ANYONE TO STARVE WOULD YOU?

OUR FINAL TALE TONIGHT DEALS WITH MAGIC, AND WHAT WOULD HAPPEN IF YOU USED IT TO BRING LIFE TO ORDINARILY NON LIVING THINGS?

I CAN TELL YOU, NOT GOOD.

ENJOY THE

THE KILLER PEANUT BUTTER SANDWICH!

IN A DARK PLACE OF MAGIC, SOPHIE THE WIZARD IS CASTING THE ULTIMATE SPELL!!

HOCUS POCUS LOST YOUR FOCUS HABLOO BLAGLAC

BUT SOON I WILL TURN YOUR WHOLE LIFE AROUND

PEANUT AND BREAD YOU SIT ON THE GROUND

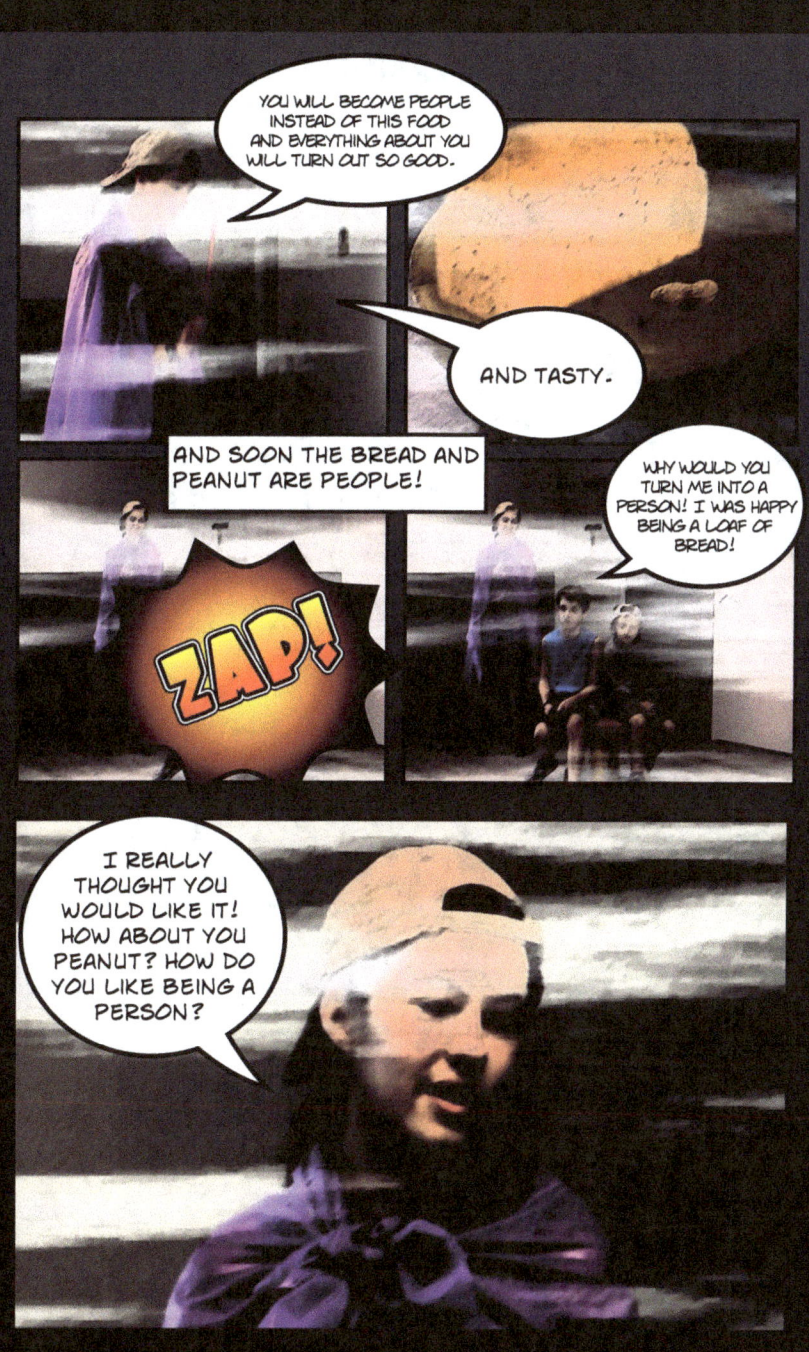

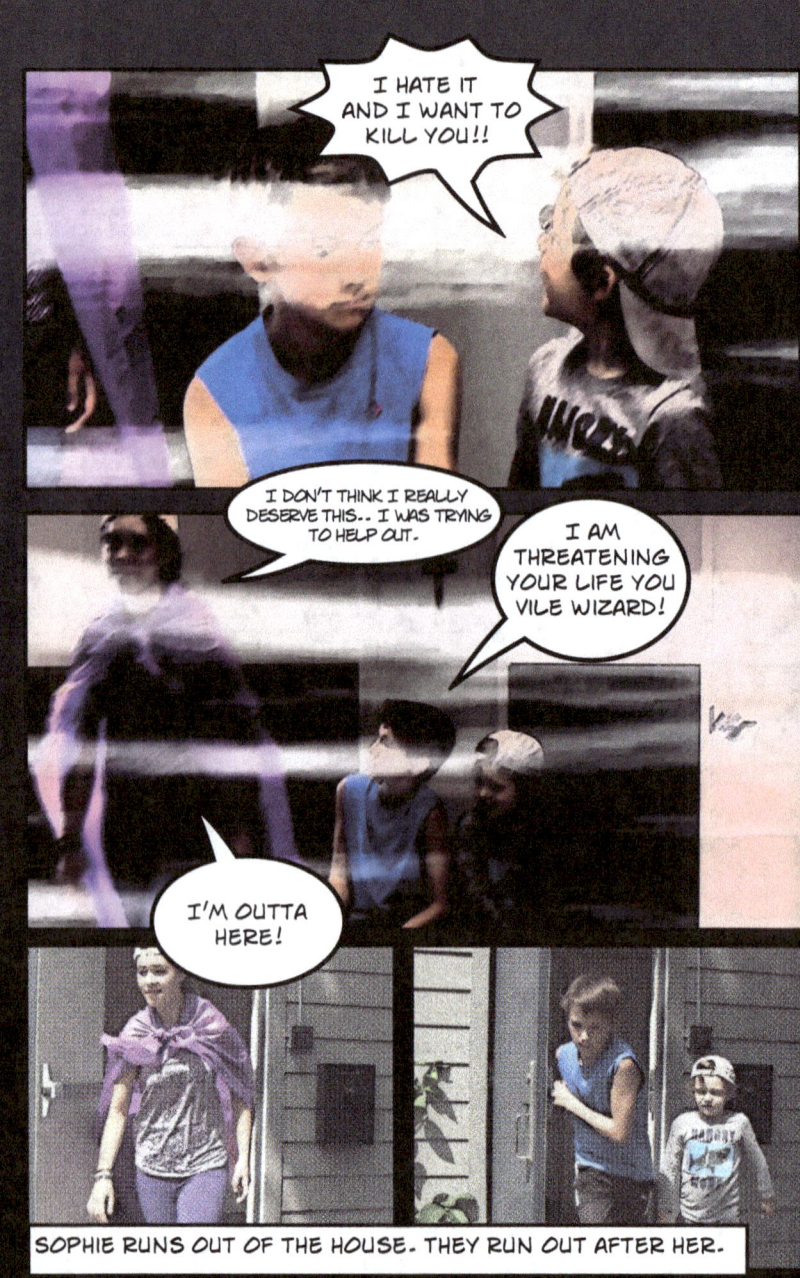

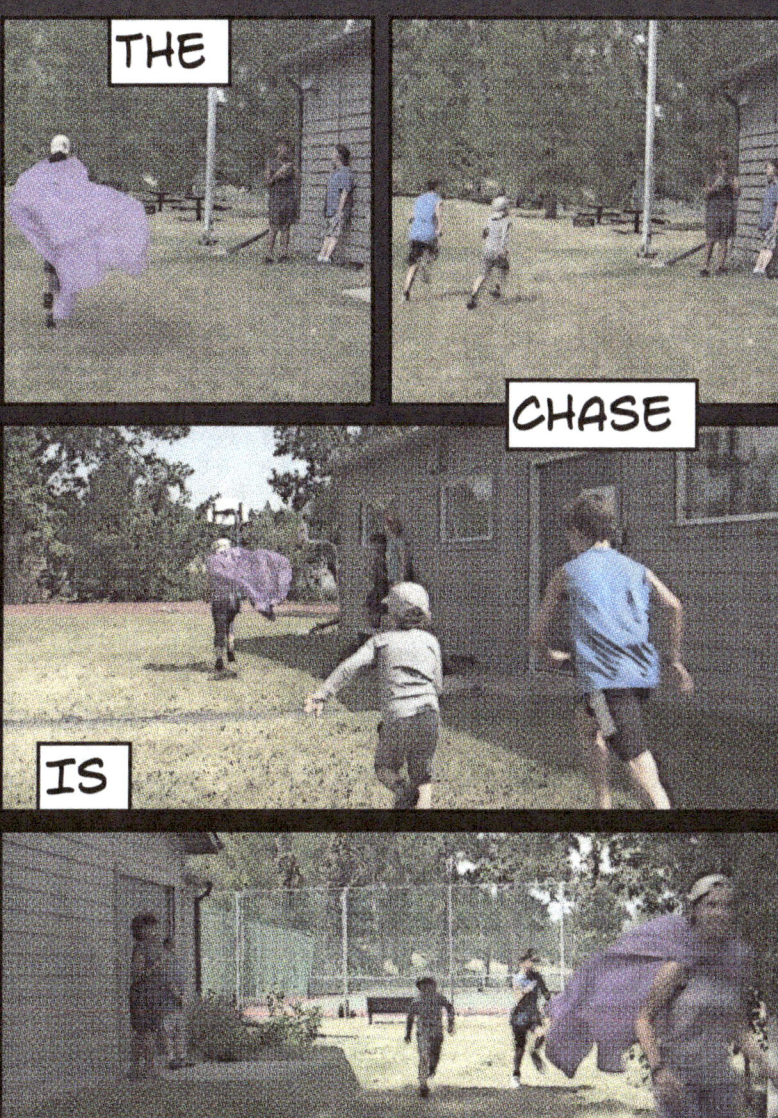

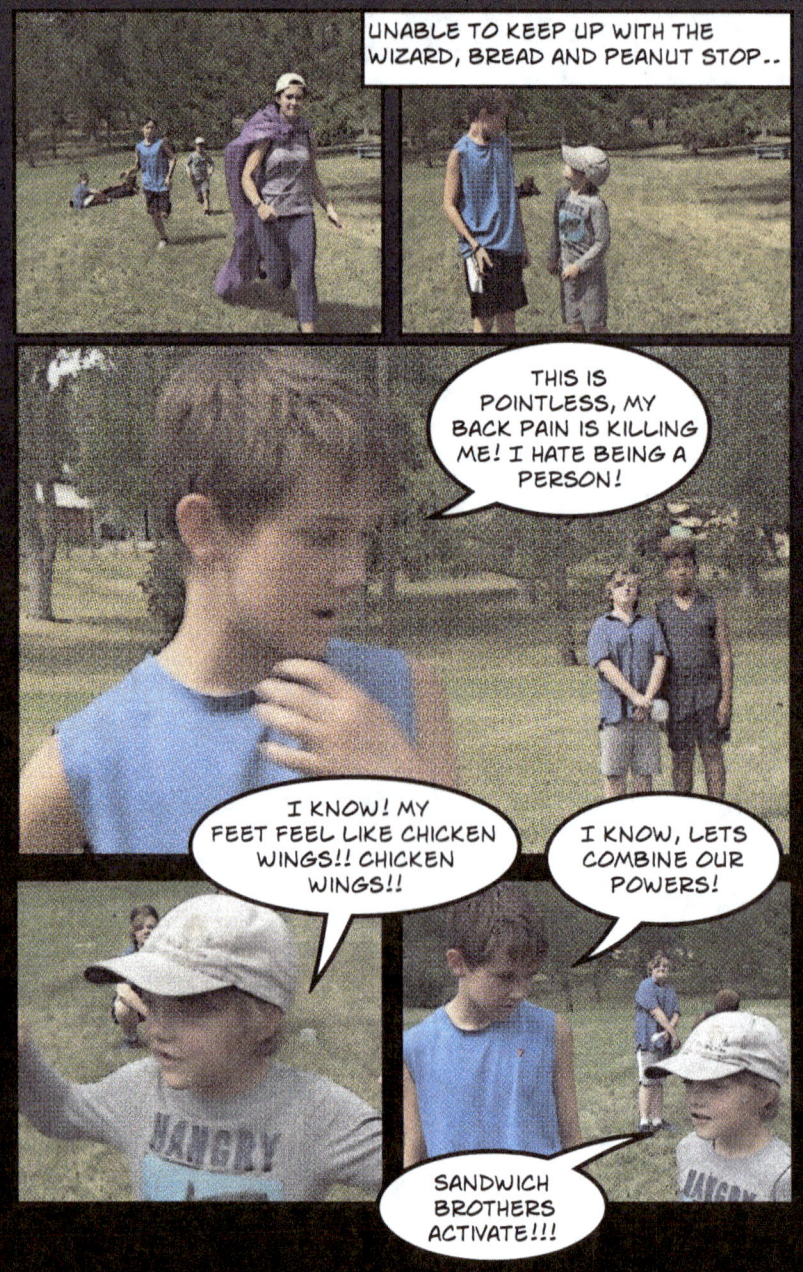

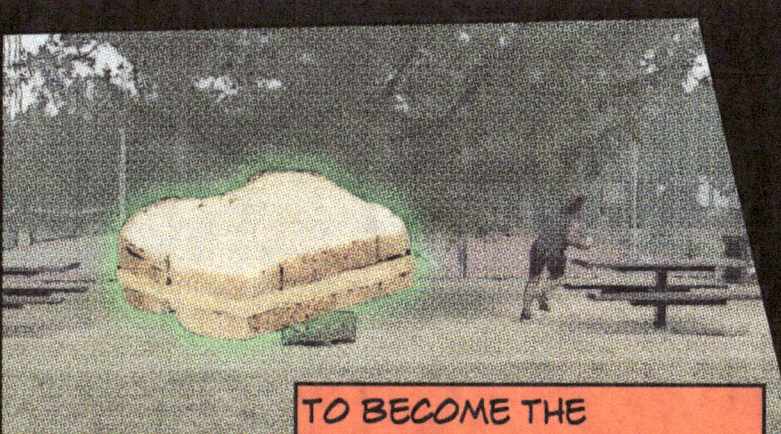

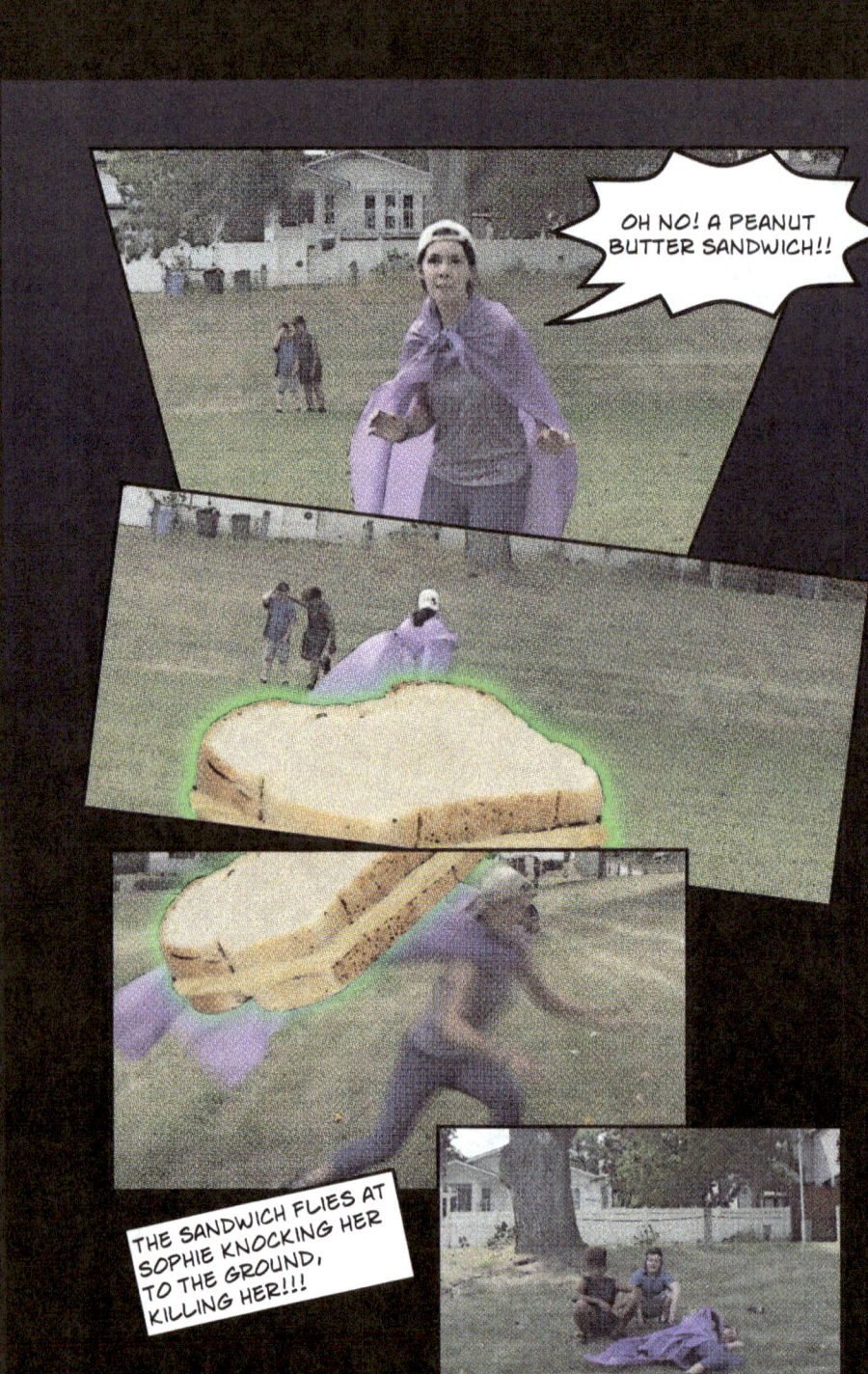

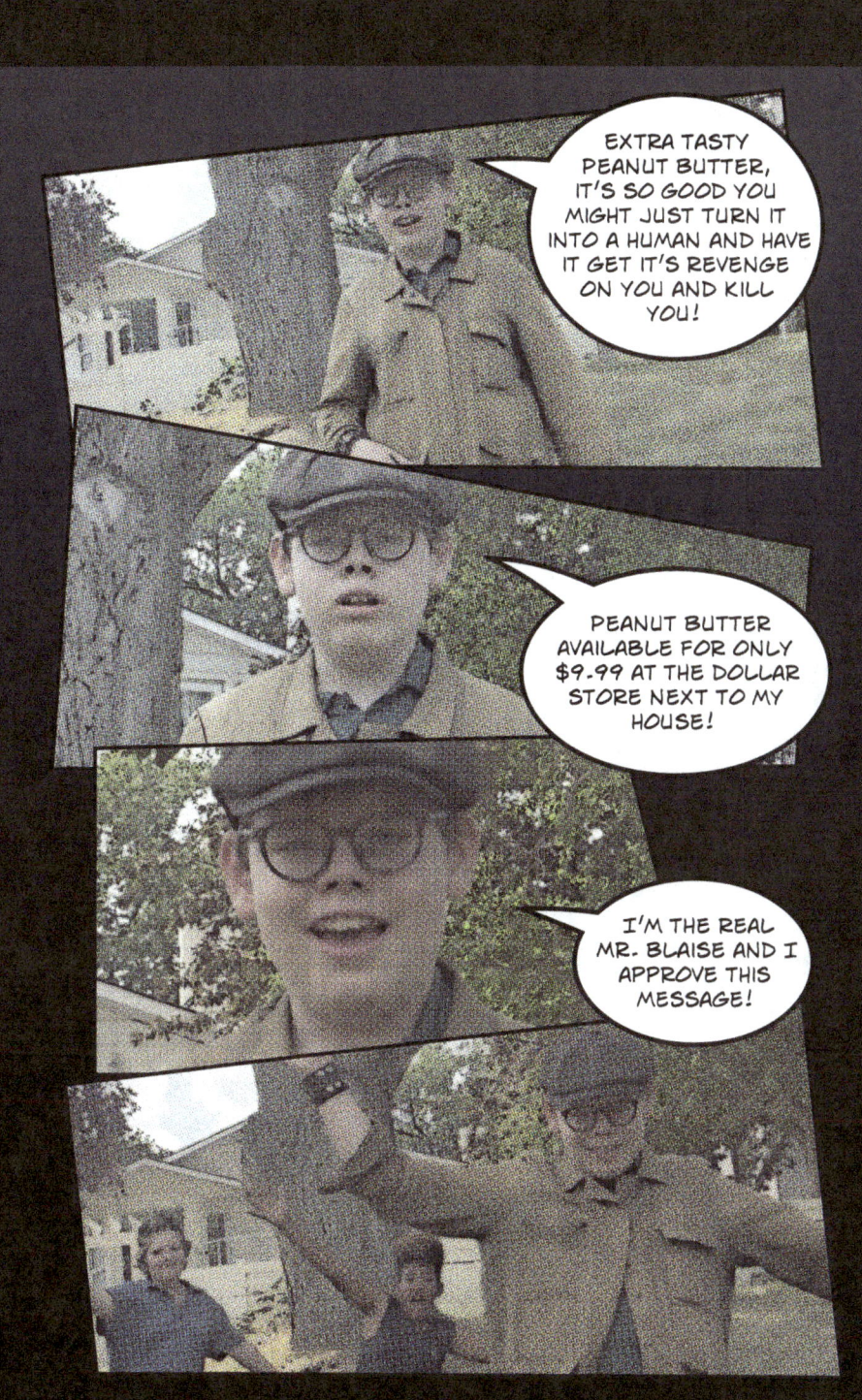

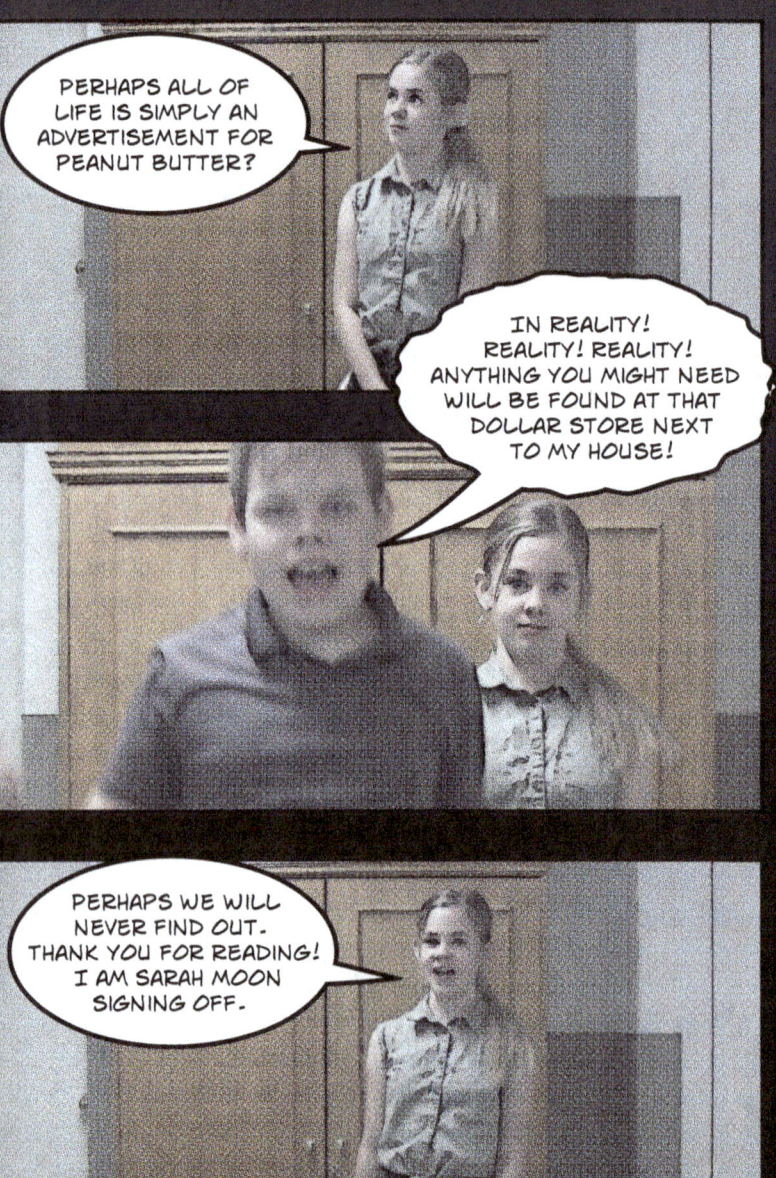

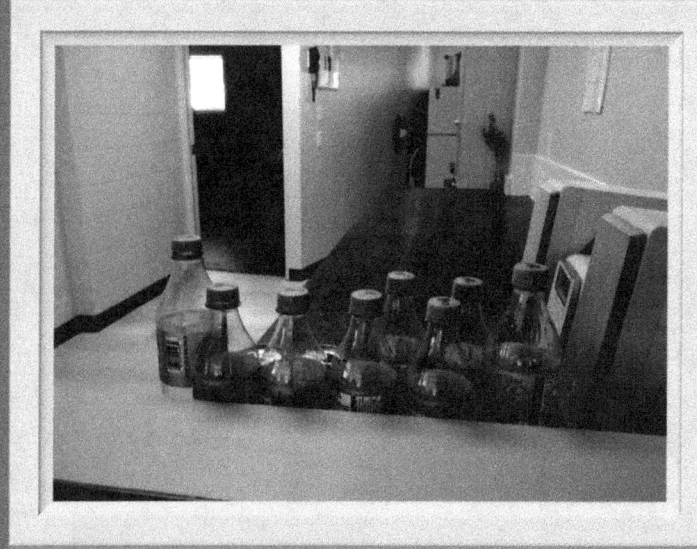

www.ingramcontent.com/pod-product-compliance
Lightning Source LLC
Chambersburg PA
CBHW052354220526
45465CB00003BA/1104